The Forgiveness Myth is **a gem**. In i
been searching for a book that expl
alternatives to, forgiveness. It is ...., respectful and
inspiring, and **full of excellent tools and strategies for hope and healing.**

Ruth Ackerman, Ph.D.,
counselor and founder of
Santa Barbara's Project Recovery

While my original intentions were to skim the book, the Preface hooked
me. Each chapter resonated more with my spirit, and somewhere along the
way, I began to be aware of the beginnings of a *personal* healing. For that
I will be eternally grateful. **If you pick up just one book to help you deal
with past trauma, abuse or hurts in your life, let it be this one.**

KathyJo Dennison, Ph.D., R.N.,
counselor, interventionist, author

If you have ever been deeply hurt by someone and find yourself unwilling
or unable to forgive, **this book is for you.** In a warm and engaging style, the
authors challenge the notion that forgiveness is the only path to healing
and wholeness, and chart what they find to be an equally fruitful approach
to getting unstuck and on to a better life. Their ideas are **encouraging,
empowering, and practical**; their book an invaluable resource for those
who long to heal from life's hurts.

Thomas Hart, Ph.D., counselor and author of
Spiritual Quest: A Guide to the Changing Landscape and
Hidden Spring: The Spiritual Dimension of Therapy

Based on the new and refreshing idea that there are many ways to heal when forgiving isn't possible or desirable, **readers will feel incredibly understood and supported** as they discover their own path to peace and happiness. A great book that will be so helpful to so many! **A huge contribution.** Bravo!

Stephanie Brown, Ph.D., author of
The Family Recovery Guide: A Map for Healthy Growth and
A Place Called Self: Woman, Sobriety and Radical Transformation

If forgiveness means acquiescing to evil or resigning yourself to being treated badly, then it is not just a myth – it is harmful. *The Forgiveness Myth* **effectively explores alternative language and ideas** for letting go, healing, and moving on, beyond the "F" word. **I recommend it.**

Rabbi Debra Orenstein, coeditor of
*Lifecycles 2: Jewish Women on Biblical Themes
in Contemporary Life* (Jewish Lights Publishing)

Employing insights from psychology, spirituality, and their own experience, Gary Egeberg and Wayne Raiter have crafted a courageous, groundbreaking book that **challenges the assumption that forgiveness is the only way** to move beyond the pain of interpersonal conflicts. By defining a path through the complexity of hurtful events and relationships, *The Forgiveness Myth* **invites us to move beyond the conventional thinking about forgiveness** that prevents us from being freely and fully alive. This book is a gentle and practical guide that will prove a valuable resource for dealing with one's own resentments, or in assisting others to cope with theirs.

Tom Stella, former Catholic priest, founder of Soul-Link,
and author of *The God Instinct* and *A Faith Worth Believing:
Finding New Life Beyond the Rules of Religion*

This sensitive, thoughtful and compassionate book brings a deeper understanding to the process of healing. It **will help many who can't or won't forgive** to move forward.

Stephanie Covington, Ph.D., author of
A Woman's Way through the Twelve Steps and
Beyond Trauma: A Healing Journey for Women

This book will be extraordinarily valuable and bring **a sigh of relief to those whose emotional healing is stunted by the untruth that forgiveness is necessary** to heal all wounds. I commend the authors for challenging the validity of a deeply ingrained concept. *The Forgiveness Myth* is full of rich examples and tools for recovery. It **will appeal to clinicians of all levels and to those on their own personal healing journey**. It is an enlightened, pragmatic, and empathetic guide.

Heather Hayes, M.Ed., LPC,
counselor, author, interventionist

From a young age I have been a victim of sexual, physical, verbal, and emotional abuse. Being raised a strict Catholic, I believed I had to just forgive my abusers, but I couldn't. They have not accepted any responsibility for their actions, nor have they admitted any wrongdoing. Yet, I believed that something must be wrong with me because I couldn't forgive. *The Forgiveness Myth* **has helped me to focus on what I need in order to begin to heal**, rather than on what my abusers need. It has given me the freedom to accept my past in a new light. I am now on my journey towards healing and true happiness.

Lynn

The Forgiveness Myth

How to Heal Your Hurts, Move on *and* Be Happy Again When You Can't – or Won't – Forgive

©2008
Gary Egeberg and Wayne Raiter, M.A., LICSW

For information, contact:

Additional copies for yourself,
friends, or loved ones: **$10** per book
$15.95
Ten or more copies for your group
or organization: **$8** per book

This book includes information from many sources and gathered from many
personal experiences. It is published for general reference and is not intended to
be a substitute for appropriate and necessary psychological or medical care. The
publisher and the authors disclaim any personal liability, directly or indirectly, for
advice or information presented within.

Cover design: George Foster, www.fostercovers.com
Interior book design: Liz Tufte, www.folio-bookworks.com
Editing: Geoff Whyte, www.whyteink.com.au
Consulting: Peter Bowerman, www.wellfedsp.com

Publisher's Cataloging In Publication
Egeberg, Gary and Raiter, Wayne

The forgiveness myth: how to heal your hurts, move on and be happy again when
you can't – or won't – forgive/Gary Egeberg and Wayne Raiter
– 1st ed.

p.   cm.

LCCN: 2007934847

ISBN-13: 9780979440007

PHONE CONSULTATIONS
COMPASSIONATE, EMPOWERING PRESENTATIONS
FOR VICTIMS & SURVIVORS OF HORRIBLE HURTS
o Reclaiming Your Personal Power & Inner Peace <u>without</u> Forgiving
o 5 Essential Rs: Remember, Resent, Release, Reclaim, Rebuild
o Loving & Caring for Yourself in the Midst of Senseless Loss & Hurt
o Helping Crime Victims Heal When They Can't Forgive

Contact Gary Egeberg at...
P.O. Box 385152   garyegeberg@msn.com
Bloomington, MN 55437   (952) 836-6504

Contents

CHAPTER I

Major Forgiveness Obstacles
1

CHAPTER 2

Six Common Reasons to Set Aside or Forget Forgiving –
at Least Temporarily
39

CHAPTER 3

Eight Common Reasons to Set Aside or Forget Forgiving –
Perhaps Permanently
63

CHAPTER 4

Healthy Alternatives to Forgiving:
What They Are and Why They Work So Well
95

CHAPTER 5

Preparing to Heal and Move Forward with Your Life
121

CHAPTER 6

Healing, Moving On, and Being Happy Again
163

CHAPTER 7

Making Peace with the Past When You Can't – or Won't – Forgive Yourself
241

Dedication

Gary

To Jeannie, a strong, courageous, and brilliant woman
who chose *not* to forgive those
who did everything in their power
to kill her spirit from the beginning, while discovering her
own unique way to heal, move on, and be happy again.
Continue to take tender care of yourself as you enjoy
your freedom *from* fear and *to* revel in the beauty
and goodness within and surrounding you.

Wayne

I want to dedicate this book to my three sons
Chris, Alex, and Nate,
and to my father, who shared his wisdom
and love of learning with me.

Acknowledgements

We would like to thank the many clients and students who have shared part of their life's journey with us over the years. We feel honored by their trust and grateful for all they have taught us. We would also like to thank our wonderful friends and wise, collaborative colleagues. They, too, have been our teachers. In particular we wish to acknowledge three individuals whose contributions to this book have been invaluable and very much appreciated: our cover designer, George Foster; our interior designer, Liz Tufte; and our editor and proofreader, Geoff Whyte. Our publishing consultant, Peter Bowerman, is owed a special word of appreciation for his passionate belief in this book from the beginning, and for his insightful suggestions along the way, most notably regarding the title. And, finally, a trinity of "angels" is owed a big thank-you hug: Peggy Egeberg for her many contributions and loving support, and Kristen and Erica Egeberg for their love.

Preface

"Forgiving is the one and only way to heal your hurts." Most of us have learned this "fact," this "unquestioned truth," from our earliest years on, perhaps from our families, through our experiences in a particular religious tradition, or by what we have read or heard from spiritual teachers and psychological experts. Yet in this book, by suggesting that forgiveness is a myth, we are challenging that which has been considered true for centuries. However, before elaborating, let us clarify our intentions right from the start:

1. We are *not* saying that people should not forgive, because forgiveness is often a noble, worthwhile, and even essential spiritual and psychological practice that has proven invaluable to millions, including both of us.

2. What we *are* saying is that forgiving does not work for all of us all of the time, and to suggest that it is the *only* way to heal is a myth, an untruth, when in fact there are many ways to recover and move on in life.

Sometimes forgiveness is the best way to heal, and at other times, a different approach will work better for you. It could very well be that you have already done something other than forgive to help you move on after some of your hurts, though perhaps unconsciously. Our goal with this book is to have you consciously choose your best path in each situation, whether forgiveness or one of the many effective alternative routes.

To propose that forgiveness is a myth, though considered the only way to heal and something a hurt person has to do in order to move on, is likely to seem sacrilegious and threatening to some. Yet, we are confident that *The Forgiveness Myth* will affirm for many what they may have already discovered through their own personal experience: forgiving doesn't always work. And rather than feel guilty because forgiving might not be something you want to do in some situations, or remain unhappily stuck in the pain of the past because you can't do it in others, we want to provide you with a variety of alternative ways to help you heal, move on, and be happy again.

If you're the type who can forgive each and every type of hurt you suffer, we encourage you to continue doing so. In your case, we invite you to read this book in order to gain a better understanding of why some people you know – whether a friend, spouse, partner, or coworker – can't always forgive like you can, and what they can do instead to reclaim their peace and happiness.

If, on the other hand, you're like both of us, as well as millions of others, and aren't always able or even willing to forgive, then our desire is that this book will help you realize that you are not spiritually defective or uniquely inept. Rather, forgiving simply isn't the best way for you to heal all of your hurts, just as aspirin isn't the best medicine for all of your ailments.

We hope that people of varying faiths and spiritual paths as well as those whose spiritual path is undefined or in flux will find this book to be a helpful resource along their journey to healing and happiness. Despite our incredibly rich diversity as human beings, one commonality we all share, even with those whose religious beliefs and spiritual practices differ most dramatically from our own, is that hurts hurt, and the desire to heal, move on, and be happy again is truly universal.

We were both raised in the Christian tradition and are well aware of the numerous passages in the Bible that seem to make forgiveness a mandatory exercise: "Forgive us our trespasses as we forgive others . . ." and ". . . If you do not forgive others, neither will [God] forgive your trespasses" are but two.[1] However, if you believe in some type of supreme being or energy, it could very well be that the deepest desire of this ultimate being or force is that we each heal and be happy again; the means, whether forgiving or some alternative method, may be of secondary importance.

Not everything in this book is likely to speak to you. We invite you to take and use what works for you and leave the rest. In fact, instead of automatically reading from front to back, you might choose to consult the chapter titles and subtitles to find the specific sections that may be most relevant and helpful to you and your situation. For example, if you are already quite comfortable with the notion that forgiving is but one way to heal and not the goal itself, you might skim, or skip over, the first three chapters and begin with Chapter Four, which is the first of three consecutive chapters on alternative ways to heal. The first three chapters, on the other hand, are devoted to explaining why forgiveness doesn't always work and the various situations when setting it aside, either temporarily or permanently, may be wise. The final chapter, Chapter Seven, is intended to help those who can't seem to forgive themselves, so if you are feeling bad because of how you hurt someone else or yourself, you might start there, and then go back and read earlier portions of the book. However you choose to use this resource, we invite you to do so in a manner that will help you to discover your unique ways to move beyond the specific hurts you have suffered, including the pain of hurting others or yourself.

Our hope for you is that as you free yourself from the pain of the past, you will regain your personal power to steer your life in a new direction of your own choosing, rather than remain a victim of past hurts that can't be undone. This newfound freedom can be yours

---

1. Words ascribed to Jesus as recorded in Matthew 6:12,15.

whether you are currently being held captive due to how someone hurt you, or because of how you hurt someone else, or both. As your healing unfolds and as you reach out for and respond to the new and exciting opportunities that await you in life, expect to be surprised in delightful ways. Personified, happiness and inner peace are eager to build a new and wonder-filled home in the deepest regions of your heart.

We hope that people of varying faiths and spiritual paths as well as those whose spiritual path is undefined or in flux will find this book to be a helpful resource on their journey to healing and happiness.

Introduction

Heather had given her husband chance after chance to amend his unfaithful ways during the course of their twenty-year marriage.[2] Finally, after endless broken promises and untold heartache, she divorced him. As is true of so many who go through the painful experience of divorce, she sought out the help of a therapist. During one particular session, her therapist told her that she needed to forgive her former husband or at least feel neutral about him, because it would be best if she sat by him at their son's high school graduation, which was scheduled to take place in about six months. Heather didn't agree, but she kept her mouth shut.

After attending one of our workshops on alternative ways to heal, she remarked, "I'll be damned if I am going to make a sandwich of my ex-husband at my son's graduation, with me on one side and his new girlfriend on the other!" Agreeing with her sentiments and intuitive sense, we recommended another therapist to her.

Conventional religious, spiritual, cultural, and even therapeutic wisdom says that you have to forgive if you want to fully recover from how you've been hurt. Even if you feel bad for harming or neglecting someone else or yourself, again, the predominant sentiment is that you must either forgive yourself or stay stuck in

2. The names and identifying circumstances of individuals whose stories are included in this book have been changed in order to protect their anonymity.

endless self-recrimination, guilt, and possibly even shame. This book, in a nutshell, refutes that age-old, deeply-entrenched and unexamined notion, and suggests instead that forgiving, whether forgiving yourself or someone who has hurt you, is always a flexible option at your disposal and not a rigid, set-in-stone obligation.[3]

Forgiving is one way to heal your hurts but *only* one; there are a variety of other ways that many of us employ quite frequently, usually without being aware of doing so. These alternatives, such as "making a fresh start," "cutting your losses," "releasing the hurt to God or your higher power or the universe," or "coming to terms with this hurt as best you can" are waiting to be named and claimed in a conscious, deliberate manner as viable options in your internal medicine chest.[4]

None of the alternatives we explore in this book will require you to forgive if you don't want to. Why? Because you have already suffered the injustice of being hurt or wrongly treated, and that may be more than enough for you to deal with, without also having to summon up goodwill or forgiveness for the person who caused you to suffer in the first place. What's more, your offender might not even be sorry for having hurt you. Yes, at some point you might choose to forgive if that is your desire, or you might consider an alternative approach that is often more effective than forgiving, so that the hurt does not rob you of your potential to be happy and at peace one minute longer than necessary.

Traditionally, forgiveness has been declared the only way to heal and recover from our hurts, yet this "only way" hasn't always worked for millions, regardless of their spiritual or religious orientation.

---

3. While the rest of the Introduction is written from the perspective of being hurt by others, we realize that many have an even greater struggle to forgive themselves. We explore ways to transcend guilt and shame in Chapter Seven.

4. We have elected to capitalize "God" and not to capitalize "higher power." Our reasoning is that "God," for most people, refers to a uniquely supreme or divine being, whereas the understanding of one's "higher power," especially among many people in recovery, may be either theistic or non-theistic. Examples of the latter include a twelve-step support group, nature, or one's true self.

Untold numbers of Christians, Jews, Muslims, Buddhists, twelve-steppers, and eclectic spiritual practitioners, as well as atheists and agnostics, struggle with this thing called forgiving for a variety of reasons. Perhaps a common denominator is the fact that forgiving has indeed been presented, often in a nearly dogmatic manner, as the only way to heal or as something we absolutely must do.

As adults, we treasure having options, which are available in just about every area of life that readily comes to mind. Even spiritual practices such as prayer and meditation, or how any of us chooses to love our neighbor or practice loving-kindness, abound with options and are wide open to personal interpretation, preference, and subsequent practice. Yet when it comes to addressing hurts, options are nowhere to be found; instead, individually and collectively, the majority of us have been locked into an either-or mindset: either forgive or stay stuck in anger, bitterness, and resentment. *And very few people have questioned why this is so, or even **if** it is so.*

To advocate that forgiving is the only "medicine" a person can take in response to being hurt is a little bit like proposing that aspirin is the only medicine available for any and all ailments. Got a headache? Take aspirin. Suffering from asthma? Take aspirin. Struggling with depression? Take aspirin. Having surgery? Take aspirin. Sounds ridiculous, doesn't it? Taking aspirin in these situations ranges from being potentially effective when it comes to remedying a headache to ineffective when treating asthma or depression to grossly inappropriate – if not criminal – were an anesthesiologist to offer you aspirin as the surgeon reached for the scalpel. Can you imagine being asked if you would prefer regular or extra strength?

So, too, there are times when forgiving is indeed highly effective, for instance in committed or endearing relationships, and when the hurts involved are neither too painful nor too repetitive. Take for example the common scenario in which one member of a household says something in a harsh manner to another, and a short time later says, "I'm sorry I snapped at you." Many times, the person who was hurt is able to respond, quite naturally and easily, with something like, "That's okay." In these types of situations, the parties involved are usually able to quickly put the hurt behind them and move on without getting bogged down. And in many cases, neither the "hurter" nor the "hurtee" finds it necessary to even ask for or offer forgiveness; it just happens in a natural and almost effortless manner.

There are other times, however, when forgiving is prone to being ineffective, especially when remorse and a relational investment with the person who hurt you is lacking. Imagine a scenario in which a rather volatile boss or co-worker snaps at you or treats you in a manner that you deem to be unfair or disrespectful. In this case you would likely feel some anger, stew a bit, and then sooner or later refocus your energies elsewhere, *even though you might not have forgiven*. In situations like these, many of us are able to move on with our lives while learning how to set some boundaries in order to protect ourselves, neither of which is dependent upon forgiving.

And then there are still other times when suggesting that someone forgive their offender runs the risk of being insensitive, even inappropriate. For instance, the person who is coming out of a marriage that was broken by habitual infidelity, as was the case with Heather, has her hands full just trying to restart her life and establish herself in the world. Devoting any effort toward forgiving her "Ex" when she is still reeling from a host of accumulated hurts may end up depleting her much-needed energy to rebuild. Trying to forgive may inadvertently sabotage rather than facilitate her ability to heal. The same is true for those who suffered some type of abuse as children. Many may find it easier to move on and reclaim their power as adults by exploring one of the alternatives to forgiving, rather than remain bound by the unexamined conventional myth which says that forgiving is the only way to break free from their painful legacy.

There are of course people who can and do forgive the most heinous of hurts, hurts that most of us could not, or would not, forgive. For example, you may have heard or read stories about surviving family members who forgave the murderer of their loved one, or an abuse victim who forgave his abuser, or a sexual assault victim who forgave her attacker. These people are truly amazing. Perhaps they have been blessed with an extraordinary ability to forgive the unforgivable, or maybe they would say that they had to work incredibly hard to get to a point where they could finally forgive. Their stories and paths to healing, like those of all of us, are unique and probably quite diverse, as is their understanding of what they mean when they say they have forgiven those who have caused them to suffer so deeply.[5]

This book, however, is for those who, like us, would not be prone to forgiving in the situations above, or in situations when other types of serious hurts are involved. It is also for those who are unwilling – or unable – to forgive certain hurts that are of a less serious nature. The common ground that all hurts share, major or minor, is that they hurt, just like a slight burn or paper cut hurts, though not nearly as much as more serious burns and cuts. So it matters not how your hurt compares to someone else's, whether it is larger or smaller, more serious or less serious, and so on. All that matters is that you choose the easiest, most effective healing strategy for *you*, so that you can overcome the hurt and reclaim your personal power to move on in life with a healthy measure of peace and happiness.

As the authors, we have no personal investment in whether you decide to forgive or choose to employ an alternative healing strategy in response to one or more of your hurts. We wrote this book in the hope that you will . . .

---

5. One of the first issues addressed in this book is the fact that there is no universally accepted definition or understanding of what it means to forgive. So when someone says they have forgiven, even something of a horrendous nature, none of us knows what their understanding of forgiveness is. How another person understands forgiveness, even if they had the misfortune of suffering a similar catastrophic hurt, can differ in significant or subtle ways. We can only hope that those who say they have forgiven the most severe hurts imaginable are truly able to experience some degree of peace and consolation. Our hearts go out to them.

1. Know that forgiving is not the only way to recover from being hurt, nor is it necessarily the primary or most effective way to heal.

2. Understand why forgiving doesn't always work, and it's not because you are somehow defective as a human being or lacking spiritually.

3. Become familiar with some of the alternatives to forgiving, and the situations in which they are likely to be both easier and more effective than forgiving.

4. Alleviate any feelings of guilt or sense of spiritual defectiveness that you may be wrestling with because you haven't been able or willing to forgive in past or current situations.

5. Heal as fully and expeditiously as possible regardless of what recovery strategy you choose to employ.

6. Learn how to make peace with your past if you are unable to forgive yourself.

In short, we are going to counter the myth that forgiving is the only medicine in town. Like aspirin, it is a wonderful remedy for some of life's hurts, especially those that are, generally speaking, neither too painful nor too chronic. It is also a beautiful and oftentimes quite doable undertaking when the person who did the hurting not only takes ownership of their behavior, but is someone you care about and want to continue being in some type of relationship with. However when these factors are not present, we intend to build a case for considering one or more of the alternatives to forgiving. Of course, you are still free to forgive in response to every single hurt you suffer, if you so choose. But maybe it will be reassuring for you to know that there are alternative ways to heal should you set out to forgive, but at some point along the way discover that you aren't willing or able to pull it off as you had hoped.

Once again, when you have been hurt, the goal is to recover, heal, and move on with the rest of your life as quickly and effectively as you can, whether via the traditional path of forgiving, or through a non-traditional, alternative way. To paraphrase the well-known passage from Ecclesiastes that begins with "For everything there is a season, and a time for every matter under heaven . . . a time to live and a time to die . . . ," we believe that there are times to forgive *and* times to employ alternatives to forgiving.[6] We are strong advocates of both; however, our focus in this book is to explain why forgiving doesn't always work in response to every type of hurt we human beings suffer, and when that is the case, what other approaches can be taken in order to heal, move on, and be happy again.

To advocate that forgiving is the only "medicine" a person can take in response to being hurt is a little bit like proposing that aspirin is the only medicine available for any and all ailments.

---

6. See Ecclesiastes 3:1–8.

～ 1 ～

Major Forgiveness Obstacles

While we will be among the first to admit that forgiving is a wonderful ideal, we will both readily concede that in most cases neither one of us is overly enthused about the possibility of forgiving after being hurt. Or when some desires to forgive are present, they are often neutralized and overpowered by even stronger desires *not* to forgive. And in those less frequent situations when our desires to forgive are actually greater than our inclinations not to, our subsequent attempts to forgive sometimes feel like they are far from successful, as evidenced by the resentful thoughts and feelings that still crop up, bidden or unbidden. We don't think these types of experiences are unique to us or to a minority of hard-headed, cold-hearted human beings, for it is our sense that at least half of the human race, perhaps including you, can relate to what we have just described.

So why is this wonderful ideal, which nearly all of us embrace when no hurt is on the table, so hard to pull off with any measure of success or sense of satisfaction when it comes to some of the real hurts encountered in life, even those of a relatively minor nature? Are ideals by their nature unattainable? Or are some of us somehow spiritually defective in comparison with those in our midst who are indeed willing and able to forgive most or all of the time? Or could it be that at least some who are quick to forgive do so because they'd prefer to avoid a direct encounter with their raw anger, hatred, and fantasies of revenge? Perhaps in some cases, their sense of self, their persona, their identity as a "nice" or "religious" or "spiritual" person does not allow them to honestly acknowledge, much less enter, the depth of painful thoughts and feelings after being hurt; hence they try to circumvent or abort emotional and mental turmoil by premature or pseudo forgiveness.

In this chapter, we will address some of the major forgiveness obstacles many of us encounter in our attempts to forgive, or even when simply contemplating the remote *possibility* of forgiving someone who has hurt us. The purpose for doing so is not to dissuade you from forgiving, for as we pointed out in the Introduction, we believe that there are times when forgiving is a highly desirable and doable undertaking, especially when one or more of the following seven criteria are present:

1. You want to continue being in some type of relationship with the person who hurt you.

2. There is a timely and genuine spirit and expression of sorrow or remorse on your offender's part.

3. The person who hurt you has taken full responsibility for their actions, without making excuses or trying to verbally soften what was done to hurt you.

4. This person is willing to listen to you and acknowledge how their hurtful actions affected you without trying to offer explanations, counter your perceptions, or discount your experience.

5. Your offender is willing to repair the harm that was done or to make amends to the fullest extent possible.

6. The person who harmed you is committed to not hurting you in the same manner again, and you feel reasonably confident that they will live up to their commitment.

7. The hurt you suffered was neither of a highly serious nor repetitive nature (e.g., betrayal, infidelity, chronic abuse, and so on).

Even if one or more of the seven criteria above are present, you can still choose not to forgive – and yet heal. What's more, as you will discover in this book, you can still choose to be in some type of relationship with the person who hurt you without forgiving, but with the help of an alternative approach.

What we hope to make clear is that your unwillingness, or your highly conflicted desire to forgive, or your inability to forgive in certain situations is *not* because you don't value the psychological or spiritual ideal and practice of forgiveness, nor is it because you are spiritually defective. Instead, you will come to recognize, perhaps for the very first time, that there are valid reasons for not always wanting, or being able, to forgive and that you are far from alone in your struggles.

While such factors as temperament, personality type, and life history certainly influence each individual's ability to forgive, what follows are ten major obstacles that are more true than not. As you read, we invite you to pay special attention to the ones that speak to you as well as to those that may be adversely impacting a friend's or loved one's ability to transcend the hurts they have suffered.

Please keep in mind that the purpose of exploring a few of the major forgiveness obstacles is so that you can be consciously aware of them and assess how significant any particular barrier is in your attempts to forgive. Then, if you decide that forgiving is still the best path for you to take in response to a particular hurt, you can try to maneuver around the obstacle or overcome it. Or if you decide that the impediment in question is insurmountable or too difficult to address, you can choose to explore an alternative and more effective way to heal that does not require you to forgive.

What we hope to make clear is that your unwillingness,
or your highly conflicted desire to forgive, or your
inability to forgive in certain situations is not because
you don't value the psychological or spiritual ideal
and practice of forgiveness, nor is it because you are
spiritually defective. Instead, you will come to recognize,
perhaps for the very first time, that there are valid reasons
for not always wanting or being able to forgive and that
you are far from alone in your struggles.

There Is No Clear, Universally Accepted Definition of Forgiving

Because this obstacle is of such critical yet often unrecognized importance, we consider it worthy of being the first one explored. Despite how forgiveness is extolled in a nearly universal manner, most have not even given thought to the fact that there is no clear, universally agreed upon definition or understanding of what it means to forgive. Yet when this issue is raised, the quandary it presents seems rather obvious.

Even though we were both raised in the Christian tradition in which forgiving was upheld and advocated, it never dawned on us to ask just exactly what this thing called forgiving is, nor did it seem to cross the minds of our parents, religion teachers, pastors, or priests to clearly explain to us, and others, what forgiving is and isn't. We were just supposed to do it. In fact, even as seasoned adults, when either of us has heard this topic addressed in various religious or spiritual settings, the message hasn't changed much at all. The exhortation is still *to* forgive, but any nuanced exploration as to exactly *what* forgiving is, much less how to go about it, remains, for the most part, missing, as is any inclination to explore healthy alternatives when a person is unable or unwilling to forgive.

In our presentations on forgiveness and alternative ways to heal, both in religious and spiritual settings and in so-called secular ones – which are also spiritual – the responses participants offer when they are asked to write down their definition or understanding of forgiveness are diverse indeed. In any group of twenty-five people, we will get twenty-five assorted responses with some commonality or overlapping of certain words and phrases.

Now if another ideal and spiritual practice such as "honesty" was considered, it is quite likely that the majority in any particular gathering would describe it as *being truthful in your words and actions with self and others,* or at least something along those lines. It is not too plausible that we would get the same smorgasbord of responses that we do with forgiving. With the latter, the responses are all over the place, including "forgetting about the hurt," "letting it go," "going back to how it was with the other person before the hurt took place," "never feeling angry or resentful again," "letting go of vengeance," or "trusting that God will give your offender their just desserts in the next life."

Not only is common agreement as to what it means to forgive lacking, specific understandings held by some are ones that others would reject in a heartbeat. In fact, because there are so many *misunderstandings* of what it means to forgive, it is not atypical for books on forgiveness to give considerable attention to clarifying what forgiveness is *not* before they go on to suggest what it *is*.

If the ideal or spiritual practice of honesty is once again considered, it's difficult to imagine that books on this topic – if indeed there are any – would need to have substantial sections on what honesty is not. Nor is it easy to envision the need for a subsequent section on what exactly honesty is. It seems quite clear, except perhaps for the chronically dishonest, as to what it means to be honest. Yet with forgiveness, it isn't clear at all as to what forgiving is, much less universally accepted, which begs the obvious question: *How are we supposed to go about forgiving, especially in each and every situation, if there is no common understanding of what it means to forgive?*

Even those professionals whom most of us might expect to have a clearer understanding of what it means to forgive, such as rabbis, pastors, priests, spiritual teachers, and therapists, are oftentimes as unsure as the rest of us. And when one of them does seem to have a clear understanding, it may not fit at all for the person who has sought their counsel, as was the case with Heather and her former therapist.

Not only is common agreement as to what it means to
forgive lacking, specific understandings held by some are
ones that others would reject in a heartbeat.
In fact, because there are so many *misunderstandings* of
what it means to forgive, it is not atypical for books on
forgiveness to give considerable attention to clarifying
what forgiveness is *not* before they go on
to suggest what it *is*.

Dictionary Definitions of Forgiving Are Not Helpful

Given the fact that wildly diverse definitions, understandings, and misunderstandings of what it means to forgive abound, what better resource to clear it all up for us than the dictionary. Usually, that is. Yet if you were to look up the word "forgive" in the dictionary, its definition may trouble you a bit. Now in defense of the dictionary, how can a few phrases possibly begin to define something as complex as forgiveness, or even other complex, multivariate spiritual practices such as prayer and meditation, especially when it seems that an unending stream of books are written on these topics? The dictionary, by its nature, has to be concise. But in our opinion, the brevity of the definition is not the problem as much as it is how dictionaries define the word "forgive," as in the following example:

1. to grant pardon for or remission of (an offense, debt, etc.); absolve

2. to give up all claims on account of; remit (a debt, obligation, etc.)

3. to grant pardon to (a person)

4. to cease to feel resentment against: *to forgive one's enemies*

5. to cancel an indebtedness or liability of: *to forgive the interest owed on a loan*

6. to pardon an offense or an offender.[7]

Now unless you are a financially wealthy individual who can cancel a loan or the interest on a loan without too much strain, you might struggle to implement this definition of forgiving in

---

7. *Webster's New Universal Unabridged Dictionary.* New York: Barnes and Noble, 2003.

response to at least some of the real hurts you suffer at the hands of others. Most of us aren't interested in pardoning or absolving our offender, especially if this person doesn't take ownership of their harmful behavior or fails to apologize or make amends. Regarding the cessation of resentments, a person who has been hurt can be free of resentments most of the time, but if she *ever* experiences resentment at any point after she has forgiven, then, according to the dictionary, she hasn't *really* forgiven.

As we will explore later on, any time the memory of a particular hurt comes to mind, even when it seems to just pop into your head, it is bound to be accompanied by some degree of painful thoughts and feelings such as resentments, even if only for a moment or two. So to be free of resentments once-and-for-all doesn't seem to be a very accurate understanding of forgiveness.[8]

Once again, most of us are not eager to offer an unconditional pardon or absolution to those who have hurt us; otherwise, we would just do it. As it turns out, the dictionary definition is not very helpful at all. In fact, its failure to factor in justice and accountability can be truly harmful to those who believe they are just supposed to forgive in an unconditional manner no matter how poorly they have been treated and regardless of how unresponsive their perpetrator may be.

Most of us aren't interested in pardoning or absolving our offender, especially if this person doesn't take ownership of their harmful behavior or fails to apologize or make amends.

---

8. We will say more about how painful memories are usually accompanied by some degree of painful thoughts and feelings in our discussion of "The Impossible Litmus Tests of 'True' Forgiveness."

Many Need a Reminder That Forgiving Is for Them – Not Their Offender

Perhaps you, like both of us, have heard someone express a sentiment such as, "When I forgive, I always remind myself that I am doing so for *me* and not for the person who hurt me." Now neither of us has any issue whatsoever with anyone who finds that such a reminder facilitates their ability to forgive and move on in life. In fact, we would fully support and applaud those who use this method as a way to help them get beyond a particular hurt. We would also encourage these individuals to keep on using this method as long as it works for them. Our concern, however, is for those who may have tried to use this reminder, or who have had other people remind them that forgiving is really for them and not for their offender, but it doesn't work in the same manner that it does for others.

If you stop and think about it, this type of reminder seems to be somewhat unique to forgiving. Neither one of us can readily think of other situations in which we have a similar need to remind ourselves that what we are setting out to do is really for ourselves and not for someone else. Of course there are times when we all set out to do something for someone else, but in those cases, we have no confusion about what we are doing and who we are doing it for.

For instance, if you set out to buy an ice cream cone for a friend, you would likely do so without any need to remind yourself that this soon-to-be-purchased ice cream cone is for your friend and not for yourself. And if you set out to buy an ice cream cone for yourself, you would do so without any need to remind yourself that you are doing so for yourself and not for someone else. There simply wouldn't be any confusion about what you are doing and no need to remind yourself of who you are doing it for.

Once again, consider the spiritual trait or practice of honesty. Those of us who practice honesty do so because it matches our values and provides us with a sense of integrity. To be dishonest would be more painful than whatever might be gained from it. Yes, others benefit from our honesty, but we choose to be honest first and foremost for ourselves, for our own spiritual wellbeing. We have no need to remind ourselves of why, or for whom, we are being honest.

Similarly, most of us don't feel a need to remind ourselves that we intend to pray or meditate or read or shower or go to work . . . because it's good for us. Yes, they are all good for us, and oftentimes good for others as well, but once again, we have no need to remind ourselves of our true reasons for doing any of these things.

The point we are making is because many people do indeed feel a need to remind themselves, or someone they know who is struggling to forgive, that forgiving is for them and not for their offender, it seems to indicate that something deep within *really believes that forgiving is for the other person*, for the person who did the hurting. Otherwise, why would they need this reminder?

As we will explain in Chapter Four, when a different word or phrase than "forgiving" is employed, this problem is no longer an issue. For example, if instead of using "forgive," as in "I am going to try to forgive so-and-so for hurting me," an alternative phrase is used such as, "I am going to make a fresh start right now despite how I was hurt," none of us would have a need to remind ourselves that we are doing so *for ourselves*. Making this fresh start, as is true of the other healthy alternative strategies, doesn't have any hidden sense of really being for our offender, as forgiving does for so many.

One reason that forgiving often feels like it really is for the other person is because the person who has been hurt is trying to direct some action, that of forgiving, toward their offender, while perhaps at the same time reminding themselves that it is really for them. This can be a bit of a difficult undertaking to say the least, whereas an alternative strategy, such as "I am going to make a fresh start" is about directing some action *toward and on behalf of the person who has been hurt*. This frees the individual from focusing on – or obsessing about – the person who hurt them, while restoring their power to take the necessary steps to be happy and at peace again as they focus on their own life.

The point we are making is because many people do indeed feel a need to remind themselves, or someone they know who is struggling to forgive, that forgiving is for them and not for their offender, it seems to indicate that something deep within *really believes that forgiving is for the other person,* for the person who did the hurting. Otherwise, why would they need this reminder?

The Head-Heart Dilemma

This obstacle is one in which your head, your intellect, may believe one thing and your heart, your deepest self, might believe something completely different. In psychological terms, your conscious mind might be trying to believe X while your subconscious mind really believes Y at a much deeper level. In the case of the previous obstacle, your head may believe–or at least try to believe–that forgiving is for you, while your heart *really* believes that it is for the other person. And despite the healthy and mature understanding or definition of forgiveness you may hold in your head, your heart might really believe that to forgive this individual means you are saying that how you were hurt no longer matters, which may not be true at all.

To give you a better feel for the power of this barrier, consider the many millions who struggle with self-esteem, whether periodically or on an ongoing basis, no matter if it is in just one area of life, such as relationships, or across the board. Perhaps you have struggled with self-esteem in the past or are currently working on fostering thoughts and feelings about yourself that are more positive.

In any case, those with low or performance-based self-esteem can be told that they are good people, and they can even tell themselves that they are good through daily affirmations. But if, somewhere deep in their heart or subconscious, they *really* believe they are somehow flawed or unworthy or not good, it is quite challenging, especially early in the self-esteem building process, to take in the truth of their inherent goodness. For those with perfectionist inclinations, if they fall short of some humanly unattainable expectation (e.g., never make mistakes or never get angry or never gain any weight), then the affirming words of others as well as their own affirming words can frequently be rendered impotent.

In this day and age, healthy, accurate, and mature insights about forgiveness are readily available through books, tapes, presentations, and on the Internet. (Of course, much of what is accessible is either simplistic or harmful, so a discerning eye is necessary.) In your explorations, you may have come across some wonderful definitions and understandings of forgiveness that appeal to you, especially when everything is going just fine and no hurt is troubling you. But when you *have* been hurt and you *are* upset and you *are* struggling with this whole forgiveness thing, your heart might have something radically different to say.

Forgiveness theories that any one of us hold to be true in "quiet times" can fall apart quite quickly in stormier moments when encountering a real hurt in life. Perhaps you will be able to relate to some of the contrasted examples of the head-heart dilemma or dialogue below. Note the use of "we" in the first column and the use of "I" in the second. Also, notice that the statements in the first column are true for many people, including both of us, who have sought to learn more about forgiveness. That is why we use the collective "we." Yet these statements tend to lose their validity – and their healing potential – when suffering a real hurt, even a "minor" one, which is the reason we use the personal "I" in the second column.

When no hurt is bothering us, and we are *not* struggling to forgive, our head may believe intellectually and theoretically:	When I have been hurt, and I am upset, and I am struggling with this whole forgiveness thing up close and personal, my heart may believe:
Forgiving does *not* mean that we are excusing the hurtful behavior of our offender.	If I forgive, it *feels* like I am excusing the hurtful behavior of my offender.

Forgiving does *not* mean that we must have warm or neutral thoughts and feelings toward the person who hurt us.

If I don't have warm, or at least neutral, thoughts and feelings toward this person, then I feel like I haven't *really* forgiven. Besides, I just can't seem to generate these types of thoughts and feelings. To be perfectly honest, I don't want to.

Forgiving does *not* mean that we will never have upsetting thoughts and feelings about or toward our offender again.

How can I have possibly forgiven my offender if I am still having vengeful thoughts and feelings of anger and hatred? Isn't that a clear sign that I *haven't* forgiven? I thought that forgiving was supposed to get rid of these negative thoughts and feelings once-and-for-all.

Forgiving means that we try to separate the hurtful behavior from the personhood of our offender.

I have no desire to separate this person's hurtful behavior from their personhood. What's more, I *can't* separate the two.

Forgiving means that we attempt to see the goodness or potential for goodness in our offender while at the same time not excusing their hurtful behavior.

As far as my offender's goodness or potential for goodness goes, why do I have to look for it in her, especially since she was the one who hurt me? She wasn't too concerned about *my* goodness when she hurt me!

| Forgiving is really for us and not for the person who hurt us. | It sure feels like forgiving is for my offender and not for me at all. It feels like I am saying that how I was hurt no longer matters, and that's not true. |

As you can see from these examples, what you may believe to be healthily and accurately true about forgiving from a dispassionate distance, when no particular hurt is troubling you, can be countered and negated quite quickly and powerfully by what you *really* hold to be true or *really* believe in your heart when wrestling with a real hurt.

When your head and heart are at odds, your heart, rightly or wrongly, tends to rule the day, hence, the head-heart dilemma. That doesn't mean you should throw out your intellect or yield to an "I'm ruled solely by how I feel" approach to life, for using your mind is mandatory, no matter if you try to forgive or if you choose to activate an alternative healing strategy.

What we recommend is that you strive for a healing path in which you can use your mind, your intellect, while also honoring your feelings, your heart, your deepest self, at the same time. When your head and heart are not on the same page – or not even in the same book or library, for that matter – then you might be wise to consider whether or not you are trying to force the round peg of forgiveness to fit into the square hole of a particular hurt. If so, an alternative approach is likely to fit better, as well as work better, for you.

Forgiveness theories that any one of us hold to be true
in "quiet times" can fall apart quite quickly in stormier
moments when encountering a real hurt in life.

Routine and Simplistic Advice to "Just Forgive" Is Often Harmful

If forgiving was something each of us could pull off with a reasonable amount of effort, we would just do it. Or if it indeed was the best "medicine" in town for each and every one of our hurts, we would just "take it." There would be no need for books on forgiveness or books like this one that challenge the unexamined notion that forgiving is the only—or even the best—way to recover from being hurt. Also, simplistic advice such as "why don't you just forgive" that is offered by so many in such a routine, automatic, and oftentimes unthinking manner, would, thankfully, become extinct. (Because both of us have lived the majority of our lives believing in the forgiveness myth, it is quite likely that we, too, have offered such "advice" to certain individuals in times past.)

Yet, is there anything—ANYTHING—less helpful to a person who has been hurt than to have someone suggest that they forgive?!! Do those who offer such easy and routine advice, oftentimes without pausing for a second to consider how it might impact the recipient, really think that this person doesn't already know that they are *supposed* to forgive—after all, they've only heard it all their life? Or do they stop and take into account that this individual may already be feeling plenty of guilt for not being willing to forgive or frustration because they can't forgive?[9]

It would be surprising to learn of someone who, upon receiving such advice, ends up slapping their forehead in a eureka-like manner while saying, "Hey, what a great idea! I never *thought* about forgiving! You are a genius. Thanks for your advice; I'll get right on it." Yet it continues to fall so casually out of the mouths of self-appointed advice-givers in an automaton-like manner, while in many cases harming rather than helping those who are already hurting. To be fair, most of us, because the forgiveness myth is so

---

9. There's an anonymous saying that points to the harmful nature of unasked-for advice: "Unsolicited advice is a curse, whereas advice that is asked for is a blessing."

deeply entrenched and its validity seldom questioned, have learned to give this type of advice. Also, many of us haven't known what else to say and do in those situations when someone has been telling us how hurt and upset they are.

Marilyn, who is in her eighties, carries hurts in her heart that are more than sixty years old. She hasn't been able to forgive or let go of these hurts even though her health is failing rapidly and death is on the horizon. Her husband Harold, in an exasperated manner, has exhorted her on many occasions, "Please let this go! Why can't you just forgive Rosie? It happened more than sixty years ago, and besides, she isn't even alive any more."

Harold, having been a loving and caring husband during their fifty-five year marriage, truly has Marilyn's best interests at heart when he makes such urgings. He wishes she could finally let it go or forgive, yes, in part because he is tired of hearing about it, but more so because he doesn't want these hurts from the past to trouble Marilyn any longer or detract from their remaining time together. Yet Marilyn isn't willing or able to forgive or let it go, or she would have done so by now. What's more, each time Harold pleads with her in this manner – and other family members and friends have also admonished her with similar sentiments over the years – her sense of guilt for not forgiving, for not letting it go, only grows deeper. In the silence of her mind, unbeknownst to others, thoughts such as these torment her:

> *What's wrong with me? Why can't I forgive?*
>
> *Besides, it really is such a little thing, but I just can't let it go like Harold wants me to.*
>
> *Harold's right. Rosie's been dead for years, but I still can't forgive.*
>
> *What would my priest think of me if he knew?*
>
> *I'm a horrible person.*

Each of us is like Marilyn when we can't forgive or let a hurt go. At such times, it would be far more beneficial if someone would offer us a sign of unconditional compassion and affirm us just as we are, rather than chide or scold or shame us, perhaps with the added weight of a scripture passage or two tossed in, because we haven't been willing or able to forgive or let it go. As was the case with Marilyn, it's often those closest to us who are inclined to offer the routine forgiveness pep talk that we don't need to hear. Instead of saying or doing the things that will let us know that we are still loved and accepted right smack dab in the middle of our reluctance or inability or failure to forgive, it's not unusual to get the automatic and unasked-for "you need to forgive" speech, which is usually of no help whatsoever. Actually, it can do real harm due to its moral overtones, which only serves to heighten feelings of guilt, failure, or inadequacy, not to mention the impression of being utterly alone – even among family and friends.

Trailing right behind this conventional advice, which is often well-intended rather than malicious, is the explicit or implicit suggestion that it's all so simple – just forgive, or just let it go. In fact, it's rather common to hear those very words: *Why don't you just forgive?* or *Why don't you just let it go?* As if it is all *just* that simple.

Yet if there's one thing that we human beings are not, and that recovering from our hurts is not, it is simple. Each of us is incredibly complex, and what enables or inhibits any of our attempts to forgive or let go is also highly complex and nuanced, even when we would admit that the particular hurt that is troubling us is of a relatively minor or inconsequential nature in the grand scheme of things.

The founder of process philosophy, Alfred North Whitehead, once said, "Seek simplicity – and distrust it." Yes, a single simple step can often help us begin to break free, but our humanity, our unique individuality, and our recovery process when dealing with a particular hurt or person who hurt us is complex. Because we are each complex individuals, simplistic solutions such as "just forgive" or "just turn it over to God" or "just pray more" or "all you have to do to forgive is _____" can be potentially insulting and imprisoning rather than liberating. Why? Because we are told by someone we may not have asked, or who may not know what they are talking about, that it is all so simple, so easy, if we would just do what they suggest. Never mind the fact that many of these individuals might not practice what they preach – unsolicited advice-givers seldom do – and that they could be even worse at forgiving, or more reluctant to forgive, than we are.

Forgiving a hurt, even a relatively minor one, is not always simple, because as mentioned, if it was, we would all just do it each and every time with each and every hurt. So perhaps we would all be wise to take a moratorium from unsolicited advice and refrain from urging a fellow sufferer to forgive, especially in such a routine and nearly mindless manner, when we know neither the wounds nor the workings of this person's heart. There are valid reasons why any one of us might resist forgiving at times or not be able to do it at other times, some of which we are addressing in this chapter and more of which we will examine in Chapters Two and Three.

Each of us is incredibly complex and what enables or
inhibits any of our attempts to forgive or let go
is also highly complex and nuanced, even when we
would admit that the particular hurt that is troubling us
is of a relatively minor or inconsequential nature in the
grand scheme of things.

Religious and Family Baggage

How ironic that religion, a key proponent if not *the* perennial champion of forgiveness, is often a major stumbling block to many people's subsequent ability to forgive. While neither one of us can speak knowledgeably about any other tradition than the Christian one, it is likely that at least a few of the other religious traditions and spiritual paths, to a greater or lesser degree, also inadvertently impede at times rather than facilitate some of their adherents' ability to forgive.

In the case of Christianity, perhaps because forgiveness is emphasized and talked about *so* much, often in glib and unexamined ways, it is bound to do real harm to some people. A saying from the Taoist tradition says it well: *Those who know don't talk, while those who talk don't know.*

And if there's one thing the average church-going or former church-going Christian – or former Christian – has heard talked about, perhaps more than any other single topic, it is forgiveness. Talking about forgiveness doesn't take a great deal of talent, as virtually anyone can do it, whereas meeting and accepting individuals in their inability or unwillingness to forgive requires pastoral skill and sensitivity as well as plain old-fashioned human decency. Sometimes that which has been held to be religiously true, regardless of how much unearned tenure it has acquired over the years or centuries, needs to take a backseat and be quiet for a change so that the deeper truth of the person who has been hurt can be heard and honored. Consider the case of Jennifer, for example.

Jennifer was adopted by a Protestant minister and his wife. Before she was welcomed into her new family, she had been sexually abused by her birth father when she was a young child. One day, her adoptive dad was preaching and said from the pulpit what so many have said throughout the ages: *We must forgive everyone everything.* Jennifer, sitting there in the front row, in her twelve-year-old wisdom, shook her head back and forth. No.

If you had been there, known her history, and seen her clinging to her truth despite the biblically supported, authoritative words of her minister father, perhaps you would have been tempted to jump up, pump your fists, and shout, "Way to go, Jenny!" Jennifer had the moxie to trust her own truth, despite the capital T "Truth" that was spoken with the best of intentions from the pulpit. Much to their credit, both her adoptive father and mother supported and honored Jennifer in her refusal to forgive the sexual abuse she had suffered.

Many others, however, have abandoned their personal truth and tried to live up to religious "truths" that have been fed to or forced on them, which may not have worked in the past, or if they did, might not work for them now. One can only imagine how many have tried to forgive at times and found no peace or relief but instead have suffered a heightened sense of anxiety or guilt, because some myopic and letter-bound religious leaders have stressed, even insisted, that they forgive at all costs and in all situations.

When a person "fails" to forgive, the model *of* forgiving is seldom if ever questioned; it's just assumed to be *the one and only way* for each and every person to recover from each and every type of hurt, from the pettiest to the most monstrous. Instead, the individual who can't or won't forgive is sometimes covertly or overtly blamed by authority figures or by pious members of a congregation or community for her lack of faith in God or in "the power of prayer" to help her forgive, or for her stubborn and "sinful" unwillingness to forgive. Sadly, it is not atypical for the dis-abled or un-able forgiver to eventually climb aboard the judgmental bandwagon and quietly denounce herself for her unwillingness or inability to forgive.

If it is tragically ironic and lamentable that so many people carry heavy religious baggage that hinders forgiving—and much more importantly, healing—it is even more heartbreaking that families, who are supposed to be the foundational source of love and support as a child grows, are often the origin of deep wounds that countless individuals cannot or will not forgive. Sometimes family dysfunction incorporates religion, as was the case in Jim's household.

Jim grew up in an unhealthy family system and was his father's scapegoat. Jim's father took the family to church every week and was as personable and sociable as could be—until he got home, that is. Then a different side emerged that was abusive and deeply scarring to Jim. Yet, Jim's father extolled forgiving and liked to talk about God's forgiveness and the human need to forgive each other in vague and general terms, while never apologizing for his abusive behavior or asking for Jim's forgiveness, or the rest of the family's forgiveness for that matter. Consequently, forgiveness has irreparably negative connotations for Jim. He often finds the very word repulsive, especially when he considers how carelessly it was, and is, bandied about. Consequently, he is at a loss as to how he can heal from his painful past. His therapist, like Heather's and so many other well-intentioned mental health care practitioners who aren't aware of viable alternatives, tells him that he *has* to forgive his father in order to be able to move on, which Jim has no intention whatsoever of doing.

Because so many carry burdensome baggage in their hurting hearts due to their experiences in a particular religious tradition, or tradition within a tradition (e.g., Baptist, Catholic, Lutheran, Methodist, non-denominational, etc., within the Christian tradition), forgiving has become an insurmountable obstacle rather than a path to and of healing. And no small number of individuals who grew up in quietly dysfunctional or overtly chaotic homes, even ones that may have looked quite normal to the casual observer, have discovered that forgiving is a virtually ruined word and option for them, which is what we will look at next.

Sometimes that which has been held to be
religiously true, regardless of how much unearned tenure
it has acquired over the years or centuries,
needs to take a backseat and be quiet for a change
so that the deeper truth of the person who has been hurt
can be heard and honored.

A Misused, Overused, or Ruined Word for Many

How sad that the very word "forgiveness" is all but ruined for many, especially since it is supposed to be *the* way, the *only* way, the *best* way to get over our hurts. How on earth did this huge gap between what forgiving is supposed to do for us and what it actually does–or too many times does *not* do for us–happen? While it is beyond the scope of this book to go into a detailed analysis, a couple of brief observations can be made.

To start, the word has been frequently misused, most often unintentionally rather than deliberately. A case in point is the saying "forgive and forget," which you may have heard on more than one occasion. It is also something that more than a few have taken to heart. Some believe that if you truly forgive you *should* forget, and if you aren't forgetting it's because you are resenting and remembering rather than forgiving and forgetting. Yet, paradoxically, you can't *try* to forget anything, for in the very attempt to do so you are actually keeping whatever it is you want to discard from your memory alive and well.[10]

This is an example of how the misuse of the word "forgive," unintentional though it may be, can do real harm to some individuals who try to forgive but end up suffering a sense of guilt or inadequacy because they haven't forgotten. What's more, even those of us who don't equate forgiving with forgetting may be surprised that this saying has taken up unauthorized residence in our heart or subconscious mind as well. Then, when the memory of an old hurt surfaces and upsets us again, we may feel guilty or question the quality of our prior efforts to forgive because at some irrational level of our being we, too, had hoped that forgiving would result in forgetting.

---

10. There's even a popular book called *Forgive and Forget*. However, the late author of this fine book, Lewis Smedes, does not suggest that to forgive means to forget. More accurately, he wants his readers to know that if they forgive they will remember the hurt differently, with less pain associated with it.

A more egregious case of misuse is evident in the following example. A minister in a non-denominational church stood up one Sunday and said to his congregation, "If a man comes home drunk one night and forces his wife to have sex with him against her will, she has no biblical grounds for divorcing him." What?! What could his point possibly be? Perhaps a comment like this might be something we could all shake our heads at in dismay if it were offered in the Dark Ages by some ignorant, mean-spirited soul, but because it was said in the twenty-first century by an allegedly educated pastor, we are left dumbfounded. Yes, it's a blatant example of how forgiving is misused, but it's not as rare as you might like to believe. And, as this case graphically demonstrates, women have been victimized by the misuse of forgiveness more so than men.[11]

Regarding the overuse of the word and concept of forgiveness, the fact that most people are not aware that healthy alternatives to forgiving even *exist* not only suggests that forgiveness has been overused, but exclusively used as well. Forgiveness, despite the fact that so many of us resist it or feel inept at it or fail at it, continues to be advocated as the *only* acceptable way to recover from being hurt. It is unlikely that many of us have ever been told that if we can't or don't want to forgive in a particular situation, we have nothing to feel bad or guilty or discouraged about because there are alternative strategies B, C, D, . . . and Z waiting in the wings to help us regain our peace and happiness.

So it seems to make complete sense that due to its misuse and overuse, the very word, concept, and practice of forgiveness is all but ruined for a significant number of people who are hurting. It literally causes some to bristle in anger when it is suggested that they need to forgive in order to move on, while for others it shuts them down entirely into a depressive-like state as their hope to get beyond a particular hurt is crushed yet again by this uncreative, unexamined, worn-out suggestion. Rather than always being an empowering and

---

11. We will explore this in more detail in the next section, "A Double Standard for Women."

liberating word and practice, it can quite often be a disempowering and imprisoning one. Fortunately, for those who find the word and concept of forgiving to be in ruins, there are viable alternatives that are very empowering and liberating, which we identify in Chapter Four.

Regarding the overuse of the word and concept of
forgiveness, the fact that most people are not aware
that healthy alternatives to forgiving even *exist* not
only suggests that forgiveness has been overused, but
exclusively used as well.

A Double Standard for Women

Remember Heather from the Introduction, and how her therapist told her that she needed to forgive her unfaithful ex-husband so that she could sit with him at their son's high school graduation? We can't help but wonder what kind of therapeutic advice her former husband would have received if Heather had been the unfaithful party throughout their twenty-year marriage. Would he have been told that he needed to forgive Heather so that he could sit with her at their son's graduation, even though Heather's new boyfriend might be sitting on the other side of her? Or would he have been encouraged to forgive but not necessarily sit with her? Or, because women's infidelity is somehow more unacceptable than men's, would forgiving have been stressed at all? Perhaps his therapist would have focused more on how Heather's unfaithful behavior had hurt him so deeply, and not been in such a hurry to have him get over his pain by forgiving. Or maybe the topic of forgiveness wouldn't have come up at all, and the therapist would have focused on what he needed to do now so that he could recover and move on in life. Somehow, we both have difficulty imagining that he would have been treated and advised in the same manner as Heather.

As numerous women's shelters can attest to, countless women have been advised, sometimes even by their religious leaders or counselors, to forgive verbal or physical abuse or completely unacceptable behavior because "he's under a lot of stress right now" or "he doesn't mean to hit you or put you down, so just be patient with him" or "he's really sorry, so you need to give him another chance" or "God would want you to forgive." Consequently, a steady flow of women end up at these shelters because they did indeed give their husbands or boyfriends another chance, many times "in the name of forgiveness" *and at great personal cost to themselves*. Unfortunately, some of the ones who didn't make it to the shelters didn't make it at all. While others, who have no need to go to a shelter, may be losing their daily-life's-energy and potential to live a happier and more fulfilling life because the types of hurts they are enduring and expected to forgive are ones that men would not. This is not to suggest that women don't hurt men, because they do. The point is that women, by and large, have been expected and encouraged to forgive when they have been hurt, whereas men have not, or at least not to the same degree.

Again, it takes quite a stretch of the imagination to picture a man being told by most therapists or religious leaders that "she's under a lot of stress right now" or "she doesn't mean to hit you or put you down, so just be patient with her" or "she's really sorry, so why don't you give her another chance." And maybe even the notion that God would want him to forgive might not be said to a man, even though it is often said so easily and automatically to women.

Because the majority of religious leaders and therapists have been men, understanding the impact of serious hurts or repetitive "minor" hurts from the perspective of women is something that a significant number haven't been capable of doing, or even pastorally or clinically interested in doing. Furthermore, even though there are many more female religious leaders and therapists these days, that doesn't mean that all of them are automatically or inherently sensitive to the forgiveness double standard. Many of these professionals, like many women in a variety of other professions and roles, are among the fiercest gatekeepers of the male-established status quo. A significant number of female therapists and religious leaders subscribe to the unexamined notion that one must forgive and that women, especially, should forgive. Heather's first therapist, by the way, was a woman.

Because it seems that women are, generally speaking, more relationally oriented and skilled than men, perhaps it was inevitable that they would be asked or expected to forgive in situations in which most men would not. Plus, because men tend to be physically stronger and more prone to violence, and because many women who have children are at least somewhat financially dependent upon men, perhaps forgiving, even unhealthy forgiving, served as a survival mechanism of some sort, both for themselves and their children.

But as the statistics on violence against women – and children – bear out, forgiving is not the way to survive at all when there is a risk of physical harm; in fact, it may put at-risk women in even greater danger. And for all the women who do not live with an overt fear of violence in their relationships, forgiving can sometimes put their human potentiality at risk and keep them from living as fully and vibrantly as they otherwise might.

As numerous women's shelters can attest to,
countless women have been advised, sometimes even by
their religious leaders or counselors, to forgive
verbal or physical abuse or completely unacceptable
behavior because "he's under a lot of stress right now"
or "he doesn't mean to hit you or put you down,
so just be patient with him" or "he's really sorry,
so you need to give him another chance" or
"God would want you to forgive."

Impossible Litmus Tests of "True" Forgiveness

A majority of us have somehow picked up the message that if we have truly forgiven we can expect to experience one or more of the following:

1. We will literally forget the hurt, as forgiving will remove it from our memory in a "forgive and forget" manner.

2. We will no longer have any painful thoughts and feelings associated with the hurt, even if the memory of it just pops into our mind without us deliberately recalling it.

3. We will have positive and warm thoughts and feelings, or at the very least neutral ones, about the person who hurt us, rather than any negative or upsetting ones, even if the painful memory should come to mind again at some point in the future.

Now perhaps most of us can't recall anyone in particular teaching us to have these forgiveness expectations, but because so many of us do believe that we should experience at least one of the aforementioned outcomes if we have truly forgiven, these messages have indeed established deep personal and collective roots within us, with or without our conscious permission. For our purposes, it doesn't really matter how any of us may have come to believe one or more of the above; what is relevant is whether or not these beliefs or expectations are valid litmus tests or signs that point to true forgiveness. And as you might safely predict by now, neither one of us believes they are. So let's take them one by one.

Regarding the first litmus test, "forgive and forget," as acknowledged in the previous section, even though you might not equate forgiving with forgetting on a conscious intellectual level, as in "I believe that to forgive means to forget," your heart or subconscious mind may indeed hold it to be true at some level of your being, at least to some degree. While it would be nice to think that the beliefs we have all consciously chosen to adopt are the sole guiding forces in our lives, it is somewhat disconcerting to discover that unapproved beliefs, irrational and contradictory though they may be, are circulating in our heart and subconscious in a far from benign manner, adding their input to the mix.

For instance, a person who has a litany of accomplishments and appears to be outwardly confident may in fact be constantly struggling with powerful doubts about herself and her abilities deep in her heart or at a subconscious level. Teresa was just such a person. She had recently been promoted to director of sales at the company where she worked. She had worked very hard to achieve this position, but was also aware that some did not support the decision of her boss and mentor. Teresa even questioned herself as to whether she was really that competent, or just lucky. Although she had an accomplished sales record, she wondered if she was simply in the right place at the right time. But by being aware of what was going on at the very core of her being, though it made no sense in light of all the evidence pointing to her success, she chose to act in a confident manner rather than yield to the subconscious power of self-doubt. This enabled her to be successful in her new, well-deserved position.

Our point regarding forgiving is that even though you might not link forgiving with forgetting in a conscious manner, it may be circulating around inside you nonetheless, and is, consequently, something to be aware of when striving to forgive. Otherwise, you might fall under its powerful spell and wrongly think that because you haven't forgotten the hurt then you haven't really forgiven, which may not be the case at all.

Regarding the second expectation that forgiving will free you from ever having painful or upsetting thoughts and feelings about a specific hurt or person who hurt you, this notion may be even more powerful and prevalent than the first one. Somehow, many have come to expect, or at least to hope, that forgiving will remove *all* of the pain associated with how they were hurt. However, this is not a true litmus test of authentic forgiveness, because it isn't always possible. So how can that which isn't always possible be a true sign of forgiveness? Consider the diagram below.

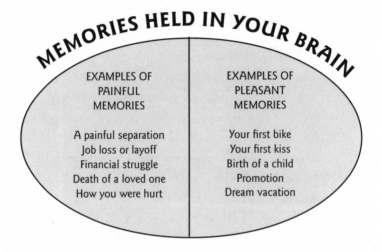

All of the painful experiences you have had in life as well as the subsequent painful memories associated with them are portrayed as being in the part of your brain labeled "Painful Memories" (see the examples on the left side of the above diagram, especially the last one, "How you were hurt"). And all of the pleasant experiences you have had in life, which produced pleasant memories, are characterized as being in the part of your brain labeled "Pleasant Memories" (see the examples on the right side of the diagram).

This is not to say that all of your painful memories are always causing you pain or that all of your pleasant memories are always resulting in you feeling joy, because it is only possible to focus on one memory at a time. Nor does it mean that a painful experience, such as a separation or divorce, did not turn out to be the best thing that ever happened to you. Perhaps you are much happier being alone than with your former spouse, partner, or significant other. Or maybe you are now enjoying a much healthier and more satisfying relationship with someone you would never have met if your previous relationship had not come to a painful end. But because the divorce or separation process itself was painful and did hurt at the time, it will always be under the category of "Painful Memories." Similarly, anything that you would include in the "Pleasant Memories" category will always be a pleasant memory. Even if your children or grandchildren have resulted in you having a few more gray hairs than planned, the happy moments you have had with them will always be a pleasant memory.

So regarding a specific hurt, when it is recalled, it's not always possible to expect to be free of *all* painful thoughts and feelings. It was painful at the time, and recalling how it hurt back then, whether the original wound occurred five days or five decades ago, may be painful now, which leads to the third expectation, that "true" forgiveness will enable the person who was hurt to think and feel warmly and positively, or at the very least, neutrally, about their offender.

Tom had his house broken into twice. During the second break-in, the thieves took everything–absolutely everything–he owned, including the fish. And even though Tom is a highly evolved, spiritually oriented, respectful human being, when he recalls these break-ins that took place more than twenty years ago, especially the second one, he is once again filled with rage and hatred. He even has reawakened urges to do some serious physical harm to those who violated the sanctity of his home.

However, because he has chosen to move on and live in a positive and healthy manner, these painful memories, for the most part, tend to rest quietly in his memory bank. But when they do rise up to conscious awareness from time to time, he temporarily suffers intensely upsetting thoughts and feelings all over again. He, as is true for most of us, cannot generate warm and positive thoughts and feelings, or even neutral ones, about and toward those who have caused him to suffer that which is not a warm and positive or neutral experience in his life. So this litmus test not only sets us up to fail at what has been deemed "true forgiveness," it also causes many to feel guilt or to suffer a sense of spiritual defectiveness for simply being a human being, for simply feeling upset about what was, and always will be, upsetting.

What Tom has learned to do, and what you may have learned to do as well, or can begin to learn if you haven't, is to become more skilled at managing the power that these memories have over you when they resurface, which is what this book is about. Over time, and as you try some of the healthy alternatives to forgiving, you can reduce the frequency and duration, and better manage the intensity, of your painful memories so that they do not rob you of your ability to experience peace and happiness in the present moment. No, they will never cross over into the "Pleasant Memories" side of your brain, but you can learn how to move on and live fully and happily, despite the fact that memories of some of your hurts will come to your conscious awareness from time to time, resulting in you feeling upset all over again.

Somehow, many have come to expect,
or at least to hope,
that forgiving will remove *all* of the pain
associated with how they were hurt.
However, this is not a true litmus test
of authentic forgiveness,
because it isn't always possible.

What about Justice and Accountability?

If there is one factor that more than any other causes millions of people to dig in their internal heels and resist forgiving like the plague, even though forgiving is supposed to be *the* way to get beyond a particular hurt, it is its perceived unfairness. Consider for a moment that you have been hurt by someone else. Forgiving implies that your healing will occur as you direct your attention toward your offender in a positive manner, even though you were the one who was hurt in a negative manner. Not exactly fair. Not always doable.

If someone deliberately kicks you in the shin, it would be ridiculous to be concerned about the condition of this person's foot rather than attend to your own bruised shin, but that's what forgiving feels like for many. Rather than caring for yourself in the aftermath of being hurt, you are encouraged to focus your attention on your offender by extending goodwill or forgiveness toward this person. This is true even if the individual who hurt you fails to apologize or refuses to get you an ice pack or, worse, lines up to kick you again.

Many have come to believe that they are just supposed to forgive, even if the other person takes no ownership or responsibility for how they hurt them and fails to do anything to repair the harm. While in the Jewish tradition a person is not obliged to forgive unless the offender has expressed genuine remorse to the injured person, repaired the harm to whatever extent is possible, and is sincere about changing their ways, those who have been most deeply influenced by the Christian and Buddhist traditions have been taught that they are just supposed to forgive or practice loving-kindness, even if justice or accountability is not forthcoming.

Though there may be something noble and even self-liberating about extending unconditional forgiveness and compassion toward our offender, especially if this person is unable or unwilling to take responsibility for their actions, in many cases it doesn't seem very fair or doable for a substantial number of us. Again, we can only

35

speak knowledgeably about the Christian tradition, while assuming that at least some Buddhists – or Christian-Buddhists or Buddhist-Christians – because they are human beings who appreciate fairness like everyone else, also struggle with forgiving without first seeking justice and accountability.

On the flip side, one could argue that to forgive unconditionally, without holding your offender accountable, or at least trying to, is not particularly noble at all. Why? Because it does not help your offender to grow as a human being, and growth often takes place when a person owns up to their wrong and hurtful behavior and tries to ease the suffering they have caused another person. What's more, if you don't hold your offender accountable, it can even stifle your own growth. How? Maybe you, like so many, fear conflict so much that you would prefer to try to forgive your offender from afar in an indirect manner rather than tell this person directly how they hurt you and what you need from them to make it right, or at least better. And as is true of most avoidance-motivated, backdoor, escapist routes, it doesn't tend to lead to a true path of liberation, enabling you to go on with your life. Instead, you may find yourself circling around right back to where you started from: suffering a host of unresolved painful thoughts and feelings about this person, all because you have tried to forgive without sticking up for yourself and saying what needs to be said.

Even when either one of us hurts another person, and we both do, we don't want this individual to forgive us unless we own up to our hurtful behavior and try to make it up to them. If we are not aware that we hurt someone, or if we are aware but hesitate to come directly to this person, then we want this person to come to either of us and confront us directly.

Though the majority of us don't like confrontation and conflict, we can learn to manage our fear of it, because it is potentially beneficial for both parties involved, the person who was hurt and the person who did the hurting. What most people tend to fear about confrontation and conflict is losing control, or getting drawn into some type of emotional escalation. And that could happen.

But with continued practice, along with the acquisition of some new skills, it is possible to learn how to respectfully confront and be confronted in a manner that leaves all of the affected parties at least somewhat intact rather than completely fragmented.

Of course, there are many times and situations in which the other person does not have the prerequisite adult skills or humanity that is needed in order to seek justice or accountability. In other words, it is simply not safe to do so, or the risk-reward ratio is not sufficiently weighted on the reward side of the equation to warrant taking the risk. At such times, it can be especially valuable to your potential healing to resign yourself to the fact that you are not going to get any justice or accountability from your offender. If that is the case, then offering unconditional forgiveness may indeed be both noble and the best way for you to heal.

Or you might decide that you still need – not only want, but need – justice and accountability in order to forgive, despite your offender's inability or unwillingness to offer it. And if that is the case, then it makes no sense to try to forgive, because you have decided that your forgiveness is contingent, or conditional, rather than unconditional, which is also a very noble and appropriate choice, *because it is right for you*. Then, it would make much more sense to explore one of the alternative strategies to forgiving so that you can reclaim your personal power to be happy and at peace again, even though your offender has failed to step up to the adult plate of justice and accountability. You can't control the other person's response; you can only control yours. Thus, the most creative and healing choice may very well be to move on with your life in some way without forgiving.

While we would both prefer to reconcile with people when we have had some type of falling-out or misunderstanding or hurt, or at least agree to part ways on respectful terms, we are well aware that doing so isn't always possible due to the other person's unwillingness or lack of skills. This is not to imply that either of us has reached the pinnacle of human and spiritual evolvement, because we are both works in progress like everyone else. It's simply a recognition that we have come to trust our ability to read other people, and when it doesn't feel safe or right or potentially fruitful to seek justice and accountability, we don't try to do so. At such times, we choose to employ an alternative healing strategy, so that we do not unwittingly give our personal power away to this person because we continue to cling to the unexamined myth that forgiving is the only way to recover, and yet at the same time we can't or won't forgive. A catch-22 if there ever was one.

Many have come to believe that they are just supposed to forgive, even if the other person takes no ownership or responsibility for how they hurt them and fails to do anything to repair the harm.

～ 2 ～

Six Common Reasons to Set Aside or Forget Forgiving – at Least Temporarily

In addition to the fact that most of us have never been told that we have nothing to worry about if we can't or won't forgive because there are alternative ways to recover our inner peace and happiness, it is also unlikely that we've ever been encouraged to hold off on forgiving or set it aside for a while after being hurt. How wonderful and empowering it might have been if someone, anyone – a parent, trustworthy friend, wise coworker, religious leader, or therapist – had ever said something like the following to you:

> *Don't be in a hurry to forgive. In fact, if I may, I'd like to suggest that you act as if forgiving doesn't exist and that you've never even heard of it. You can always revisit the*

*possibility of forgiving later on if you'd like, but for now don't even **think** about forgiving the person who hurt you. Your first job is to be very tender and gentle with yourself, because **you** are the one who has been hurt. I invite you to focus exclusively on yourself and on what you need in order to begin to heal. Although you are very upset right now, and it is no fun to feel as angry and outraged as you do, I am here with you and for you. I promise that I won't try to fix you, and your pain won't make me go away. Do you want to tell me what happened?*

But no, many people, including a fair number of mental health care professionals and clergy, are more than a bit uncomfortable when someone is upset and angry as a result of being hurt. The tendency is to rush the process—sometimes even avoid the process altogether—and do whatever it takes to get, or talk, the hurting person out of their pain as quickly as possible. The would-be helper may not like being around someone who is so angry, so hurt, so filled with bitterness. In fact, this person's anger, especially if it is not softened or toned down within a reasonable number of sessions, could even be a threat to the helper's sense of competency. Consequently, it is not uncommon to be counseled to forgive way too early after being hurt. Or an individual may tell herself that she must forgive, and do so as quickly as possible, because what she is thinking and feeling about her offender is wrong, not spiritual, unladylike, or what have you. Whether from within or without, or both, the message remains crystal clear: hurry and forgive in order to expel or silence these "ugly" thoughts and feelings, because other people simply don't want to be around someone who is so visually, vocally, and perhaps even vociferously upset.

But as many of us have discovered through our own personal experience, it's not quite so easy to get rid of these painful thoughts and feelings, even by forgiving. And if there's ever a time when forgiving seems almost predestined to fail completely, it is when there is a rush to forgive in order to squelch or expel upsetting thoughts and feelings.

It's analogous to suffering a severe ankle sprain. If you try to go back to your normal routine of walking a mile or two each day or playing eighteen holes of golf or going to your aerobics or yoga class without first allowing for some convalescence and rehabilitation time, you are setting yourself up to further aggravate your ankle. Your rush to get back to your regular, pre-injury activities actually postpones your healing.

The same is true of forgiving. If you rush to forgive, your painful thoughts and feelings are not likely to go away; in fact, personified, they will interpret it as an invitation to stay, because they have yet to be acknowledged and validated. And your hope to recover the peace and happiness you were enjoying before you were hurt tends to get delayed, while your potential to heal more deeply and completely gets pushed further and further into the future, all because you attempt to circumvent painful thoughts and feelings by premature forgiving. We both know, because we, too, have tried in vain to forgive too quickly many times in our lives.

In this chapter, we will be exploring six common reasons to set aside or forget forgiving, at least temporarily. There are likely many others reasons, and you may very well have your own, so please keep in mind that these six are *not* the only ones to consider when discerning whether to put forgiveness on hold for a while. Always trust yourself rather than any outside authority or resource, including us.

The point we want to make is that rushing to forgive, as with rushing in general, tends to be less effective than when you choose a more deliberate and well-planned response. While it's upsetting to have lost your inner peace in the aftermath of being hurt, and it is certainly understandable that you want to do whatever it takes to become un-upset as quickly as possible, there is no instant solution or magic potion to spare you from suffering the painful thoughts

and feelings you might wish to banish forever. You may simply need to table forgiveness for a while and pick it up again later on. By not rushing to forgive, no matter how much internal or external pressure there may be to do so, you might come to the realization that an alternative approach will work better for you.

As many of us have discovered through our own personal experience, it's not quite so easy to get rid of . . . painful thoughts and feelings, even by forgiving. And if there's ever a time when forgiving seems almost predestined to fail completely, it is when there is a rush to forgive in order to squelch or expel upsetting thoughts and feelings.

Troubling Feelings Such as Anger, Hatred, and Rage Are Overwhelming You

Steve, like many of us, grew up in an era in which his family, along with most of society, did not have ready access to helpful information and skills with which to handle emotional pain. Since this information abounds today, he has read several books and attended workshops on how to cope more effectively with painful feelings. He is trying mightily – perhaps even too hard at times – to be okay with the upsetting emotions that are a part of life, especially when he has been hurt. But because these emotions were so taboo and poorly managed in his family system during his formative years, he wonders if he will ever be able to make peace with them.

While Steve now believes on an intellectual level that these emotions are acceptable, at least when *he* is not under their influence and someone else is, at a much deeper heart or subconscious level they are still unacceptable, wrong, and to be gotten rid of as quickly as possible when he is the one who is feeling them. Not only is the head-heart dilemma from Chapter One at work here, so is a reverse double standard that says it is okay for other people to be human and to experience these normal human emotions, but Steve must be something other than human, so it is definitely not okay for him. We suspect that he is far from alone in wishing to be exempt from painful emotions that are inherent to the human condition.

During your earliest years, you, like many of us, may have been taught that some emotions are "bad" or wrong or to be suppressed and avoided at all costs. Some of us even had these so-called negative emotions silenced and shamed out of us whenever they surfaced in the presence of our parents, caretakers, or teachers. Consequently, millions learned at a young and impressionable age that these emotions were unacceptable, and if this is what *you* learned during your childhood, it can truly be an epic-like undertaking to begin to accept, feel, and let these emotions be, rather than continue to reject, deny, and resist them, even after suffering some type of hurt.

No matter how wrong your heart or subconscious mind might deem these types of emotions to be, your conscious mind needs to counter this untruth and begin, or continue, to give you permission to accept and feel them. Because of Steve's earliest experiences in life, it is likely that his struggles to accept what is completely normal are going to continue for a while. He will need to repeatedly put his conscious mind in charge, despite the fact that his heart or subconscious mind might be kicking and screaming every step of the way: *These feelings are bad, wrong, unacceptable! Get rid of them! Help! I'm dying!*

The fact is that when any of us has been hurt, it is normal to feel anger, hatred, or rage, as well as other painful emotions. Once again, no matter how opposed to them you may be at the core of your being, they are inevitable when you have been hurt or wronged. None of us has to like or embrace painful emotions; maybe all that we can do at times is simply endure their upsetting presence and hang on without lashing out at others or lashing inwardly at ourselves until they pass—which they always do, but usually not as quickly as we would like.

What both of us as well as countless others have learned along the way is that trying to forgive in an attempt to get rid of these emotions as quickly as possible simply doesn't tend to work. If it did, we would advocate quick forgiving or any other technique that could free you in short order from their power. But as human beings, we need to feel them or endure them, and at the same time give ourselves conscious permission to set aside or "forget" forgiving for a while, because their very presence indicates that we are not ready to forgive.

If you consider being angry or upset in other situations in life, you would probably think it wise if that person were to take some time to collect themselves and regain their composure before proceeding with whatever task is in front of them. If your surgeon, for example, was really upset about something, you would probably want him to calm down a bit before operating on you. Or if you had a friend who was a business owner and she had an important decision to make, but she was feeling angry and frustrated about something, you might encourage her to buy some time rather than make an emotionally-based decision. And those of us who are parents learn by trial and error the importance of regaining our emotional equilibrium rather than setting reactionary, unenforceable consequences (e.g., "You're grounded for the rest of your life!"). As these examples illustrate, it is usually wise to delay any important action when feeling emotionally upset. Similarly, when painful emotions such as anger, hatred, and rage are at their most intense because of how you were hurt, it may be wise to delay or postpone any attempts to forgive.

As you set forgiving aside for a while and feel and accept your emotional pain, you will be better able to forgive – or employ an alternative healing strategy – in the future, all because you honored and abided by your emotional truth today, rather than trying to escape it by premature forgiving. In Chapter Six, we will offer a number of suggestions as to how you can better manage upsetting emotions, so that you do not feel so powerless, and perhaps overwhelmed, in their presence.

The fact is that when any of us has been hurt, it is normal to feel anger, hatred, or rage, as well as other painful emotions. Once again, no matter how opposed to them you may be at the core of your being, they are inevitable when you have been hurt or wronged.

Painful Memories, Vindictive Urges, or Arguments Are Upsetting You

The typical remedy for those times when any of us is experiencing a painful memory, vindictive urge, or argument–both real and imagined–with our offender has been to forgive. Yet this remedy doesn't tend to work very well precisely *when* we are upset. It is akin to suggesting that someone who is very angry go to sleep in order to calm down. Yet falling asleep is about the last thing that can be done at the height of emotional turmoil.

When the remedy of forgiving, or an alternative strategy, is more likely to be effective is *after* a healthy measure of serenity and the capacity to think clearly has been regained. Being upset, by its very nature, means that a person's emotional equilibrium is for the most part gone, replaced by constricted and cloudy thinking. For this reason, it seems to make more sense to hold off on forgiving for a while rather than try to forgive when caught in the throes of a painful memory, vindictive fantasy, or argument with an offender.

Painful memories seem to have a life of their own. A hurt that is decades old and that hasn't been that big a deal over the years can come to conscious awareness at the oddest times out of nowhere and shatter the tranquility you were enjoying just a moment ago. While some painful memories do indeed die, if for no other reason than the fact that other painful memories have replaced them or because most of us have simply forgotten them as the years have passed, other painful memories seem destined to accompany us until our final breath.

Sheri, who is well into her fifties, can recall a relatively minor hurt she experienced when she was about eleven years old. She was walking home from school with Kate, who lived just a few houses down the street from her, when Kate broke the silence and said to her out of the blue, "You're ugly." While this comment hurt at the time, it didn't appear to have any lasting effect on Sheri. However, this memory resurfaces about once every year or so, and is accompanied by some surprisingly intense feelings of anger. Why does this particular memory crop up every year for Sheri when other hurts, perhaps even more substantive ones, don't? Neither one of us knows the answer, but it seems that most people, like Sheri, do indeed have certain painful memories of hurts, both large and small, that revisit them on a seemingly random, periodic, or regular basis.

Of course, it is normal to have some reawakened anger and vindictive urges when a painful memory comes to mind. Even regarding the "You're ugly" comment above, Sheri has fantasized all sorts of responses over these past decades, ranging from "Thanks for sharing" to swearing. The good news is that she is not alone in having vengeful fantasies about something relatively inconsequential that happened long ago, and neither are you.

What may lead many of us to question our own sanity, or at least raise doubts as to whether or not we fall within the parameters of normal human behavior, are those times when we are having a full-blown argument or conversation with our offender in the not-so-silent silence of our mind. But maybe the normalcy of those who *haven't* had such arguments or conversations with phantom opponents is more subject to debate.

And then, of course, some of us have real arguments with people who have hurt us in the past, simply because we must continue to interact with these individuals at work or in our families or in some other aspect of our lives. For example, a significant number of those who are divorced or separated need to have some contact with their "Ex" in order to work out the details of raising their children in two different homes. Because there is often a long and deep history of hurt, it is not at all uncommon for some to find themselves having real arguments with this person. Even if you would like to communicate in a mutually respectful manner, your "Ex" may not have a similar desire – or the skills – to do so. Your former spouse may actually enjoy upsetting you, and it's oh-so-easy to take the bait when it's dangling there right in front of you. Of course, once the verbal sparring begins and the low road is embarked upon, it is almost inevitable that even the most centered person's best intentions can go out the proverbial window, as the temptation to revert to an almost knuckle-dragging stage of human interaction may take over.

The thrust of all this is to strongly suggest that you hold off on forgiving when painful memories are plaguing you, a vengeful urge is sweeping through you, or you are having a real or imagined argument with your offender. Let the memory or urge or fantasized argument play itself out, for it will pass in due course. If you are caught in the midst of a real argument with the other person, try to remove yourself from the situation, so that it doesn't take a deeper toll on you than it already has. Just cut your losses, and if at all possible, walk away or hang up the phone.

If you try to forgive when you are upset, you may be setting yourself up for plenty of frustration, for *it simply isn't the best time to forgive.* Set it aside for a while and redirect your energy toward doing something you have a much greater chance of being successful at: going for a walk, talking to a supportive friend, participating in something you enjoy (e.g., a hobby or activity), or completing a task that needs doing (e.g., shopping or paying a few bills).

Rather than chastising yourself because you can't forgive at such times, consider being very gentle with yourself instead, even – or especially – if you just lost your composure and got into a serenity-shattering, heated argument with your "Ex" or someone else who has hurt you. Allow the passage of time to come to your assistance and befriend you as the intensity of your upsetting thoughts and feelings begins to decrease. For now, forget forgiving and remember to take tender care of yourself by doing something kind or constructive for yourself in the same manner that you would so readily do for a friend if they were suffering in the same way that you are.

Painful memories seem to have a life of their own. A hurt
that is decades old and that hasn't been that big a deal
over the years can come to conscious awareness at the
oddest times out of nowhere and shatter the tranquility
you were enjoying just a moment ago.

You Were Hurt Quite Recently and Your Inner Peace Has Been Shattered

Most of us have experienced more than one occasion in which everything was going just fine and then someone says or does something that is highly upsetting or hurtful, which turns an enjoyable day upside down. If it happened at work, we may still be reeling and very angry on our commute home, because what had been a predominantly peaceful day has now become one in which a torrent of upsetting thoughts and feelings are dominating our consciousness.

So in an attempt to regain our previously held sense of peace, which we desperately want back because everything was just fine a short time ago, some of us try to forgive. We may think that if we can only get ourselves to forgive this person or "consider the source" or pray for this individual or practice loving-kindness, we can quickly get over the hurt and recapture our tranquility. But alas, it doesn't tend to work that way, all because the hurt is so very fresh and some passage of time still needs to take place. It doesn't matter if that which hurt or upset us was relatively minor, it still hurts. And as you'll recall, even though paper cuts and minor burns are also relatively insignificant in comparison with more serious injuries, they still hurt enough to bother us for a period of time afterward.

So let's assume that you have suffered a recent hurt that is not too large in nature, for if it was, it would be so upsetting that you wouldn't even be *thinking* about the possibility of forgiving. But it's with the so-called "lesser" hurts, or even the midsized ones, that we want to forgive as quickly as possible, not so much because we are trying to live up to or out of our religious or spiritual beliefs, but because *we simply want our serenity back*. However, as is true with a minor cut or burn or a midsized sprained ankle, some time needs to pass before the majority of us can forgive or let go or employ some other strategy that will enable us to reclaim a healthy measure of our previously enjoyed peace and happiness. Take the case of John for example.

John teaches middle school and truly loves his profession. However, as is true for many teachers, the hardest part of teaching is not the students, not even the ones who act up, but a few of the parents. One parent in particular, who had gone through a bitter divorce and was using his children as a way to continue to hurt and aggravate his "Ex," targeted John for his perceived flaws as a teacher and his alleged mistreatment of one of his kids. Needless to say, this was upsetting to John, who is a very good teacher, respected by students and staff, and who readily admits his mistakes in the classroom and seeks to learn from them.

One Friday afternoon, this parent verbally harangued John, who went home for the weekend very angry and upset. Being a spiritual person, he tried to meditate and pray so that he could forgive this parent, regain his inner peace, and have a good weekend. But because his feelings of anger and fantasies of revenge were overpowering him, he quickly gave that up and tried to do some reframing instead. He told himself to "consider the source," as he dispassionately recognized that this parent was transferring his own unhappiness and failures as a husband and father on to John. While that was certainly true from an intellectual standpoint, his anger and vindictive urges were not quieting down as he had hoped. So as a last resort, he finally headed to the basement to take out his anger on his punching bag. (Normally his punching bag is simply a part of his aerobic exercise routine along with his stationary bike and treadmill, rather than something he uses to release his anger.) While working out on the punching bag, in his imagination he punched his attacker and said aloud, actually yelled aloud, what had been circulating in his mind since this unsought upsetting encounter had occurred earlier that afternoon.

John is neither a primitive nor violent person; he simply has his better and worse moments like the rest of us. In this case, because his attempts to meditate, forgive, pray, and intellectually reframe the situation weren't working, he knew that he had to own his true feelings and release the anger and outrage that were circulating in his heart and mind. He told us that because he finally got around to honoring and expressing the violence that he felt toward this particular parent who had violated him, he *was* able to begin to let it go and pray and intellectually reframe the situation more successfully.

John still went back and forth with his anger throughout the weekend, although he felt no need to punch the parent out again on his punching bag, and it took him about a month to pretty much "get over it." During this month, he recalled that hurts of this nature have typically taken him anywhere from one to four weeks to pretty much run their course, so he was right on track. And because the parent never took ownership of his behavior, John is not surprised or thrown when the memory of this hurt, along with some reawakened anger, resurfaces from time to time.

John's situation reminds all of us that it can be very wise to set aside or forget forgiving for a period of time, especially when recently hurt, for there is a process we must each go through that cannot be rushed, whether via our hurried attempts to forgive or an alternative healing strategy. Yes, most of us would like to regain our serenity as quickly as we can, but forgiving doesn't tend to work that fast in light of a fresh hurt, especially when our offender makes no effort to apologize or repair the harm that was done.

And while time does not necessarily heal all of your wounds, it certainly has a critical role to play in making them more manageable, even when so-called minor or petty or mid-range hurts leave you feeling very upset. Perhaps you won't need to take out your anger on a punching bag or pillow, but you might be wise to engage in some type of physical activity and say, or yell, what you really feel. Honoring your truth (i.e., your angry feelings and violent urges) and working with it as best you can tends to be more liberating in the long run – even if it requires you to do so in a less than pretty way – than does trying to recover from an ugly or intrusive hurt or incident in a dignified or "spiritual" manner when you are feeling neither dignified nor spiritual.

However you choose to respond to a recent hurt, you may find that giving yourself permission to set aside or forget forgiving for a while is an important, self-liberating step you can take on your journey toward recovering the peace and happiness you were enjoying prior to being hurt. Paradoxically, it is often true that if you don't rush to forgive but, instead, table it for a while so as to honor your upsetting thoughts and feelings, you can forgive or let go of the hurt more quickly than if you try to forgive while you are still "bleeding."

While time does not necessarily heal all of your wounds, it certainly has a critical role to play in making them more manageable, even when so-called minor or petty or mid-range hurts leave you feeling very upset.

A Significant Change or Transition in Your Life Is Pending or Underway

How many of us have said, perhaps on several occasions, "I hate change!" It wasn't too many years ago that changes took place much more slowly than they do today, and consequently we were more resistant to that which threatened the status quo. We could count on things to be relatively stable and enduring, and so when a change occurred, such as a new boss, it tended to rouse all sorts of fears in us, most of which proved to be either groundless or blown way out of proportion. However, all that was needed was for someone to say, "There's going to be a change around here," to throw most of us into a defensive, hyper-vigilant tizzy, as our fear-prone imaginations took flight.

But nowadays, things not only seem to change overnight, they appear to change *every* night, and there's really no time to protest or get too defensive about it. The relative stability that was once a part of society seems to be increasingly absent as family life, politics, religion, business, and society as a whole continue to undergo changes at such a rapid rate that many of us feel somewhat overwhelmed by it all. Factor in the relatively recent phenomenon of 24/7/365 "news" to the mix, and we may want to scream, "Time-out! Enough already!" In fact, recent studies have revealed that today we receive the same amount of stimulation in one day that previous generations got in a year, and that it is growing exponentially.

Because the stress and strain of the unique personal changes or transitions we each go through during the course of our lives can take such a persistent toll, it is a wonder that any of us keep our balance at all, even in the best of times. And it is absolutely no surprise that when an important personal change or transition is pending or underway, coping becomes more difficult and emotional equanimity more elusive.

When you are contemplating the possibility of making a significant change, or when you are in the midst of a major transition, it requires a great deal of energy and focus. It simply might not be the best time to try to forgive, because whatever is changing in your life, whether it is something pleasant (e.g., marriage, promotion, having a child, retirement) or unpleasant (e.g., divorce, separation, loss of a loved one, health challenge) or that which could go either way or be a mixture of both (e.g., starting therapy, moving, empty nest, new job or boss) is likely to throw you off to a certain degree. Your equilibrium is going to be shaken to a certain extent, because in a sense you have left – or are about to leave – your familiar terrain and are headed toward an unknown land through uncharted waters. And it's the time in the waters, between what was and what will be, that is often so challenging and disorienting.

Change, even positive change that you may have initiated or longed for, such as a job promotion or returning to school or moving into a bigger house or apartment, by its nature, leads you into something you have not experienced before. The stability and familiarity of what was, for instance your previous job, is gone, and the challenge and unfamiliarity of your new job awaits you. This is true even when choosing to leave a toxic relationship: the familiarity of it, though painful, is gone, and your life without that relationship is yet to be experienced.

Times of transition and major change are inherently destabilizing, and it is human nature to feel stressed and be prone to overreacting. Your center has shifted or is even temporarily absent, and forgiving, even in the best of circumstances (e.g., when your offender is accountable and is someone you want to continue being in relationship with, etc.), requires that you be centered and somewhat rooted. Once you have adjusted to the change and have reestablished some normalcy in your life, then you have a much better chance of forgiving in a way that leaves you feeling personally satisfied. In the interim, you may discover that by simply postponing any efforts to forgive, you will be able to devote all your attention to dealing with the transition, without the added weight of feeling guilty because you can't forgive at the same time. Complete your transition, and then devote your energy to forgiving, or to employing an alternative approach to deal with the particular hurt that is bothering you.

When you are contemplating the possibility of making a significant change, or when you are in the midst of a major transition, it requires a great deal of energy and focus. It simply might not be the best time to try to forgive, because whatever is changing in your life, whether it is something pleasant . . . or unpleasant . . . or that which could go either way or be a mixture of both . . . is likely to throw you off to a certain degree.

Fatigue – Mental, Emotional, Physical, or Spiritual – Has Drained You

It seems to make sense that if you are tired or fatigued, you might not have the necessary energy to forgive; therefore, it may be wise to take a "forgiveness sabbatical" in order to recharge your batteries and regain your vitality. Among the questions to consider as you assess your energy level are these:

1. Is the memory or repercussions of how you were hurt, though it may have happened long ago, draining you at this point in your life?

2. Are your attempts to forgive exhausting you?

3. Is your inability or unwillingness to forgive taking its toll, perhaps because you feel that you should forgive but you can't or don't want to?

4. Are there other factors in your life that are sapping your energy such as your responsibilities at home, at work, or your concerns about an aging parent, spouse, or partner?

5. Are you mentally, emotionally, physically, or spiritually spent or worn out?

Hurts are like earthquakes in that they have aftershocks. The hurt itself could be a very brief one-time event, such as a belittling comment that took all of ten seconds to upset you to the core of your being. Yet the effects or reverberations of this single putdown can stay with you for days, months, or even a lifetime in some cases. Of course, when degrading comments or behaviors are par for the course, then it would be quite surprising if you had any energy, much less willingness, to forgive at all.

It is not uncommon for many of us to discover that our attempts to forgive, which are supposed to set us free and restore our energy, can end up trapping us in a loss of personal vitality because we aren't always able to pull it off in a successful or satisfying manner. Nonetheless, we continue trying to bring about something that we either can't do or don't want to do, all because we have subscribed to the unexamined myth that forgiving is the only way to heal. This myth says that we won't be able to move on *until* and *unless* we forgive, which isn't true.

We can be like toddlers who become upset because the round peg (of forgiveness) does not fit into the square hole (of a particular hurt). As a competent and caring adult, you would likely step in and say to a frustrated toddler, whether she was your own child or someone else's, "Here, sweetie, let me show you where the round peg goes." Then you would simply guide her hand to the round hole where, after a bit of effort, she is able to deposit the round peg. If, however, she now picks up the square peg and tries to place it in the round hole due to over-generalizing, and becomes highly upset as a result, you would simply redirect her attention (e.g., read her a story or play with a ball). Perhaps in a couple more weeks, or in a month or two, she will be able to find the proper location for each of the various-shaped pegs with little or no frustration. For now, however, this task is beyond her capabilities.

When you have been hurt and your subsequent attempts to forgive are draining you, then you have to be – actually, you *get* to be – the wise adult who steps in and redirects your own attention (no other adult can do this for you, though they might offer encouragement). You can say to yourself something like, "My attempts to forgive are not working right now, so I am going to stop forcing it. I will set forgiving aside and take a break. I need to focus on taking care of myself. Then, when I feel more centered and relaxed, I will either renew my efforts to forgive or choose one of the other ways to address this particular hurt, so that I can move on with less pain and more freedom."

The consequence for not redirecting your energy elsewhere is not pleasant. You can sit there and spin around endlessly – and childishly – as you try to force what can't be forced and feel frustrated because you can't forgive, or guilty because you won't forgive, all because you cling to what you may have learned long ago: forgiving-is-the-only-way-to-heal-and-you-must-forgive-no-matter-what. Or you can unlearn this myth and learn a new truth: there are other ways to heal when you can't or won't forgive.

**TRYING TO
FORCE FORGIVENESS**

**GUILT BECAUSE YOU
WON'T FORGIVE OR
FRUSTRATION BECAUSE
YOU CAN'T FORGIVE**

You can also learn to "read" the times and seasons of your life. If your "reading" indicates that you have so much going on that you are already stretched to a breaking point, perhaps due to demands at home and work, you might forget forgiving for a while. It just might not be a prudent undertaking at this point in time. If so, then you can choose to take some "down time" in order to regain a semblance of balance. Perhaps a nap, a relaxing bath, lunch with a friend, a vacation, or a three-month "forgiveness moratorium" might renew you so that you can then try to forgive from a position of strength. Being more centered and refreshed will likely increase your chances of being able to forgive in a way that is satisfying for you. Or you might decide that an alternative approach is called for. In either case, you will be able to choose what is best for you at a time that is best for you.

It is not uncommon for many of us to discover that our
attempts to forgive, which are supposed to set us free
and restore our energy, can end up trapping us in a loss
of personal vitality because we aren't always able to pull
it off in a successful or satisfying manner.

Religious Beliefs and Old Expectations Are Getting in the Way

Carol was raised in the Christian tradition and has continued to attend church services on a weekly basis throughout her adult life. Her faith, a source of comfort, meaning, and community, is absolutely central to who she is. She generally feels good about herself and enjoys her identity as a Christian, though because she is somewhat quiet and respectful by nature, she is not the type to talk about her faith with others or try to convert them. She simply tries to be a good and loving person, and indeed is both – though she often feels like she is neither as good nor as loving as she should be.

One aspect of her faith that has troubled her over the years has to do with forgiveness. She feels a need to be forgiven by God, and by others, yet she is unable to forgive some of the hurts that she has suffered in life. What's even more disturbing is her honest realization that it's not just the bigger hurts, but a number of smaller ones as well, that she hasn't been able to forgive. In fact, she becomes most critical and harsh with herself because "some of the pettiest hurts imaginable" irk her so much. At times, intense feelings of pure hatred over something that "just isn't that big a deal" engulf her, which she feels very bad about because she knows that she is supposed to love her enemies and forgive them.

She has sought out the counsel of her pastor, who encouraged her to pray more. Taking his advice to heart, she has prayed more, even pleaded with God out of a sense of desperation to "take her bad thoughts and feelings away," but still hasn't been able to forgive as she thinks she should. Carol has also read several books on forgiveness, a couple by Christian authors, and has tried to implement their suggestions, with mixed results. At times, she feels like she has finally succeeded in forgiving, only to discover that upsetting thoughts and feelings about a person she thought she had forgiven come back, without her permission, to haunt and taunt her. Then her inner critical voice scolds her, "You are *such* a hypocrite. You want God to forgive you, yet you don't forgive others like he commands you to. How can you expect God to forgive you, especially when you can't forgive the littlest things?" Her guilt and sense of inadequacy is compounded by a faith crisis of sorts, as she fears the eternal consequences of disobeying God's command to "forgive as he has forgiven you."

Needless to say, Carol is far from alone. Many people, especially those who have been most influenced by the Christian tradition, have beliefs and expectations circulating in their hearts and minds that are impacting their ability to forgive. Many others of varying faiths and no particular faith are influenced by beliefs and expectations that have their origins in religion, family life, school, or society as a whole. Some common ones that make forgiving–and simply being a human being–more difficult include:

- ❧ Nice girls don't get angry.
- ❧ It is wrong and bad to have such emotions as anger and hatred.
- ❧ God just wants you to obey his command to forgive.
- ❧ If you are truly a person of faith or at all spiritual, then you should forgive.
- ❧ Turn the other cheek.
- ❧ Don't rock the boat.
- ❧ Don't make such a big deal out of your hurts. Look at how Jesus suffered!
- ❧ Having "bad" thoughts and feelings means you are bad.
- ❧ You should be over it by now.

> ◈ Just give it to God and forgive or let it go.
>
> ◈ Forgive and forget.
>
> ◈ Others have been hurt much worse than you, and they have forgiven. . . .

As adults, we have the capacity to take a long hard look at our beliefs, especially those that may be operating beneath our conscious awareness, and make some choices about them. If you are unable to forgive, you might need to set this whole forgiving thing aside for a while in order to examine the validity of some of the beliefs and expectations that you have about forgiveness, anger, and what it means to be a human being with a mixture of strengths and weaknesses.

For instance, if you believe that anger is bad and something to rid yourself of as soon as possible, your efforts to forgive are going to be hampered, because feeling angry is natural and normal when hurt. Or if you believe that God won't forgive you if you don't forgive others, you can ask yourself if that is truly how you think God is. Or, if you believe that you can't work a good twelve-step program and enjoy freedom from addiction or codependency unless you forgive, you can ask yourself if that is indeed true.

Beliefs are just that: beliefs. And expectations are just that: expectations. Both can be challenged and changed, because each of us has changed since we first took them on. Getting beyond our hurts, even some of the ones we might sheepishly acknowledge are candidates for "Petty Hurt of the Year" honors, is often challenging enough without having outdated, unattainable, or inhumane beliefs and expectations getting in the way.

If you are unable to forgive, you might need to set this
whole forgiving thing aside for a while
in order to examine the validity of some of the beliefs and
expectations that you have about forgiveness, anger, and
what it means to be a human being
with a mixture of strengths and weaknesses.

～ 3 ～

Eight Common Reasons to Set Aside or Forget Forgiving – Perhaps Permanently

Some of the hurts that many millions of people suffer in life may never be forgivable. Even if you hear about someone who was able to forgive a serious hurt that is similar in nature to one that you suffered, it doesn't mean that you have to do so as well. Nor does it mean that you are inferior or lacking in any way, certainly not spiritually, to this person who did forgive. It also doesn't mean that because you can't forgive, you can't heal.

Remember, each person's understanding of forgiveness differs, so this other person, in all likelihood, has a different understanding of forgiving than you do. What's more, you may not agree with their understanding at all. They may have decided that forgiving means "to let go of the hurt" or to "give it to God," even though their offender has refused to be accountable. You, on the other hand, may absolutely need accountability and justice in order to even *think* about the possibility of forgiving your offender. So in your case, you can't "let it go" or "give it to God," and you shouldn't, because to do so would require you to deny your truth and neglect your needs. This would not only be unfair to you, it would likely add to the pain you have already suffered as a result of the original unasked-for hurt.

The myth that is so prevalent, both in religious and spiritual circles and in society as a whole, is that if one person can forgive a huge hurt, then everyone should be able to. Strong proponents of "forgiveness as the only true way to heal" are sometimes quick to refer to cases in which certain individuals have forgiven those who have caused them or their loved ones to suffer the most catastrophic hurts imaginable. For instance, they will cite an example of how a family that was devastated by a murder found some degree of peace and healing by forgiving the perpetrator. Yet they fail to mention the many other families who have not been able, or not even interested in *trying,* to forgive the murderers of their loved ones. They also neglect to mention that when some family members are able to forgive and others within the same family are not, irreparable rifts can result. Not only has the murderer taken their loved one away, the surviving family members may split into two camps and become estranged from each other, as some favor and others oppose forgiving the perpetrator who has split all of their hearts wide open.

Yet the most ardent advocates of forgiveness continue to support their case by suggesting that because a relatively small number have forgiven the most serious hurts imaginable, *everyone* who has been devastated by such hurts should be able to do so as well. However, this doesn't make sense if we consider other areas of life. If one person can write a great novel, does that mean we all can—or should be able to? If one person can run a marathon in less than three hours does that mean we all can—or should be able to? If one person can climb a steep mountain, does that mean we all can—or should be able to?

For every person who does forgive such serious hurts as abuse, assault, exploitation, or murder of a beloved family member – again, as this individual understands forgiving – there are probably at least nine who can't or won't. Instead of exploring alternative ways to heal with the nine who are left behind, these countless individuals are indeed left behind by advocates of the forgiveness myth.

In this chapter, we are going to take a look at eight types of hurts that may be outside the range of most people's ability to forgive, or even their desire to do so. This is not intended to be an exclusive or exhaustive list; rather, these are but a handful of the common reasons to set aside forgiving, perhaps on a permanent basis.

You are the sole authority when it comes to deciding whether or not to forgive. What's more, you can certainly choose not to forgive hurts of a substantially less serious nature than the ones explored in this chapter. You are also the only one who knows how deeply a hurt has affected you. Even if your offender offered an apology, repaired the damage to the fullest extent possible, and met all seven of the forgiveness criteria that we cited in our introductory comments to Chapter One, as well as any other stipulations you might have, you can still choose *not* to forgive. Once again, the goal is to heal and move on as best you can, not necessarily to forgive. Healing may require you to close the door of forgiveness on a permanent basis, so that you can open up another door and discover your own unique way to recover and rebuild your life.

The myth that is so prevalent, both in religious and spiritual circles and in society as a whole, is that if one person can forgive a huge hurt, then everyone should be able to.

Abuse or Neglect Has Made
Forgiving Impossible

One of the main characteristics of abuse is the flagrant, intentional misuse of power. Generally speaking, two people of equal power cannot abuse each other, though they can certainly hurt each other in a deep and serious manner. The very nature of abuse, however, is such that the abuser has more power than his or her victim, and this individual deliberately misuses their power, frequently instilling fear as a means of control. In the case of child abuse, the perpetrating adult has more power than the child, for one of the key characteristics of childhood is relative powerlessness. When it comes to spousal or domestic abuse, one person, most often the male in heterosexual relationships—but an increasing number of females—has more power than the other. In abusive homosexual relationships, the more physically or verbally intimidating or aggressive person tends to have more power than their partner.

Abuse is often characterized by its repetitive nature, although a single incident of abuse (e.g., a child who is sexually assaulted by a child molester) can have a deeply scarring impact. In either chronic or isolated incidents of abuse, the needs and wants of the victim are virtually irrelevant to the abuser. In fact, the abuser sees the victim as an object, as not even being human.

It is quite likely that most of us who are parents have said or done things to our children that we regret, perhaps in a moment of anger. Sometimes we may even be shocked or dismayed by our own behavior, wondering if we have acted abusively. And it could be that on one or more occasions, some of us either crossed the line or came very close to doing so. But if or when we did, we felt very bad about it, apologized, tried to repair the damage we had done, and took steps to improve our parenting skills. Not too many parents have avoided doing and saying a few things that they regret with all their heart.

Abusive parents do not tend to be shocked or disheartened when they mistreat their children, because their very objective is to exercise power, abusive power, at the expense of their child, often in a misguided attempt to feel more powerful in their own lives. Oftentimes they see the child as the one who caused or instigated their behavior or reactions. The child is at fault because he or she is being "naughty" or "provocative" or "not measuring up," or what have you. Non-abusive parents, on the other hand, do not seek to gain power at the expense of belittling, intimidating, or otherwise hurting their children. Furthermore, non-abusive parents, rather than blaming the child, take *full* responsibility for their wrongful behavior and reactions.

The types of abuse, of both children and adults, are manifold, including:

Spiritual and religious abuse	*Sexual abuse*
Physical abuse	*Verbal abuse*
Emotional or psychological abuse	*Domestic or spousal (partner) abuse*
Harassment, bullying, or intimidation	*Cyber-stalking and cyber-bullying*

A failure to provide children with basic kindness, respect, love, and opportunities to grow and develop by those who had more power than them can be as devastating – and unforgivable – as overt forms of mistreatment or abuse. While the abuse or neglect that a person may have suffered as an adult (e.g., in an abusive marriage) can be unforgivable, not to mention disabling and difficult to recover from, the abuse that children suffer is particularly devastating because it takes place during the most formative and vulnerable years of their development. Yet, the very good news is that victims of abuse can and do recover, and more can and will recover as they set aside their attempts to forgive what may be unforgivable for them and seek alternative ways to heal, which is what Anne did.

Anne grew up in a family in which her parents divorced when she and her sister were quite young. Her father had virtually nothing to do with the two girls once the divorce became official and he had moved out. Her mother remarried another man who ended up adopting Anne and her sister. Unfortunately, he was a sex abuser and an addict. He started to abuse Anne when she was eleven years old and continued off and on until she was a teenager. He also abused her younger sister, despite Anne's best attempts to protect her. What's even worse, many of the men who associated with her stepfather were also abusive toward the two girls; in fact, the girls were sometimes traded for drugs.

Years later, when she was seeing a therapist for anxiety and depression, she finally talked about the abuse. Quite understandably, she was having an extremely difficult time continuing any type of relationship with her stepfather, and she was terrified to have her own children around him. Her mother told her that his abusive behavior was in the past and that she should try to forgive him. Besides, he was getting old, and her mother was sure that he was sorry for what he had done. Nonetheless, Anne was not able to forgive what was completely unforgivable. She still felt traumatized by him, and her fear of him, and her even greater fear of his potential to abuse her children, made it truly impossible to have him in her life, much less forgive.

With the help of her therapist, Anne was finally able to confront her stepfather and clearly state that she did not wish to have any further contact with him, and that he was *not* to contact her. After taking this brave step, which was no easy thing for her to do, the anxiety and depression lessened substantially and she started to recover. She even mentored her sister, who set similar no-contact boundaries.

Instead of forgiving her stepfather, Anne, with the help of her therapist, chose to free herself from the legacy of her terrible childhood. She brought closure to this pain-ridden chapter, which had seemed like it would haunt her for the rest of her life. She chose to move on and be a loving and protecting parent to her own children. As she focused on her needs, on her life, and on the lives of her children, she was able to move forward and discover peace and happiness. She refused to forgive, and not only survived, but thrived. She faced the pain of the past with the help of a skilled therapist, and courageously confronted her stepfather.

Anne's story is inspiring for those who can't forgive the abuse or neglect they suffered, yet who at the same time have an insatiable desire to heal and taste happiness again – or for the very first time. She is currently writing new and better chapters to her life and would no doubt encourage others who have suffered abuse or neglect to do the same. To which we would add: *no matter what type of neglect or abuse you have suffered – be it sexual, verbal, physical, emotional, religious, or something else – you, too, can heal, move on, and be happy again when you can't or won't forgive.*

The very nature of abuse . . . is such that the abuser has more power than his or her victim, and this individual deliberately misuses their power, frequently instilling fear as a means of control.

You or Someone Close to You Has Been Victimized by Crime

Because criminals tend to be narcissistic and overly, if not completely, concerned with themselves, they tend to see others as objects to gratify their desires. Their victims are not even viewed as being human, but are something—not someone but some *thing*—to be exploited.

Other serious hurts that occur in a committed relationship or in the work arena or among friends are at least somewhat understandable, because they involve our human nature, our limitations, our weaknesses, and so on. Crime, however, is beyond understanding—and in many cases beyond forgiving as well—because of its purposeful, callous, and serious violation of another person. A criminal doesn't just find himself in someone's home or apartment, for example, and wonder how he got there; no, he willfully and deliberately sets out to break in. Yes, there are crimes of passion that occur spontaneously in the heat of the moment, but the overwhelming majority of criminal activity is preplanned.

There is nothing about crime that points to one's humanity; in fact, crime is indicative of a lack of human decency. It is simply the careless and selfish disregard of the rights and needs of others. This is true of all types of crime, even so-called minor property crimes such as vandalism and graffiti, and nonviolent crimes such as auto theft or identity theft.

If you have been a victim of crime, as is true of any kind of hurt, you are certainly free to forgive if you so choose. However, if you cannot forgive, or don't want to forgive, we want to reassure you that your decision is just as valid and laudable as those who do choose to forgive. More importantly, you can still heal and go on with your life. The goal is to recover as best you can from the traumatic experience of being a victim of crime—not to forgive if you don't want to.

Many, including both of us, would not be prone to forgiving a criminal because of the following characteristics of criminal behavior:

- **Its inherent wrongness.** There's little gray area in the realm of crime, like there is in relationships in which people experience short- or long-term rifts due to any number of reasons that are fairly normal to the human condition. Crime, however, including the crime of different types of abuse, is inherently and fundamentally wrong.

- **Its total disregard for people and their property.** Those who commit crimes have a criminal mindset in which other human beings, the personhood of any and all of us, and the things that belong to us – our property, the physical and emotional wellbeing of our loved ones and ourselves, even our lives – are irrelevant. The criminals get to take or destroy what they want, when they want, and none of us has any say in the matter.[12]

- **Its impact upon victims is often devastating and long-lasting.** Crime victims respond in a variety of ways. Some whose homes are broken into may be able to recover relatively quickly, while many others might not ever feel as safe as they did prior to the break-in, despite having state-of-the-art security technology installed. Common symptoms that crime victims experience include:

  ∾ A loss of a sense of safety

  ∾ Feelings of helplessness/hopelessness

  ∾ Crying

  ∾ Depression and anxiety

  ∾ Overwhelming anger, rage, and vindictive desires

---

12. If you would like to learn more about how criminals think, a good place to start might be with Dr. Stanton Samenov's book *Inside the Criminal Mind*.

- ∼ Replaying the crime over and over again in their minds

- ∼ Second-guessing themselves and wondering what they should have, or could have, done differently

- ∼ Inability to function well at home or work

- ∼ Excessive fears (can't stop thinking about it)

- ∼ Having to move, and going through all the stress that moving entails

- ∼ All sorts of scars, ranging from emotional to financial to spiritual.

Some who have been victimized might be able to forgive if there is a sincere, heartfelt expression of remorse along with a total commitment by the offender to live in a respectful, law-abiding manner. For others, remorse and a commitment to change may not be good enough. It does not restore what they lost, and so they may need to set forgiving aside permanently, as was Brenna and Martin's choice.

Brenna and her husband Martin were awakened at 4:00 a.m. by a phone call that every parent fears. The police informed them that their son had been involved in a violent incident and had died on the way to the hospital. Aaron and his friends had been in a public setting, celebrating the fact that they would soon be heading off to college, when he was caught in the crossfire of two rival gangs. Aaron, who had many plans for his life and was excited about making a contribution to society, had his life snuffed out.

After the initial shock and numbness wore off, Brenna and Martin were consumed by an overwhelming sense of hatred and rage. How could this have happened?! Because they were very religious Christians, they turned to their minister for help. He told them that they must forgive and move on. He said that Jesus turned the other cheek, and they should do the same. But how on earth could they when the shooter had smiled at them during the trial and showed no remorse for what he had done.

After a number of years, the intensity of their pain did decrease considerably, though it was never completely gone. They had experienced some degree of healing, but they still could not – would not – forgive. Though their son had been taken from them, they found comfort in the fact that their love for him was *not* something the criminal could take. They redirected their energy toward helping other families who had suffered similar traumas. They discovered that while they couldn't control the bitter thoughts and feelings that came and went, they could manage their pain to some extent, rather than be totally devoured by it. What's more, they decided for themselves that they could still be good Christians and not forgive.

No matter what your spiritual or religious beliefs may be, if you have been victimized by crime, you may discover that your ability to heal will happen as you "forget forgiving" and activate one of the alternative approaches. The sense of anger, fear, helplessness, and outrage that many crime victims suffer is a big enough price to pay for something that never should have happened in the first place. Trying to forgive might be an additional cost that is simply too much to bear. Once again, this may be true even if you suffered a nonviolent yet highly violating crime such as vandalism, car theft, identity theft, burglary, and the like. You were victimized once, and you don't have to be victimized again by the forgiveness myth, when there are other ways to heal and take back your personal power after having suffered crime's hugely upsetting impact.

There is nothing about crime that points to one's
humanity; in fact, crime is indicative of a lack of
human decency. It is simply the careless and selfish
disregard of the rights and needs of others.
This is true of all types of crime. . . .

An Accident, Negligence, or Wrongful Behavior Has Resulted in a Major Loss

Accidents happen. By their nature, they are unexpected and unintentional. Yet accidents that could have been prevented are far more difficult to forgive – if a person tries to recover by forgiving – than those in which nothing could have been done. Regarding the latter, a seasoned driver who is proceeding in a prudent and cautious manner in the wintertime could come upon some hidden ice and suddenly lose control of their vehicle, which could cause them to slide into another car or pedestrian, resulting in permanent injury.

Then there are accidents that take place because of a moment's lapse in vigilance or an error in judgment. Someone forgets that they are burning a candle, resulting in a fire that quickly spreads to nearby apartments in the same building. Other tenants end up losing their home and possessions through no fault of their own.

Regarding negligence, which may be even harder to forgive than a preventable accident, a doctor or someone in any profession or trade can make a mistake or overlook something that has far-reaching consequences. The doctor misses something in a routine exam and a cancer that could have been – and should have been – caught and successfully treated in its earliest stages becomes much more serious, perhaps even life-threatening. Or a housing inspector fails to notice a structural flaw that ends up costing the unsuspecting new homeowners thousands of dollars and a great deal of inconvenience and stress as repairs are made.

In either the doctor's or the housing inspector's case, this person may be (1) generally competent but adversely affected by some type of personal problem that impacted their performance (e.g., problems with their teenager, financial difficulties, or a divorce), or (2) generally competent but they simply made an error that comes with being a fallible human being. Perhaps they have an impeccable reputation in their field, but for some unknown reason, they didn't do their normal stellar job on this one occasion and missed or overlooked something

74

that they never have in the past and never will again. Yet, *you* may have been the one who suffered as a result.

For many of us, wrongful behavior is most unforgivable due to the fact that it is done with knowledge and intent. The nature of its wrongfulness ranges from being unethical to criminal. It can be especially devastating because the victims placed their trust in another person's expertise and competency, only to have it trampled on.

Yes, there is always the human factor to account for when dealing with others, and mistakes are made, but we are not talking about mistakes here. We are talking about people in various trades and professions who have had training as well as a code of ethics to guide them in their practice or profession. And for those who do not have a professional code of ethics, such as car mechanics and sales people, they are well aware of the unwritten code of ethics most of us try to abide by: treat other people as you would like to be treated (i.e., fairly and honestly).

Major losses can be financial, as in the following examples:

- A person of very limited means is taken advantage of by a car mechanic.

- A person nearing retirement age who has limited savings is sold a high-risk product by an aggressive investment broker, resulting in the loss of half their savings.

- The head of a company accepts a large bonus at the same time that employees are being laid off.

- A company does not fully fund the retirement account, which results in a reduction or loss of benefits for faithful, dedicated employees who were counting on the company to provide them with a good pension and full health care benefits.

- A person, due to company politics, is passed over for a well-deserved promotion, while someone less qualified is offered the position.

Major financial losses such as the ones just mentioned can also exact a physical, spiritual, and emotional toll and cause individuals to lose their faith in the goodness of humanity. While that which constitutes a major loss can vary from person to person, its common ground is the serious, even life-shattering, impact it has on victims.

While we all know intellectually that life isn't fair and that an accident, negligence, or even wrongful behavior is a possibility in this world, if it happens, forgiving may be neither possible nor desirable. The last thing any of us needs to hear at such times is, "Well, no one said that life would be fair." Nor do we need to be told that we should "forgive and move on" or that "other people have it worse" or that "it could have been worse" (e.g., a person who has lost his ability to walk due to a drunk driver is told that at least he isn't dead by someone who also isn't dead, yet who can still walk). These platitudes tend to create more angst and confusion for those whose lives have already been turned upside down, as was the case for Tony and his wife.

Tony was driving home from work late at night. He was looking forward to a skiing weekend with his wife, in which they were going to celebrate their recently discovered pregnancy. Life could not have been better: he had a loving family, a great job, and was about to enjoy a wonderful weekend with the love of his life.

At that very moment, a woman driving a truck passed another vehicle and hit Tony's car head-on, paralyzing him from the neck down. Meanwhile, the woman, who had no insurance, suffered only minor injuries. The life that Tony was living was now over. His wife would not only have to care for their new baby by herself, she would also have to take care of him as well. And his needs, unlike the baby's, would be ongoing. Tony could no longer work, and their financial life was severely compromised. He fell into a deep depression, and his wife was overwhelmed by her around-the-clock responsibilities.

Although the other driver expressed remorse and served a minor sentence, she had no financial means with which to begin to adequately compensate Tony and his wife. Neither Tony nor his wife could reconcile how abruptly and unfairly life had turned on them. Well-meaning friends and family pointed out that he was still alive, and that things could be worse. Not surprisingly, such comments resulted in Tony and his wife feeling even more alone in life's unfair turn of events. Adding to their wounds, many who had once been in their lives began to drift away, in part because they didn't like to be reminded so graphically of life's fragile and tenuous nature.

Tony and his wife came to realize that despite the other driver's sincere and tearful expression of remorse, they could not forgive her. They also had a hard time believing in a God who would allow this to happen, especially when comments such as "everything happens for a reason" or "God has his reasons which remain a mystery to us" were made in their presence. Their faith in God and the goodness of humanity was shaken to the point of bitterness and despair. While Tony and his wife did rediscover some meaning and joy in life again and were able to adapt to their radically changed circumstances, theirs is a powerful example of how a serious accident can result in a multitude of major losses that may be beyond forgiving.

While we all know intellectually that life isn't fair and that an accident, negligence, or even wrongful behavior is a possibility in this world, if it happens, forgiving may be neither possible nor desirable.

You Have Been Harmed by Religious Rigidity and Ignorance

Religious rigidity and ignorance not only abounds, it seems to be on the rise. Perhaps it is inevitable given the fearful and tumultuous times we live in, although it could be argued that every generation from the dawn of humankind has lived with a significant measure of fear and instability.

Religious rigidity and ignorance hurts both individuals and groups. It can occur when members of one religion oppress, persecute, or demonize the members of another religion or lifestyle, or when members of one religion vilify, dismiss, or otherwise hurt other members or groups who claim to be of the same religion.

Religious rigidity and ignorance, regardless of which religion or sect within a religion is perpetrating it, in its most callous manifestations, has several prevailing characteristics, including:

1. A fear-based intolerance of those who think, believe, and act differently.

2. An unyielding claim to know the mind and will of God, oftentimes by quoting, misinterpreting, and misusing isolated passages from their particular scriptures (e.g., the Bible, Koran, or Tanak) to support *their* understanding of the mind and will of God.

3. Rigid, black and white thinking that is dualistic in nature.

4. A literalist approach to scriptures, and an obsessive attentiveness to the letter of the law or a specific teaching while missing the deeper spiritual meaning.

5. An us-versus-them mindset, in which their group has *the* truth, *God's* truth, and others simply do not, even if these others feel passionately about their own beliefs.

6. A neurotic preoccupation with sex and sexual behavior.

7. The use of shame and guilt to control human behavior.

Ironically, some who are most passionate about their religious beliefs act in the most passionately unloving ways that adversely impact the wellbeing of minority groups, including that of gays and lesbians. Rather than being proponents of human rights and tolerance, they frequently stifle human rights and are agents of intolerance. In many cases, this intolerance of those who are different—which is really all of us as we are each different in our own unique ways—is due to fear run amuck, rather than because they are seeking to act in hateful and hurtful ways. Tyler's parents are a prime example of the devastating power of fear-based religious rigidity and ignorance rather than blatant ill will.

Tyler was raised by parents who belonged to a very strict religious sect. He and his siblings were home-schooled so that they would not be "infected" by the corrupt teachings of those outside of their tradition.

When Tyler was a teenager, he met some other kids his own age who were not of his faith. He ended up spending more and more time with them, and quickly discovered that they were not the "frightening and unholy people" he had been taught to believe they were.

When Tyler finally worked up the courage to tell his parents about his new friends, they were extremely upset and took him to see the elders of their faith community. The elders, who had no interest in hearing what Tyler had to say, told him in no uncertain terms that he must sever all contact with these "outsiders." Intimidated in the presence of his parents and authoritative elders, he agreed to do so, but secretly he kept getting together with his new friends. He simply enjoyed hanging out with them. They talked about all sorts of things that seemed both natural and normal to him—despite what he had been taught.

Several years later, Tyler met a woman through his friends with whom he fell deeply in love. One day he announced to his family that he was going to marry her in *her* church, rather than the one in which he had been raised and to which his parents still belonged. The church elders told Tyler's parents that if they attended the wedding at this "heretical" church, they would be expelled from their own church community. They were also told that they must no longer have contact with their son until he came back to the faith community "where he belonged."

Tyler refused to come back, as he no longer believed what his former church taught. When he got married in his fiancée's church, his parents disowned him. Even when he and his wife started up their own family, his parents still refused to have anything to do with him. In fact, to this date, they have yet to meet his wife and children.

Sometimes departing from the religious tradition in which you were raised comes with a price. You might be overtly rejected, like Tyler was, or shamed and badgered because you are no longer attending religious services or because you have joined another tradition. Or you could be met with loud "silent" disapproval, perhaps from a parent, that is far from subtle.

In such cases, you can choose to move on and live your life without forgiving those who have hurt you out of religious rigidity and ignorance. In fact, if you can visualize them as acting out of fear rather than consciously choosing intolerance or hatred, you might be able to set yourself free more quickly, because it really isn't about you at all. It's about their fear, and you are perceived as a threat.

Ironically, some who are most passionate about their religious beliefs act in the most passionately unloving ways that adversely impact the wellbeing of minority groups, including that of gays and lesbians.

Your Sexual Orientation Has Resulted in You Being Hurt

When Tim was a teenager, he realized that he wasn't like the other boys who hung out in the school hallways. He was not attracted to girls in the same way that they were, and he had interests that most of his peers did not share. His father, who had yet to learn of his son's sexual orientation, frequently made "queer" jokes during dinner, which caused Tim a great deal of discomfort. Because he lived in a small town, Tim felt that there was no one he could talk to.

One night Tim went to a party and drank too much beer. He told one of the boys at the party that he was attracted to him. This boy, who had also been drinking, reacted poorly and called him a "fag" in front of everyone else. Once the news of this incident got out at school, Tim became a victim of all the bullies and an outcast in his own community. His father, ashamed and embarrassed, brought him to a minister who guaranteed that he could turn his son into a heterosexual. Within a short time, Tim tried to commit suicide.

Shortly thereafter, Tim moved away and developed a long-term relationship. About a month before he and his partner were going to take a cruise to celebrate being together for ten years, he received a standardized letter informing him of a forthcoming class reunion, which caused Tim to feel quite anxious. His partner was confused as to why Tim was so upset about the possibility of attending it, and suggested that Tim "forgive and forget" the homophobia and verbal gay-bashing he had experienced. Besides, he was convinced that these people had all matured in the decade since the unfortunate incidents took place.

Tim, however, chose to honor his own intuition. He came to realize that he had moved away for a reason. He had freed himself from the persecution he had experienced as an adolescent and had come to feel at home with himself, his lifestyle, and his partner. He did not go back, nor did he choose to forgive what for him was unforgivable.

Brittany realized that she was a lesbian when she developed a relationship with another woman while in college. Struggling with feelings of guilt because she knew that homosexuality was against the tenets of her religion, she sought out the counsel of her pastor. He told her that if she continued this relationship she would surely go to hell. He sent a few members of the church, which Brittany attended and where he served as the pastor, to her house in an attempt to coerce her to change her ways.

Brittany felt betrayed by these church members and her pastor. She could not forgive them for their prejudicial attitudes toward gay people. Yet at the same time, she wrestled with the notion that God would never forgive her and that she was going to end up in hell because of her "sinful" lifestyle. She came to realize that this particular faith community was no longer hers. She had not wanted to leave them, but they had rejected her. Fortunately, she found a new community and continued her spiritual journey. She grew into a deeper understanding of a compassionate God who had created her as she was, and who was calling her to be true to herself. She came to see her sexuality as a blessing, as a gift, rather than as something that was sinful and for which she would be punished.

Suffering discrimination due to one's sexuality can be so harmful that it may be beyond forgiving. Attacking or discriminating against people for who they are at the core of their being and for how they identify themselves in terms of their sexuality is simply wrong. And it matters not how many scripture passages are taken out of context to support the attackers' point of view.

If you have been a victim of homophobia, discrimination due to your sexual orientation, or some form of gay-bashing, you have likely suffered enough without trying to forgive those who have caused you so much needless pain in the first place. Of course, you can still choose to forgive as you understand forgiving, but if you are not inclined or able to do so, we would both support you in exploring alternative ways to take back your personal power and get on with your life. You cannot necessarily change the opinions and behaviors of those who are bound by ignorance or prejudice, but you can set yourself free from their extremely harmful influence, as much as possible, oftentimes through an alternative approach to forgiving.

Attacking or discriminating against people for who they are at the core of their being and for how they identify themselves in terms of their sexuality is simply wrong. And it matters not how many scripture passages are taken out of context to support the attackers' point of view.

You Have Been Victimized by Racism

Racism is at or near the top of humanity's ugliest spiritual and psychological illnesses. It has resulted in unfathomable suffering on every level imaginable – including physical, spiritual, emotional, and psychological suffering – for millions upon millions of people in times past, and is still taking its toll upon countless numbers of individuals and groups today. It can, and does, have malignant reverberations at the economic, institutional, and systemic or structural levels of a society or country, and a crippling impact upon those who personally encounter discrimination, racial slurs or epithets, or even violence in their daily lives. Philip is but one of many innocent victims who has suffered needlessly and cruelly due to racism.

The white family that adopted Philip moved to a small town where there were very few African Americans. As he grew up, he had to fend off the usual stereotypes, including inquiries as to whether he planned to be an athlete or a musician when he got older, though he was interested in neither.

When it was time for him to go to college, he decided to attend a university in a large city in the South. While he had encountered some discrimination while growing up in his small town, often of a subtle nature, what he suffered as a college student is, in our estimation – and more importantly, in Philip's – completely beyond forgiving.

Philip was having a conversation with a white woman in a bar and grill when he was confronted by a group of young white men, who threatened him and called him every racial slur imaginable. At first, he had trouble believing that this was happening to him. He had heard about such ugly incidents, but he thought they were part of a bygone era. Tragically, the verbal assault escalated into a physical one. Severely beaten by these men, he suffered permanent injuries, forcing him to discontinue his schooling.

Quite understandably, Philip grew to fear groups of young white males and became extremely bitter toward them. His bitterness nearly consumed him when the men who had attacked him got off with a light sentence at the trial. He rejected any and all advice that he forgive his attackers, even that which came from his fellow African Americans. Unable to forgive and unaware of any alternative ways to begin to heal from this life-shattering event, his anger and rage grew and grew. Trying to disengage from the memory of how he had been attacked was not working for him. He only wanted to hurt them like he had been hurt.

Eventually Philip set aside the whole notion of forgiving, and with the help of a mentor worked toward managing the power of outrage that he felt toward these men. He was sorely tempted to let bitterness control him for the rest of his life, and on some days it did indeed overpower him. But gradually, and with a great deal of inner strength and discipline, he spent less time and energy in the lifeless land of bitterness toward those who had caused him to suffer so deplorably, and more and more time and energy in the life-giving land of inner freedom.

He freed himself from the crippling power of hating these men, partly through an attempt to understand why they were the way they were. No, he wasn't excusing their behavior, but by trying to understand it, coupled with seeing them as a product of their environment, he was able to focus more on his life in the present moments of each new day, rather than on his attackers and that horrible day gone by, which he could do nothing to change. They had to live with what they had done; he, however, wasn't going to continue to give his power away to them for the rest of his life by self-destructing.

Philip had every reason in the book to yield to the seductive call of lifelong bitterness and self-destructiveness, and if he had gone that route, no one could have blamed him or stood in judgment of him. Instead, he developed his power of choice to move on and rebuild, which is not only an inspiration to others who have suffered racism, but to all of us.

We need to acknowledge that because we are both white males, we have no firsthand experience with racism. Historically, we, and other white men in the United States, especially those of us with educational and economic opportunities, have had access to unprecedented power and privilege just because we are white and male, which isn't right. However, we have the highest admiration for those who, like Philip, have been victimized by racism and yet have found a way to move on and make a contribution, even though they have chosen not to forgive those who have caused them to suffer so grievously.

Racism is at or near the top of humanity's ugliest spiritual and psychological illnesses. It has resulted in unfathomable suffering on every level imaginable . . . for millions upon millions of people in times past, and is still taking its toll upon countless numbers of individuals and groups today.

Betrayal of a Serious Nature
Has Left You Devastated

Few wounds hurt more deeply than that of betrayal. While most of us tend to think of betrayal in terms of intimate relationships, it can also happen in many other arenas in life. Employees can feel betrayed by an employer or company for any number of reasons, such as an executive decision to close a plant and outsource operations, resulting in hundreds or thousands of faithful workers losing their jobs. Voters who help to elect certain candidates can feel betrayed when these individuals do not follow through on their campaign promises, or when they act unethically, even scandalously. However, in this section, we limit our focus to the impact that betrayal has on intimate relationships, on those who have given their trust or confidence – and oftentimes their heart as well – to another person, only to have it violated or broken.

Sally and Tom had been married for many years, and though Sally knew that their marriage was difficult at times, she did not think it was in serious jeopardy. Sally had been a stay-at-home mom, but as she and Tom had agreed upon years ago, she went back to work as the kids began to head off to college. She got a job in a local business, but Tom was very uncomfortable with her working there. She soon found out the reason why: he had been having a long-term affair with one of the employees.

As devastating as this discovery was, Sally was crushed when she learned that this affair was common knowledge to pretty much everyone except her. When she asked various people in her life if they had known about it, she was devastated to learn from her in-laws that this affair had been going on for almost eighteen years and that most of the family had been aware of it for quite some time. Even her sister had known about it for several years. Not only had she been betrayed by her unfaithful husband, a man she had loved through the ups and downs of their marriage, now she felt betrayed by her own family, by his family, and by several friends as well.

Sally had been betrayed by most of the people she had trusted. The life she had been living for some twenty years had become a lie overnight. Her family and her children were of paramount importance to her, and she felt she had lost them all due to betrayal and selfishness. Feelings of rage and hurt overwhelmed her, and she felt like she had been walking around with a neon sign proclaiming her the world's biggest fool, obvious to everyone but her. Adding salt to her wounds, including her unremitting sense of embarrassment, was the fact that, because of her children, she felt obligated to interact with the people who had betrayed her at several family and social functions.

Like many who have been betrayed, Sally internalized her hurt and rage and became anxious and depressed as a result. She started therapy, where she began to process the depth of her pain and anger. Although she thought it would be wise to forgive and forget, she couldn't do it. Every time she thought about her husband with this other woman and her family and friends knowing about it for years, her painful feelings overwhelmed her, making it impossible to forgive and move on.

Fortunately, her therapist encouraged her to explore alternative ways to begin to heal that did not require her to forgive. Sally found that the discipline she had developed during her years as a stay-at-home mom was something she could call upon now. She started to see the managing of her painful emotions as similar to that of managing her home, and all the skill that that 24/7/365 role had required of her. She took each emotion one at a time, and made a decision about how she wanted to handle it. As a result, she regained a measure of control and personal power over her life.

When she had to interact with the other members of her soon-to-be former husband's family, she was just cordial to them, while focusing her energy on her kids or on the event itself (e.g., a concert or graduation ceremony). She also limited her interactions with Tom as she went through the divorce proceedings.

As the months and years passed, Sally continued to develop her personal power and cultivated more trusting and authentic friendships. Yes, she still felt angry and hurt about what had happened to her, but it did not have the final say in her life. She learned to let the waves of painful thoughts and emotions wash over her, and then moved on with her life as best she could. She became increasingly skilled at moving on, although every so often the pain of the past came back with a fury, but never for very long. Although she would have been happy to live the rest of her life without being in any type of serious relationship, she did eventually meet someone with whom she shared a mutually loving – and faithful – relationship.

While Sally chose to divorce Tom, some who have been equally devastated by betrayal may desire to reconcile with the person who was unfaithful and rebuild the relationship. In our opinion, an alternative approach to forgiving may be more doable and healing in these cases. Why? Because, once again, the betrayed person may believe in their heart or at a subconscious level that to forgive means they are saying they are now somehow okay or at peace with how they were hurt, which may not be true at all. They might not want to have anything to do with forgiving, because in their estimation, how they were hurt will always be unforgivable. So, perhaps instead, they choose to see a therapist together to process the impact of the harm done, learn some ways to rebuild trust, and develop a blueprint of sorts to help them move forward into a new and stronger relationship.

The betrayed person, along with their beloved, may decide that the best way to proceed is to "clear out the wreckage from the past and make a fresh start," which may be more doable than forgiving. Maybe they come to an agreement in which the unfaithful person is told quite bluntly that if they repeat their behavior, the relationship will be over for good. This one incidence of betrayal, especially if it was a brief event and not an eighteen-year exercise in deception, might not have totally ruined the relationship. It may have come close, but perhaps there is still enough love, and the risk-reward ratio may still offer plenty of potential rewards for the betrayed person to warrant giving the person who hurt them so deeply continued access to the inner regions of their heart.

Conventional wisdom suggests that "it takes one to forgive and two to reconcile." While that may be true, the one who is betrayed can move on and rebuild without forgiving, and without continuing any type of relationship with the person who did the betraying. Similarly, both people might agree to work toward reconciling and rebuilding their relationship, with the one who was betrayed taking the lead in setting new ground rules. This reconciling/rebuilding process might be much more doable when one of the healthy alternatives to forgiveness is used as the foundation.

The betrayed person may believe in their heart or at a subconscious level that to forgive means they are saying they are now somehow okay or at peace with how they were hurt, which may not be true at all. They might not want to have anything to do with forgiving, because in their estimation, how they were hurt will always be unforgivable.

Religious Help or Professional Therapy Hasn't Enabled You to Forgive

Many people who have difficulty forgiving seek assistance through their faith tradition. Some may even set up a meeting to talk with their pastor, priest, rabbi, or imam about their inability or reluctance to forgive. Others might read a book on forgiveness written by an authority from their tradition or ponder passages from their Bible, Hebrew Scriptures, or Koran. And still others might choose to discuss their forgiveness difficulties with someone from their church, synagogue, or mosque, or perhaps even join a study or support group to help them learn more about forgiving and how to go about it.

It seems to make sense that included among the many people who struggle most deeply with forgiving are those who were raised, or who are still active, in one of the three monotheistic religions that trace their roots to Abraham: Judaism, Christianity, and Islam, because forgiving is important to all three traditions. Because it is deeply valued, no small number of Jews, Christians, and Muslims feel guilty or troubled by the fact that they can't – or won't – forgive in some situations, even when the hurts involved are of a relatively minor or petty nature rather than something more serious.[13]

Others who were not raised in one of these three traditions, or in any religious tradition at all, may not struggle with forgiving or wrestle with guilt because of their inability or unwillingness to forgive in the same manner or to the same degree at all. We suspect that how these people respond to their hurts runs the same gamut that it does for Jews, Christians, and Muslims, ranging from clinging to bitterness to striving for new freedom and everything in-between.

---

13. If any of us who are not Muslim were to base our understanding of Islam upon the distorted creeds and violent acts of "Muslim" terrorists, we might come to the conclusion that forgiveness is not important to the Islamic faith. Nothing could be further from the truth. True Muslims seek forgiveness from God when they have offended the divine, and they seek forgiveness from both God *and* the injured party when they have harmed another person. Islam teaches that the person who did the harm needs to do whatever is possible (within reason) to repair the damage, while making a commitment to not repeat the offense.

As we mentioned earlier, a Jewish person is not obliged to forgive unless the person who hurt them expresses sorrow and remorse, repairs the harm to the fullest extent possible, and is committed to not repeating the offense. The one who did the harm, according to Jewish law, is required to seek the offended person's forgiveness up to three times.

In contrast to Judaism, and Islam (see the footnote on the previous page), Christians are expected, taught, and exhorted to forgive even if their offender does *not* express remorse, repair the harm done, or make a commitment to not repeat the injurious behavior. For this reason, forgiving can be even more difficult – if not impossible – for many Christians than it is for some Jews and Muslims.

It is not uncommon for a significant number of Christians to be under the influence of such religious notions and advice as:

- ◦ Forgiving is at the center of our faith, so you have to forgive.

- ◦ God wants you to forgive, no matter what.

- ◦ You don't deserve God's forgiveness, so you should forgive others even when they don't deserve yours.

- ◦ Jesus forgave from the cross and he was totally innocent, so you should too, because you are not only *not* innocent like him, you are a sinner who caused his death by your sinfulness.

- ◦ Your suffering pales in comparison to what Jesus endured.

- ◦ If you want God to forgive you, you must forgive others.

Yet when there is no justice and accountability, or no remorse – or even when there is – forgiving isn't always possible. Even with the help of prayer.

Ironically, an overwhelming number of Christians ranging from the most liberal to the most conservative, including the majority of pastors and priests, seem to be bound by the forgiveness myth. When some can't – or won't – forgive, Christian clergy seem to be somewhat stumped as to what alternative counsel they might offer to these individuals to help them get beyond their hurts.

This doesn't mean that the majority of Christian clergy are not compassionate and supportive of those who can't forgive. Countless pastors and priests, especially those who are not scriptural literalists, fundamentalists, religionists, or doctrinal dogmatists, would not cite scripture passages or church teachings in an attempt to coerce or shame a reluctant or un-able forgiver. Instead, they would be – and indeed often are – very kind, tactful, and compassionate with those who struggle to forgive.

Yet at the same time, these caring and competent pastors and priests seem to be unaware of healthy alternatives to forgiving that could be helpful to these individuals. They, too, seem to have unintentionally mistaken one path, that of forgiving, with the goal, that of being able to heal and move on in life. Aloud they may say something like, "I know how hard it is for you to forgive, and I might not be able to forgive either if I had suffered the same hurt that you did," while silently they are at a complete loss: "I don't know what else to tell this person. We're all supposed to forgive, but we often can't – even when we ask for God's help."

Professional therapists also seem to be bound, by and large, by the forgiveness myth, for many people who still cannot forgive after seeking religious help, as well as those who do not seek religious help to begin with, often turn to therapists, as was true for Paul.

In therapy, Paul found himself returning time and again to the hurts and abuse he suffered as a child from his parents. For most of his adult life, he had sought help from a variety of therapists, psychiatrists, and therapy groups. He also met with his priest on several occasions. In all these various settings, he was encouraged to forgive.

Paul was told that his parents had done the best they could, and it was now time to forgive once-and-for-all and move on with his life. Yet he couldn't. He wondered what was wrong with him. Although he realized that his inability to resolve these early wounds was keeping him from having a full life, including a healthy relationship with a woman, he simply could not forgive.

Paul was raised to believe in forgiveness, and intellectually it made sense to him. Yet he couldn't feel it in his heart; it never felt genuine or freeing. What made forgiving even more impossible was the way he continued to be hurt by his parents even as an adult. Still, his current therapist, who is a very compassionate and skilled practitioner, like all those of the past, is confined by the forgiveness myth and does not know of any alternative ways to heal.

When you are unable or unwilling to forgive, for whatever reason, you do not need to persist in your attempts to forgive or feel guilty because you can't. Nor do you need to abandon your religious tradition or stop working with your therapist, for there are other ways to heal that are oftentimes more doable than forgiving.

Our basic position is that forgiving should be both a relatively easy and natural endeavor, and if you are resisting it or are reluctant to forgive, it may be because it is too difficult and unnatural, at least in terms of that particular hurt and person who hurt you. If that is the case, then you might be wise to consider one of several alternative ways to recover your personal power to move on and be happy again. In the next chapter, we explore what these alternatives are and why they work so well.

It seems to make sense that included among the many
people who struggle most deeply with forgiving are
those who were raised, or who are still active, in one of
the three monotheistic religions that trace their roots
to Abraham: Judaism, Christianity, and Islam, because
forgiving is important to all three traditions.

$\sim 4 \sim$

Healthy Alternatives to Forgiving: What They Are and Why They Work So Well

Life by its very nature is incredibly resilient and regenerative. Even after devastating natural disasters such as hurricanes, life tends to reemerge out of the ruins left by wind, rain, and sea. Nothing seems to be able to keep Mother Nature down for very long.

As a part of nature, we human beings have this incredibly resilient and regenerative life-force within us as well. We can suffer some awful hurts in this world, yet somehow find the strength to hang in there. The goal, of course, is not just to hang in there and survive, but to be able to thrive and be happy again, or for the very first time.

A young man who was studying for his GED while incarcerated was asked by his English teacher to write about a happy moment in his life. Having grown up in a constantly chaotic home where crime, violence, drug dealing, and his mother's addiction and endless stream of "boyfriends" were the norm, he wrote, "I haven't had one yet, but I'm looking forward to having one." His admission, "I haven't had one yet," is heartbreaking enough, but when he goes on to say, "I'm looking forward to having one," we are both rendered speechless. This young man models what it means to be resilient and to continue to hope for something better, for a taste of happiness, despite the fact that his life has been a steady stream of one hurt after another.

Just as he is pursuing his high school diploma in a non-traditional manner, through a GED program in a less than ideal setting, you too can pursue your dreams of being happy again and break out of the prisons of your hurts in a non-traditional manner and in a less than ideal setting or situation (e.g., following a divorce, a painful situation at work, wounds that are due to a loved one's addictive behavior, and so on). When forgiving is something you can't do, or won't do, you can say "yes" to life's beckoning, regenerative life-force within by seeking other ways to heal and be happy.

After being hurt, you *can* live again and go on with your life, though you may still be suffering some painful thoughts and feelings from time to time. Bitterness comes and goes, as does anger and hatred and all sorts of pleasant emotions as well: happiness, excitement, contentment, and so on. Your emotional landscape within is constantly changing, and when painful memories surface, accompanied by painful thoughts and feelings, they will pass – though it may feel like they are here to stay. Again, your experience may already support this.

To prove our point, what kind of thoughts and feelings were you experiencing two years ago? If you're like both of us, the details of last week may already be fading, a month or two ago is becoming blurry, and two years ago might as well be ancient Greco-Roman times. Whatever we thought and felt then is not what we are thinking and feeling today. Even if you were in a lot of emotional pain two years ago and are still hurting today, your painful thoughts and feelings and how you are experiencing them are not exactly the same.

In this chapter, we begin by identifying what these healthy alternatives to forgiving are. Then, we explore several reasons why these alternatives work so well, including the fact that they come with little or no baggage, especially when compared to the religious and personal baggage that so often accompanies forgiving. The alternative approaches are simply intended to help you reclaim your personal power as quickly and effectively as you can after being hurt. And because we are operating from the assumption that the criteria which make forgiving both natural and easy are not always present, these healthy alternatives have a much greater chance of helping you to heal, move on, and be happy again.

The alternative approaches are simply intended to help you reclaim your personal power as quickly and effectively as you can after being hurt.

Some of the Healthy Alternatives to Forgiving

Language is powerful. Words can either lull us to sleep due to their over-familiarity, or awaken us because of their less frequent and more care-full use. They can entrap us as they diminish our sense of choice, or liberate us as we realize that there are several viable possibilities from which we can choose. Sometimes a single word or phrase can change the direction of our lives.

For instance, many of us have discovered that when we consciously choose to focus or meditate upon a word such as "abundance" we reap some near-immediate payoffs. We find ourselves able to break out of the habitual fear and scarcity mindset that is so stifling, immobilizing, yet oftentimes familiar, and into a lighter and more effective way of engaging others, life itself, and our own life.

Choosing a mindset of abundance, especially when thoughts of fear or scarcity have resulted in a loss of perspective and possibility, changes everything. We are able to see the world with fresh eyes, and abundance, which just a short time ago was nowhere to be found, suddenly seems apparent everywhere. A surge of energy begins to flow within, and a renewed sense of possibility stirs us to take some action to make life better for ourselves and others. What changed? Nothing outside of us, only our inner outlook on life, as a single word, "abundance," came into our conscious awareness and inspired us to try a different and more effective way of living.

So it is with the use of alternative language to "forgiveness." These alternatives are brand new ways to reframe what you are trying to do: heal, move on, and be happy again. They are simply different ways to heal when you have decided that forgiving is not something you want to do or can do.

The healthy alternatives to forgiving that follow are in no particular order. They are numbered solely for easy identification purposes. For instance, if you are discussing these alternatives with someone else, you can refer to them by number, rather than saying the sixth one down, and so on. As you read them, please keep in mind that they are primarily about language, and as we said at the beginning of this section, language can be powerful and liberating. Healthy alternatives to forgiving include:

1. Moving on as I keep the focus on myself and my needs.

2. Freeing myself from the person who hurt me and for a new beginning in life.

3. Releasing the pain of the past to God, my higher power, or the universe.

4. Coming to terms with this hurt as best I can.

5. Cutting my losses and "divorcing" myself from this person (or family of origin).

6. Bringing some type of closure to this chapter of my life.

7. Accepting that how I was hurt cannot be changed, so that I can begin to move on.

8. Taking tender care of myself, just like I would if I had suffered a physical injury or illness.

9. Making a fresh start right where I am and just as I am.

10. Grieving what I lost, naming what's left, and envisioning what's possible.[14]

11. Affirming my strength to survive this hurt and to recreate my life anew.

12. Choosing to take positive, constructive action on my own behalf each day.

13. Letting the past be in the past and opening up to something new this day.

---

14. Dr. John Schneider, in his book *Finding My Way: Healing and Transformation through Loss and Grief*, poses three poignant questions for consideration: What's lost? What's left? What's possible?

14. Disengaging from this person who hurt me.

15. Moving forward each moment in a fully conscious and intentional manner.

16. Embracing new opportunities.

17. Responding to life's invitation to rebuild.

18. Letting go of this hurt each day so that I can reach out for something better.

19. Creating a self-care plan to guide me in fostering my healing and happiness.

20. Managing my pain while taking small steps and risks to help me move forward.

21. Identifying what is—and isn't—within my power to change and positively impact.

22. Choosing to be responsible for the quality of the rest of my life, starting now.

23. Reclaiming my power of choice to take positive and constructive action each day.

24. Making a firm and disciplined choice to move on, even though I am still hurting.

25. Affirming that I *can* move on with some pain, which will decrease *as* I move on.

These words and phrases are not meant to be a comprehensive or exclusive list; rather, they are intended to show you the possibilities as well as the potential power of using new and different language other than "forgiving." We invite you to experiment with other words and phrases. Perhaps you will come up with something that is not on the list above.

The particular phrases that may appeal to you regarding one of your hurts aren't intended to set you free by themselves. Instead, they are meant to provide you with a new framework or foundation with which to approach the healing of your hurts so that you *can* move on and be happy again. For example, let's say that number four, "coming to terms with this hurt as best I can," and number twenty-three, "reclaiming my power of choice to take positive and constructive action each day," are two that attract you and seem much more doable than forgiving. One of the reasons they may be so appealing – and healing – is the fact that they come with little or no religious or personal baggage, which is very freeing and empowering in and of itself. We address this freedom from unnecessary and cumbersome baggage next.

The particular phrases that may appeal to you regarding one of your hurts aren't intended to set you free by themselves. Instead, they are meant to provide you with a new framework or foundation with which to approach the healing of your hurts so that you *can* move on and be happy again.

No Religious or Personal Baggage

We suspect that most people have none of the baggage, or at least nowhere near the same amount of baggage, with any of the alternatives to forgiveness that they so often do with forgiveness. As we have already explored in previous chapters, many of us have acquired heavy "forgiveness baggage" through our experiences in a particular religious tradition, from our families, or both. Thousands, if not millions, of us have been taught that we must forgive in each and every situation, and that God won't forgive us if we, in turn, don't forgive others. These teachings, rather than setting us free, have tended to weigh us down with baggage that is quite cumbersome, making forgiving all but impossible in many cases.

It is our opinion that the one alternative phrase to forgiving that indeed does have some baggage attached to it is "let it go," as this dictum, like that of "just forgive," has been overused and oftentimes a bit too quickly, even automatically (e.g., "Why don't you let it go?"). And of course, letting it go is not always such an easy thing to do, otherwise we would just do it. There are many valid reasons why you might hang on to your hurts, one of them being that "letting it go" doesn't seem to be the best way to heal, especially if you haven't done everything within your power to obtain some justice and accountability. But because most if not all of the other alternative phrases are not used regularly, much less casually, it makes sense that they have no accompanying baggage.

For instance, it's difficult to imagine that if a therapist, counselor, member of the clergy, or even a friend were to suggest to you in a gentle, timely, and highly respectful manner, that "Instead of trying to forgive in this case, I invite you to consider moving on by keeping the focus on yourself and your needs" your response would be, "I am so sick and tired of being invited to move on by keeping the focus on myself and my needs! I've been invited to do this all of my life! I don't know how many sermons and lectures I've heard on this topic!" The reason this reaction would be unlikely is because a phrase such as "moving on as I keep the focus on myself and my needs" is fresh, alternative language, as opposed to the tired, baggage-laden, and overly familiar word and concept "forgive." Besides, instead of being told that you *can't* move on *until* you forgive, as if that were empirical, set-in-stone truth, you have been invited to *consider* moving on by keeping the focus on yourself and your needs. And most of us appreciate being invited to consider doing something rather than being told that we absolutely have to do it—much less that it is the only way or the best way.

Regarding the alternatives to forgiving, it can be like hearing the word "abundance" for the first time in a fresh way that fills you with a sense of energy, excitement, and personal power you may not have experienced in a long time. A voice within may say:

> *Hey, I want to try this abundance approach to life. I've mastered a fear-based and scarcity mindset, and it just isn't paying off. I have nothing more to gain from it, and everything to lose, including my potential to be happy and at peace. I just end up feeling more and more worried, and that which I long for seems to be increasingly scarce. I wonder what might happen if I started looking at things, at life itself, even at my own life, through the lens of abundance. I'm going to try it. It can't hurt.*

With "moving on by keeping the focus on myself and my needs" or "making a fresh start" or "freeing myself from the person who hurt me and for a new beginning in life" or any of the other healthy alternative phrases, many of us feel a similar sense of energy, excitement, and personal power bubbling up within us. A voice within might say:

> *Hey, I want to try a couple of these alternative approaches or come up with one of my own. The word 'forgive' turns me off. I can't or don't want to do it, at least not when it comes to this particular person who hurt me. I feel stuck. I wonder if using some different language and trying a different approach, such as*

> *"making a fresh start right where I am and just as I am," might work, at least better than forgiving has. It can't hurt to try.*

Now whichever alternative words and phrases appeal to you, applying them is not necessarily going to be as effortless as a walk in the park. It can still be quite an undertaking to "move on" or "make a fresh start," depending upon the nature of the hurt you have suffered, who hurt you, how accountable they are, and so on. What's more, the passage of time still has a critical role to play in the healing process, and so these alternatives are not an instant cure.

Yet even though activating an alternative approach does not work immediately or magically, it is likely to work better for you than forgiving, at least in some cases when the criteria that are conducive to forgiving are absent. And for those times when forgiving is impossible for you because you can't or won't do it, then it makes sense that at least one of the alternatives will be at least marginally possible, which is better than *impossible*. Oftentimes, they are significantly more possible and liberating than forgiving, for the simple reason that they place the focus on *you*, rather than on the person who hurt you, which is what we will look at next.

Regarding the alternatives to forgiving, it can be like
hearing the word "abundance" for the first time in a fresh
way that fills you with a sense of energy, excitement, and
personal power that you may not have experienced
in a long time.

The Focus Is on You and on Your Needs – Not on Your Offender

Keeping the focus on yourself and on what you need in order to begin to heal, move on, and be happy again is one of the main reasons why the alternatives to forgiving work so well. Forgiving, by its nature, implies that the focus is on the other person, as in "I need to forgive so-and-so," which is then supposed to set the person who was hurt free. As we mentioned before, many who have been hurt feel a need to remind themselves, or someone else, that forgiving is for them and not for their offender. The need for this reminder may point to something deep within that really believes that forgiving is for the other person. Otherwise, why would such a reminder be necessary?

When it comes to forgiving, most of us don't tend to say, "I need to forgive" in the same manner that we might say, "I need to exercise." The phrase "I need to forgive" or "I want to forgive" or "I don't want to forgive, but I guess I'd better forgive or God won't forgive me" always begs the question: "Forgive *who?*" or "Forgive *what?*" And when we use the word "forgive" in a sentence, it is always followed by either the name of the person who hurt us, as in "I need to forgive so-and-so," or the behavior of the person who hurt us, as in "I need to forgive such-and-such," or both. Hence the questions that are implied in forgiving are:

Who do I need to forgive?

or

What hurt do I need to forgive?

or

Who do I need to forgive *and* what hurt do I need to forgive?

The traditional model of forgiving places the focus on your offender, on how they hurt you, or on both your offender and how they hurt you, which instead of always setting you free from your emotional pain as it is intended to do, may inadvertently keep your feelings of anger and bitterness alive and well. It makes sense that instead of invariably liberating you from your pain, attempts to forgive can actually exacerbate your wounds and entrap you more deeply, *because you are focusing your attention on the person who hurt you and how they hurt you. And where you consciously place your focus is where your energy is going in the present moment.*

Depending upon what your unique understanding of forgiveness is, you might be trying to let go of the hurt – even though the other person refuses to be accountable, or you may be trying to extend some type of goodwill or warm or neutral feelings toward your offender – despite the fact that this individual is not in the least remorseful. As you try to forgive, you might find yourself wondering why they *aren't* being accountable or remorseful, which could very well heighten your anger and outrage, making forgiveness all but impossible, at least in that moment. Despite the fact that you might not be willing or able to forgive in some situations, forgiving continues to be advocated as the only "medicine" for any and all of your hurts, regardless of the nature of the relationship you may have with your offender, and no matter how accountable or unaccountable this person may be.

All of the alternative approaches, on the other hand, keep the focus on you, which is where your power lies. The person who hurt you has already done so, and this hurt is in the past – though it may still be impacting you in the present. You can't do one darn thing to change it, and you can't make your offender be accountable or remorseful. What's more, trying to extend goodwill or forgiveness toward this person in order to set yourself free might not be something you want to do or can do. If that is the case, then it makes sense to leave your offender out of the picture and *focus on yourself and on what you need.* To help you do so, you can ask yourself the following questions:

> **What do _I_ need so that I can begin to heal?**
> or
> **What do _I_ need so that I can begin to move on?**
> or
> **What do _I_ need so that I can begin to be happy again?**

As you live into the answers, the frequency and duration of your painful thoughts and feelings toward and about the person who hurt you will begin to decrease of their own accord, and the intensity of your emotional upset will become more manageable. This is because you are keeping the focus on you and your needs, and again, whatever you are consciously focusing on is where your energy is going in that particular moment.

This doesn't mean that you won't ever feel angry or upset about how you were hurt, nor does it mean that you don't have to face the pain of the past head-on and address it. However, by keeping the focus on yourself, you will be better able to deal with how you were hurt in a truly effective and self-liberating manner. When you find yourself feeling angry or bitter about this particular hurt and person who hurt you, and getting stuck again in the pain of the past, you can return to the "What do _I_ need . . ." questions time and time again. You can also ask yourself other specific self-liberating questions of your own design, such as: "What is something enjoyable that I can do to help me break free from focusing on this person who hurt me?" or "Who can I reach out to and connect with so that I can break the connection of focusing on this past hurt, which is only causing me to feel upset?" Doing so will enable you to manage and ease your painful thoughts and feelings, so that you can, once again, move forward with your life in that particular moment or in the very near future.

As you keep the focus on yourself and on what you need, you will also have more inner resources to call upon, including one of the most powerful resources in your arsenal: _your personal power to choose._ You will be able to make effective choices as you deal with the pain of the past because you are continually re-turning your attention to yourself, by discerning what *your* needs are in this moment, instead of endlessly rehashing upsetting thoughts and feelings about your offender. Once more, the frequency and duration of your bitterness and anger, etc., toward your offender will reduce, and the intensity of your emotional pain will become more manageable, as a natural byproduct of focusing on your needs. Even during those earliest hours and days after being hurt, when your painful thoughts and feelings are at their most intense, zeroing in on your needs and taking tender care of yourself will make your pain a bit more tolerable.

The traditional model of forgiving places the focus on your offender, on how they hurt you, or on both your offender and how they hurt you, which instead of always setting you free from your emotional pain as it is intended to do, may inadvertently keep your feelings of anger and bitterness alive and well.

Activate as Often as Needed to Manage or Alleviate Painful Memories

There's no way to avoid emotional and mental upset after being hurt. Painful thoughts and feelings are natural byproducts of being hurt, just as some degree of physical pain is normal after an injury or surgery. Even so-called little hurts have the surprising capacity to throw many of us off balance and disrupt our normal daily routine in a profound manner. They can even cause our previously enjoyed poise and emotional equilibrium to take an unauthorized leave of absence.

One reason why forgiving is so hard for so many of us to pull off in a satisfactory manner, especially when the criteria that make forgiving relatively natural and easy are not present, is because *there is an expectation that we are supposed to complete it at some point in time.* Not only are we to eventually complete the forgiving process, we are to do so in a once-and-for-all manner. After we have forgiven, whether it takes us a few weeks or a few years or even a few decades, the expectation is that the particular hurt will no longer bother us again. And if it does, perhaps years or decades after we thought we had put it to rest, then we may question the quality of our prior efforts to forgive. "Did I *really* forgive so and so? I thought I did. But if I did, why am I feeling upset again?"

The alternatives, however, do not have this same expectation that you complete them in a once-and-for-all manner. For instance, there's no expectation, hidden or otherwise, that you must complete "moving on as I keep the focus on myself and my needs" or "freeing myself from the person who hurt me and for a new beginning in life" or "embracing new opportunities" in the same way that there is with forgiving.

Now, admittedly, one reason for this lack of expectation is because most of us have not been aware that healthy alternatives to forgiving even exist. Therefore, it's quite difficult for any expectations to have accumulated when we didn't realize that there were any other options to forgiving in the first place! Despite the fact that a significant number of us have likely employed one or more of the healthy alternatives to forgiving several times in the past, such as "moving on" or "cutting our losses," we have usually done so in an unconscious rather than conscious, intentional, and deliberate manner. Most of us haven't said or acknowledged to ourselves, "Instead of forgiving, I am choosing to move on as I keep the focus on myself and my needs." It is much more likely that we simply moved on in an unconscious manner because we either couldn't or wouldn't forgive. But because we didn't realize that "moving on" was an acceptable alternative, we may have experienced some guilt or shame whenever the memory of how we were hurt resurfaced, as we became aware that we had yet to forgive our offender like we were supposed to.

Though it is likely that these alternatives are new for most people, there is no covert or overt expectation that we must complete them at some point in time and in a once-and-for-all manner. Why? *Because they are present moment approaches to healing, and living, that can be activated on an as-needed and as-often-as-needed basis.*

You, like all of us, are living with a history of hurts in your memory bank. Some of these hurts will remain dormant for the rest of your life, while others will come to your conscious awareness on a periodic or regular basis. When any hurt, large or small, comes to mind again, you will likely feel some degree of emotional and mental pain as well. The alternative approaches simply help you to manage this reawakened pain in the particular present moment in which you are experiencing it. And as you become more skilled in managing your pain, you will also become better at refocusing your energy in a positive and creative direction in a timely manner, rather than becoming trapped for an inordinate period of time in the grip of a painful memory. For instance, you might choose to "make a fresh start right where I am and just as I am," even though the memory of this hurt has surfaced and troubled you again, perhaps when you least expected it to.

The alternatives have no accompanying sense of having failed to pull them off successfully in a once-and-for-all manner, as is so often

the case with forgiveness. Again, when painfu
we thought we had forgiven, many of us ten
or guilty because we thought that forgiving
memories never bothering us again. An
simply allows you to manage the painful mem
attention in a direction of your own choosing,
guilt or confusion. In that sense, they are like a cough drop you take
only when you have a cough, or a couple aspirin that you take only
when you get a headache. You probably don't get down on yourself
for getting a cough or a headache; instead, you reach for something
to manage or alleviate the discomfort so that you can go on with
your life, which is exactly the purpose of the alternatives.

How might this play out in a real life situation? Let's say that
Kim, instead of trying to forgive, chooses the alternative strategy
of "managing my pain while taking small steps and risks to help me
move forward" to help her heal and rebuild after her divorce. As
she makes this choice to "manage her pain and take small steps and
risks to help her move forward" over and over again, even many
times each day early on in the process, she gradually experiences a
significant degree of healing and newfound freedom. She is able to
recreate her life anew and enjoy being happy once again.

Even when years have passed since her divorce and painful
memories about her "Ex," though infrequent, still crop up from time
to time and cause her to feel upset again, she can consciously re-
choose to "manage her pain and take small steps and risks to help
her move forward" *in that particular moment of reawakened emotional
upset.* However, most days, because she *has* learned to manage her
pain and she *has* taken hundreds, even thousands, of small steps and
risks that have resulted in her being happy again, she has no need
to deliberately call upon this alternative strategy. The majority of
time she is simply living – and enjoying – her new life. But on those
less frequent days when a painful memory of her "Ex" arises, she can
choose to consciously and deliberately activate a chosen strategy
that has worked well for her in the past, or employ a different one
to help her quickly reclaim her personal power.

her self-talk might go like this: "Okay, for whatever reason I am really feeling angry again about how my 'Ex' hurt me. It's probably because the anniversary date of our divorce is coming up. Even though I am feeling upset right now, I will use the tools I have gained to manage my pain. Instead of focusing on him, I am going to get up and take my dog for a walk and pay full attention to the various sights and sounds along the way." And though she is hurting in that moment, she moves forward by choosing to do something specific, by refocusing her attention in a deliberate and intentional way, rather than wasting her energy wondering why she can't forgive him in a once-and-for-all manner. What's more, she has accepted the fact that she is probably never going to have positive thoughts and warm feelings about him, which is another advantage to the healthy alternatives to forgiving, which we will say more about in the next section.

When any hurt, large or small, comes to mind again, you will likely feel some degree of emotional and mental pain as well. The alternative approaches simply help you to manage this reawakened pain in the particular present moment in which you are experiencing it.

Positive Thoughts and Warm Feelings Are Not Required

In addition to believing for most of our lives that forgiveness is something that we should be able to complete at some point in time, many of us also believe that we should have certain thoughts and feelings if we have truly forgiven someone. We have an expectation that forgiving will enable us to think positive thoughts about our offender and feel warmly toward them. At the very least, we should have neutral thoughts and feelings, but certainly not negative or painful ones.

Yet when the memory of how we were hurt by this person comes to mind again, whether it does so ten days or ten or more years after we have forgiven, we are often dismayed to discover that some powerful negative thoughts and bitter feelings toward our offender tag along as well. Because we are not only *not* thinking positively or feeling warmly about this person, but are having some fairly intense negative thoughts and bitter feelings, we may decide that (1) we deceived ourselves when we thought that we had forgiven or (2) we are somehow uniquely inept at forgiving and are "forgiveness failures."

The healthy alternatives, however, have no expectations that we think or feel in a certain way, least of all positively or warmly toward our offender. *In fact, the alternatives allow you to think and feel — and accept — exactly what you are thinking and feeling at any point in time, even when it is not what you would **like** to be thinking and feeling.*

You can be having the most bitter thoughts and painful feelings imaginable, and that is perfectly acceptable. And it matters not whether you are experiencing them three days or thirty years after you were first hurt. Conventional understandings of forgiveness, on the other hand, do not allow you to think and feel what you are thinking and feeling, unless you are thinking positively and feeling warmly toward and about your offender, which is hard to do when a memory of how you were hurt comes to mind again.

Thoughts and feelings by their nature are transitory; they are changing all the time, and changing rather quickly at that. So how

113

can what any of us are thinking and feeling at any point in time be an indication of how successfully we have forgiven? Yet this expectation that we think positively and feel warmly toward our offender – or at least neutrally – if we have truly forgiven has deep roots. We can try to tell ourselves that it is okay to have bitter thoughts and feelings even after we have forgiven, but in our heart or at a subconscious level, we are not buying it, because "true forgiveness" is supposed to get rid of these types of sentiments once-and-for-all. But once again, the healthy alternatives free us from having to think and feel in a certain way.

The range of our thoughts and feelings can be quite wide, as portrayed by the continuum below:

• . . . . •

Extremely	Incredibly
negative and	positive and
painful	enjoyable

You can start out the day suffering some painful thoughts and feelings, not necessarily in regards to someone who has hurt you, but about something else in your life (e.g., perhaps some sharp or impatient words were exchanged with your teenager, or you got caught in a traffic jam). Later in that same day, you could find yourself in a much more upbeat frame of mind and feeling quite good (e.g., maybe you received an unexpected word of appreciation or a compliment).

Regarding someone who has hurt you, the healthy alternatives to forgiving allow you to feel whatever you are feeling, whether it is complete bitterness and hatred toward and about your offender or an overwhelming sense of compassion for them, or something in-between. Of course, if you are feeling compassion for this person, it is a more pleasant experience than when you are feeling reawakened hatred. But that's all it is: a more pleasant experience. Whether you are experiencing bitterness or compassion, both are but thoughts and feelings. And, once again, thoughts and feelings change.

What matters, and all that matters in the final analysis, is how we each respond to what we are thinking and feeling. For example, if you are feeling reawakened bitterness and are having vengeful thoughts and then choose to act out in some way, perhaps by drinking too much, or by lashing out at your offender in an attempt to make them hurt in the same way that you are hurting, then you might suffer some painful consequences. You may feel bad for drinking excessively, because you don't normally do that, and you may suffer the consequence of a hangover or getting sick as a result. If you lash out at your offender, you may feel bad about it when you are in a more centered state of mind. There might be other consequences as well, perhaps even of a legal nature (e.g., a restraining order or loss of custody or visitation privileges).

Otherwise, feeling bitterness or having thoughts of revenge are morally neutral. The only consequence they have is that they tend to be upsetting, for none of us says, "I'm having a great day today because I am filled with hatred and fantasies of revenge." No, when you are caught in their grip, you are not having a great day. *You are upset, and that's when employing an alternative approach to forgiving can help you break free from the power of these painful memories so that you can redirect your energy in a more positive and creative direction.* And since you were the one who was hurt, you get to choose the specific alternative that you think will work most effectively for you, rather than do what others have decided is best for you: forgive, when in fact that may be something you can't or don't want to do at all.

Regarding someone who has hurt you, the healthy
alternatives to forgiving allow you to feel whatever you
are feeling, whether it is complete bitterness and hatred
toward and about your offender or an overwhelming
sense of compassion for them, or something in-between.

Since You Suffered the Hurt, You Get to Decide How to Heal

A well-known quote about prayer that is attributed to the Benedictine monk Dom Chapman goes like this: "Pray as you can, not as you can't." Regarding the hurts we all suffer in life, this quote could be adapted as follows: "Heal as you can, not as you can't," or "Move on as you can, not as you can't," or "Be happy again as you can, not as you can't."

Yet forgiveness continues to be advocated by well-intentioned people as the only way to heal. According to their line of reasoning, if you can't forgive, then you simply can't heal, move on, or be happy again. Period. You're out of luck. End of discussion.

Instead of "If you can't forgive, heal as you can," the spoken or implied message is: "If you want to heal and move on, you *have* to forgive," or "Forgiving is the *only* way to heal," or "If you don't forgive, God won't forgive *you*," and so on. Nonetheless, millions of individuals are not able to forgive, at least not in some situations. Perhaps even the best forgivers in our midst would admit that there have been a couple of occasions during the course of their lives when they weren't able to forgive, at least not as well as they would have liked.

This notion that forgiving is the only possible way to heal your hurts is an extremely deep one that has largely gone unquestioned. Even some excellent clergy, spiritual teachers, and therapists are taken aback at first when it is suggested that people don't necessarily have to forgive in order to heal, move on, and be happy again. They, like most people, including both of us for most of our lives, believe that forgiving is the only way to genuine healing.

On the one hand, it seems to be a radical departure from what has been held to be inexorably true for centuries to suggest that there are other ways to heal in addition to forgiving. On the other hand, it seems rather obvious that countless people have gone on with their lives in a positive manner even though they have not forgiven certain hurts or specific people who have hurt them. You, or someone you know, might be such a person.

In keeping with the spirit of Dom Chapman's wisdom, it makes no sense to continue advocating that forgiving is the only viable and authentic way to recover from being hurt when . . .

1. There is no universal understanding of what it means to forgive.

2. Countless numbers of individuals have been able to recover and be happy again though they haven't forgiven.

3. It is something that many of us can't – or won't – do, at least in some situations.

To suggest that forgiving is the only way to heal is like suggesting that one's favorite spiritual practice is the *only* practice, and the *best* practice at that, for everyone. While some enjoy the practice of silent prayer or meditation or mindfulness, and for them it is indeed the best spiritual practice, for others, conversational prayer or going for a walk or gardening might be more satisfying and spiritually enriching. It is human nature to sometimes think that *our* way is the best way, when in fact it may not even be the best way for us a couple months or years down the road, much less the best way for everyone else for all time.

This is probably a good time to reiterate that we are not advocating the alternatives to forgiving over forgiving. As we said earlier, we would encourage those who can forgive in each and every situation to continue doing so. Neither one of us would even *think* about suggesting that these individuals should do something other than forgive. Why? Because forgiving is working for them, and as the saying goes: "If it ain't broke don't fix it." *But for countless others, forgiving is broken. What's more, for some it is broken beyond repair.*

Some who are able to forgive think that because they can forgive, then others should be able to do so as well. Yet none of us knows what these "able forgivers" even mean when they say they have forgiven or that they are always able to forgive. Do they mean they have "let the hurt go" or that they have "refrained from vindictive actions" or that they are "filled with compassion for their offender" or "that they have decided to part ways with their offender" or that "they are now best friends?" Or none of the above?

Unfortunately, some of the strongest advocates of the "forgiveness mono-path" are those who invoke the name of God or "religious truth." Yet many millions are turning away from the religious tradition in which they were raised, and perhaps to which they belonged during a portion of their adult life as well, because the "truths" that were—and still are—assumed to be true are no longer plausible or credible. They don't seem to be so unquestionably true after all, especially in light of their life experiences. A case in point are those who were taught, and perhaps once believed, that their religious tradition had unique or special access to "truth" or God or life after death, but have walked away as a result of meeting wonderful people of different faith traditions as well as "non-believers."

One "truth" that no longer seems plausible to both of us as well as many others is that a person who has been hurt . . .

1. Has to forgive in all cases.

2. Will not be able to move on with their life until they forgive.

3. Will not be forgiven by God (their higher power, the universe, or what have you) if they do not forgive.

Millions of individuals who have turned away from religious authority are discovering that they are the true authorities of their own lives and that they have the power to author, to write, the remaining chapters of their lives as they so choose. They are seeking to live meaningful lives in which they can make a contribution to our wounded and wondrous world by exploring spirituality and by honoring both their intellect and their intuition. And for many, neither their head nor their heart can buy in to the forgiveness myth any longer.

As the one and only person who has suffered your particular hurts and who knows how your hurts have impacted your life, *you are the only one who gets to decide how to heal*, whether by forgiving as you understand forgiving or by an alternative approach. There simply isn't just one way. In fact, the way that you choose to get over a hurt today may not be the approach you choose to deal with a different hurt a couple of years down the road—or even with the same hurt revisited.

This is not to say that you might not need some type of professional help, especially if a particular hurt or a hurtful relationship has taken quite a toll on you. But if the helper insists that you have to forgive when you would prefer to employ an alternative strategy, you would be wise to walk away and seek out someone else who will respect what you have decided is the best route for you to take. Since you suffered the hurt, you get to decide how to heal—as you can, not as you can't.

As the one and only person who has suffered your particular hurts and who knows how your hurts have impacted your life, *you are the only one who gets to decide how to heal,* whether by forgiving as you understand forgiving or by an alternative approach.

～5～

Preparing to Heal and Move Forward with Your Life

If a person wants to get in better shape but is unsure how to proceed, she might be wise to consult a fitness trainer as a preliminary step, rather than jump into specific exercises on her own in a haphazard **and o**verzealous manner. With a trainer's guidance, she can learn how to get started in a manner that will minimize her soreness and reduce the likelihood of injury. That way, she will be more likely to stick with it, rather than end up quitting because her body is aching from doing too much too soon or because she is not seeing results fast enough.

When it comes to healing your hurts, we think that it is important for you to have an understanding of the healing or recovery process prior to introducing you to specific ways to heal and reclaim your personal power—which we will do in the next chapter. Jumping into a specific practice or exercise without having an idea of what the journey entails would not only be similar to starting to exercise in a random and overly enthusiastic manner, it would also be like setting out on a two-week vacation without selecting a destination or making any other preparations for your trip. While being so spontaneous might turn out to be fun, it might also set you up to experience a "vacation from hell," as you encounter unexpected road closures, fully booked airlines, or packed hotels.

In this chapter, we want to prepare you for the healing journey so that you do not get too discouraged along the way. Just as importantly, we want to set you up for success as you apply the specific alternative approaches to some of the hurts you have suffered. But first, we would like to take a moment to emphasize that these healthy alternatives to forgiving are *not* second class citizens in comparison with forgiveness. In other words, they are not a second, or last, choice only to be activated in those situations when you can't or won't forgive. Instead, you might intuitively sense, almost as soon as you suffer a hurt, or shortly thereafter, that an alternative approach is the best way for you to recover your peace and happiness. That way, you don't waste any time or energy trying to forgive because some believe that it is the one and only way to heal, when you have already decided that an alternative approach will work more quickly and effectively for you.

Once again, the myth is that forgiving is the best way to heal, or as we once heard it poetically described, "Forgiving is the royal road to healing." And, of course, forgiving is indeed *a* "royal road" to healing that many of us travel in response to some of our hurts, however it is not the *one and only* path to healing that we must all take in response to all of our hurts. In this abundant universe of ours, of which each of us is a vital, interconnected part, there are many "royal roads" and healing paths, and forgiving is but one of many possibilities from which we can choose. Though it is the oldest and most well known – at least by name, if not in successful practice – it is not necessarily the best or even the primary way to recover from being hurt.

The "royal road" for each of us is simply the one that enables us to heal, move on with our lives, and be happy again as quickly, fully, and effectively as we can. Your "royal road" is the one in which you are loyal to yourself, to your intuitive sense as to what is the best path for you to take in order to recover from a specific hurt or person who hurt you. Sometimes your "royal road" might be that of forgiving, and at other times it might be one of several alternatives.

As we have said several times, we are not advocating the alternative approaches to healing over forgiving. It is a "both-and" world; there are times to forgive, and there are times to set forgiving aside and try something else. What we are encouraging you to do is to travel the easiest and most effective path to healing in each and every situation so that you can move forward with your life.

An analogy might be helpful here. If the easiest way for you to get to your car or to the bus stop is to walk, it would be absurd to crawl. Yes, theoretically, and perhaps even physically, you could crawl. But why would you do so if you can walk? Not only would you look ridiculous, it would be an incredibly slow, arduous, and exhausting way to reach your destination, not to mention hard on your clothes and a bit painful.

Sometimes an alternative approach will be like walking to your car or to the bus stop, whereas trying to forgive would be akin to crawling. When that is the case, why would you try to forgive? Yes, you might be able to do it eventually, but if it's ten times harder, more exhausting, and slower than an alternative approach, it makes no sense.

The goal is *to heal* as quickly and fully and effectively as you can – not necessarily to forgive. The goal is *to move on* again with your life as quickly and fully and effectively as you can – not necessarily to forgive. The goal is *to be happy* again as quickly and fully and effectively as you can – not necessarily to forgive. *Forgiving, as is true of each and every one of the healthy alternatives to forgiving, is but one way to reach your goal, not the goal in and of itself.*

Having said that, and because many fine books on forgiving already exist, in this chapter, we want to provide you with a basic understanding of the healing journey and what it entails. That way, you will be better equipped to successfully implement the suggested practices and ideas that appeal to you in the next chapter, because you are familiar with "the big picture" or "blueprint" of the process.

We begin by reminding you that healing is indeed a process rather than an event.

Your "royal road" [to healing] is the one in which you are loyal to yourself, to your intuitive sense as to what is the best path for you to take in order to recover from a specific hurt or person who hurt you. Sometimes your "royal road" might be that of forgiving, and at other times it might be one of several alternatives.

Healing Is a Process – Not an Event

Processes, as opposed to events, take place over a period of time and entail a series of actions and phases or stages. An obvious example of a process is the one whereby we each began life as a baby and eventually reached physical adulthood some twenty years later. We went through a remarkable series of stages, ranging from being entertained by the discovery of our own toes to standing on our own two feet, first literally and then metaphorically, as we ventured out into the world to find our way.

Some processes have a well-defined goal or endpoint, such as when a person enters college in pursuit of a degree and graduates a few years later, or when a worker who has been laid off decides to pursue some type of vocational training and becomes newly skilled and certified, sometimes within as little as six months or a year. Other processes are more open-ended, as is typical when someone enters therapy. A person may seek therapeutic help to deal with a particular issue (e.g., how to handle their teenager), only to discover that other issues need attending to as well. Then there are processes that are ongoing, even lifelong, as is true of the growing numbers – including both of us – who are striving to establish healthier eating and exercise habits in order to manage their weight and safeguard their health.

An event, in contrast, is something that happens in a particular place and at a specific time and, generally speaking, is shorter in length. Events can be "big" or significant happenings such as when a person graduates, gets married, receives a promotion, or attends a long-awaited concert. They can also be quite ordinary: attending a class or therapy session on any given day, going to work, getting a dental checkup, or eating a meal.

When it comes to recovering from your hurts, it is critically important to understand that healing is usually a process rather than an event. It is something that:

1. Takes place over time.

2. Encompasses several phases or stages that are often repeated or revisited.

3. Requires you to take action.

At one point in your life, your developmental task was to discover and play with your toes. Doing so was something you did before rolling over, which was something you did before crawling, which was something you did before walking, and so on. While you did these things automatically and even willingly as a baby and toddler who delighted in your newfound locomotive abilities, they *did* require you to be an active participant. Fortunately, you didn't have an understanding of the process much less the wherewithal to say to yourself at the time, "Crawling is too much work. It really exhausts me. I'm going to sit out this stage and just wait until I can walk."

However, as an adult who desires to recover from your hurts, just as fortunately, you now have the capacity to gain a better understanding of the healing process and what it requires of you. Instead of passively sitting out the rest of your life because of how you were hurt earlier in your life, or because you haven't known what to do if you can't or won't forgive, *you can choose to be an active learner and an adult participant in your own recovery process.*

As most of us have learned through our experiences with doctors and other health care providers, when we gain a thorough understanding of a particular medical condition or challenge we may be facing—whether it is diabetes, depression, high cholesterol, or cancer—we can engage it more proactively, creatively, and successfully. Yes, wishing that we didn't have this particular medical condition or challenge, or wishing that we had never been hurt so deeply by this other person, is part of the process. But in and of itself, wishing will not ultimately help any of us to heal, move on in life, and be happy again, whereas having an understanding of the healing process and what it entails will begin to set us free.

So, once again, the first thing you need to know is that recovering from your hurts and regaining your ability to heal, move on, and be happy again is a process. There are no shortcuts. But there is a map of sorts, which we will provide you with in this chapter, and a method, *your* method, which you will discover or refine as you try out some of the suggestions we offer in the next chapter. As you do some experimenting, we trust that you will quickly set aside those that don't work for you, while remaining open to trying or modifying others – or creating your own – that do end up working for you.

Before providing you with an overview of the healing process, which we will do in the next section, it is also important to understand that the very nature of a process consists of an ongoing cycle of progress, setbacks, and comebacks.

1. **Progress** – You *will* make progress as you honor and work with your unique healing process, and as you gain and employ new skills and insights.

2. **Setbacks** – You will likely suffer some setbacks along the way, which tend to be disappointing and discouraging, but on the positive side, they are oftentimes precursors to renewed growth as well as opportune times to reevaluate and make some adjustments.

3. **Comebacks** – You will be able to make courageous comebacks after suffering discouraging setbacks, and continue to heal and make even more progress – again, in part, because you are willing to reevaluate and make a few changes.

As opposed to the physical development of a child, or the sequential order that is inherent in earning a college degree or vocational certificate, the process of healing your hurts is *not* linear; instead, it is circular or spiral-like. Each time around the process, you develop a greater understanding and appreciation of the alternatives, while discovering how they can set you free in a timely manner. While setbacks tend to be discouraging and disappointing, they are not fatal. In fact, they are often learning opportunities that are invaluable to your overall healing process. Revisiting an old way of dealing with a hurt (e.g., obsessing about your offender, or believing that your life is ruined, and so on) is often necessary in order to move further along the journey of healing and happiness.

When any of us regresses, which, as human beings, we are prone to doing, we often re-learn that some degree of misery is waiting for us as we give our power away to the unchangeableness of the past. This can be a highly valuable re-learning. Spending a little more time with misery, along with paying the price that misery exacts from you, may motivate you to take renewed actions on your own behalf, which quite often results in a surge of progress. In that sense, a setback is like an argument a couple gets into, only to move forward into a greater appreciation of each other as they mend the rift and see each other through fresh eyes – which would never have happened without the argument.

Instead of passively sitting out the rest of your life because of how you were hurt earlier in your life, or because you haven't known how to heal if you can't or won't forgive, *you can choose to be an active learner and an adult participant in your own recovery process.*

An Overview of the Healing Process

In very broad terms, the healing process is one in which you will move *from* being stuck or trapped in the pain of the past because of how you were hurt *to* a growing sense of freedom, possibility, and hope in the present moment. Below, in no particular order, you will find twelve additional ways of expressing this movement. We invite you to pay special attention to the ones that appeal to you.

FROM feeling power-less about your ability to get beyond how you were hurt . . .

TO feeling increasingly **power-filled** as you take small steps to heal and move forward with your life.

FROM feeling stuck when the memory of how you were hurt upsets you again . . .

TO gaining an experientially-based sense of **confidence** in your ability to break free from your reawakened emotional pain within a reasonable timeframe.

FROM feeling helpless and hopeless about your life as a whole, or perhaps in just one area such as the relationship realm, . . .

TO feeling **energized and hopeful** about the possibilities in front of you as well as the ones that are yet to come.

FROM feeling like, and perhaps even identifying yourself as, a victim . . .

TO seeing yourself as someone who, unfortunately, was victimized by your offender but who now chooses to be a **strong and capable adult** rather than a permanent victim.

FROM spending an excessive amount of your finite time and daily-life's-energy "playing" the can't-win "blame game," despite how blameworthy your offender is, . . .

TO **taking full responsibility** for the quality of the rest of your life as you choose to aim for something new and better.

FROM wishing that things had been different in the past . . .

TO **taking consistent action** to *make* things different – and better – for yourself in the yet-to-be-lived present moments of each new day, which will result in a brighter future.

FROM feeling guilty or bad about having negative thoughts and upsetting emotions with regard to the person who hurt you . . .

TO **recognizing that such thoughts and feelings are normal** and to be expected whenever a painful memory resurfaces.

FROM rejecting yourself for what you are thinking and feeling, especially when it is not what you would *like* to be thinking and feeling, . . .

TO **accepting yourself** exactly as you are (e.g., even when you are struggling with bitterness, hatred, and anger, etc.).

FROM being a passive bystander in your life . . .

TO being an **active agent** with the greatest influence on your own healing process.

FROM clinging to "reasons" why you cannot heal, move on, and be happy again . . .

TO **affirming that you can't help but heal**, move on, and be happy again as you discover your **unique way**, honor your process, and take consistent and creative action.

FROM emotional reasoning in which you are bound by how you feel about the past . . .

TO calling upon **your intellect, your spirituality, your attitude, and your other intrapersonal allies** to help you temper painful emotions and live with more balance.[15]

---

15. See the section "Activating Your Seven Intrapersonal Allies."

FROM getting trapped for an inordinate amount of time in black and white, all or nothing thinking (e.g., "my life is ruined" or "no one would want me") . . .

TO **finding yourself – your true self** – in more flexible and resilient thinking (e.g., "Yes, I was hurt badly, but the next chapter of my life is waiting to be written" or "Why *wouldn't* someone want to be in a relationship with me?").

To summarize, the healing process is one in which you will spend less time trapped in your head as you *think* about and replay the hurtful events of the past over and over, which tends to result in a host of painful feelings and a steady loss of personal power. At the same time, you will find yourself *living more and more fully in the present moment*, which is where your true power resides, while learning to manage the emotional pain that comes and goes.

However, while all this sounds good and perhaps even simple on paper, it is a highly complex and nuanced journey that entails some ups and downs, progress and setbacks. Perhaps it is best conveyed by a circle. While it is typical to proceed in a clockwise manner – from being completely stuck to periodically stuck to largely free to completely free – especially early on when how you were hurt is most upsetting, over time you can reverse direction and go from being completely stuck to completely free, sometimes in a matter of hours or even minutes.

COMPLETELY STUCK,
POWER-LESS & UNHAPPY

COMPLETELY FREE
POWER-FILLED & HAPPY

YOUR EXPERIENCE
IN THE
PRESENT MOMENT

PERIODICALLY STUCK
POWER-LESS & UNHAPPY

LARGELY FREE,
POWER-FILLED & HAPPY

At any given time on any given day, you might be at any particular point on the circle (or cycle). If it is a painful spot, then you can choose one or more of the alternative approaches from Chapter Four, and a couple of insights or suggested practices from this chapter as well as Chapter Six, to help you move toward a less painful place.

When you have been hurt, it is normal to feel powerlessly stuck in the pain of the past on some days, perhaps with a sense of helplessness, unhappiness, and negativity as well (see the top of the circle on the previous page). On other days, you may feel like you are completely free from this hurt forever, as you enjoy a powerful sense of hope, happiness, and positive energy flowing through you in the present moment (see the left side of the circle). While on many, if not most, other days you will be at other points on the circle.

Because the very nature of life is dynamic, characterized by movement and change, it makes sense that in response to how we have been hurt, most of us will find ourselves at different points on the cycle at various times. However, as you discover your unique healing process, work with it, and take consistent action, the power that the pain of the past has over you *will* decrease. At the same time, you will find yourself spending more and more time living fully and freely in the now. First, however, you can expect to get or feel partially or completely stuck on a regular or periodic basis.

In the next section, we will identify some other expectations to keep in mind, for if you know what to anticipate, you will be less likely to succumb to discouragement during difficult times. Just as importantly, you will learn to *expect healing and happiness*, which will increase your attentiveness to the "little things" in your life that point to the fact that you *are* breaking free from the pain of the past and moving forward with your life once again.

As you discover your own unique healing process,
work with it, and take consistent action,
the power that the pain of the past has over you
will decrease. At the same time, you will find yourself
spending more and more time
living fully and freely in the now.

What to Expect Along the Way

Expectations play a big role in life. We can expect something that is unreasonable and end up feeling disappointed by the subsequent reality we encounter. We can also be unaware of what to expect and then become discouraged or frustrated when encountering unforeseen, yet completely normal, obstacles or challenges that are not worth fretting over. And, of course, we can have expectations that are too low, which may keep us from living as fully and vibrantly as we otherwise could.

With regard to the process of healing your hurts, your expectations might be unreasonable. For example, you might expect that one of the alternative approaches to forgiving will free you from ever feeling upset again when a painful memory comes to mind. Or you might not know what to expect and become discouraged, perhaps even tempted to give up, as you encounter some rough spots you had not foreseen. For instance, you might not know that it is normal to experience some intensely upsetting thoughts and feelings whenever a memory of how you were hurt comes to mind, even after making significant strides toward reclaiming your inner peace and happiness. Or you might hold expectations that are too low and not really expect yourself to heal and be happy again, perhaps because forgiving hasn't worked all that well for you, so you are doubtful whether the alternative approaches will make much of a difference either. Consequently, your energy level and subsequent efforts may be a bit too low in terms of what recovering from your particular hurts really needs.

We want to dissuade you from having unreasonable expectations such as no more pain ever again. For most of us, we have two tasks or invitations: (1) learning how to manage our pain concerning past hurts, and (2) learning how to move forward with our lives at the same time, even on those days when we are hurting. They feed and complement each other. As you learn to manage your pain, you are able to move forward with greater energy and effectiveness; as you learn specific ways to move forward into each new day and live as fully as you can, the pain associated with past hurts loses its power to hinder you for any extended length of time.

Because we do not want you to become overly discouraged and possibly even quit along the way, we have identified ten expectations that will help you walk that wide middle path between being blindsided by the unexpected and not expecting enough because you have lost sight of your capacity to heal and move forward. Regarding the latter, we believe that your potential for healing is in direct correlation to how deeply you have been hurt. So if you have been hurt in a deep and serious manner, your potential to heal and be happy again, or for the very first time, is equally deep. What follows are ten expectations you may wish to keep in mind:

1. Expect to experience a multitude of upsetting thoughts and emotions such as rage, bitterness, anxiety or depression, especially early on in your recovery process as you actively address the hurt and its impact on you.

2. Expect to be highly uncomfortable with these upsetting thoughts and feelings, especially early on, and to want to escape, numb, or avoid them in some way that may be less than healthy (e.g., eating sweets, chemical usage, staying extremely busy, excessive sleeping, and so on). Keep in mind that upsetting thoughts and feelings, by their nature, are upsetting, but you *can* learn to manage them more skillfully and send them packing a little more quickly than in times past.

3. Expect a lot of ambivalence or fluctuation as portrayed by the inner voice of powerlessness and the inner voice of power in the examples on the next page:

Inner Voice of Powerlessness	Inner Voice of Power
I can't move on with my life.	I want to move on with my life.
I can't stop thinking about my offender.	I need to focus on myself.
I don't know how or where to start.	I know that I can take one step today.
I am a victim and my life is forever ruined.	I have the strength to rebuild.
My offender is responsible for my past pain, present misery, and future happiness.	I am responsible for the quality of the rest of my life.
I can't accept how badly I was hurt in the past, and I can't do anything to bring about peace and happiness today.	I cannot change the past, but I *can* take steps to begin fostering a return of peace and happiness today.
I am bad – or it is wrong – if I don't forgive.	I can heal without forgiving.
Upsetting thoughts and feelings are simply too much for me: I can't tolerate them at all, much less begin to manage them.	I *can* handle upsetting thoughts and feelings and learn to manage them more skillfully.

4. Expect emotional pain and upsetting thoughts, that may be quite intense at times, to accompany memories of how you were hurt whenever they come to mind.

5. Expect the passage of time to contribute greatly to your overall recovery process, but not to heal your hurts in a "time heals all wounds" manner if you yield to passivity and do nothing to help yourself.

6. Expect to get stuck in the pain of the past from time to time, even to feel like you have made no progress whatsoever, especially during the holidays or at other times of the year that have significance for you such as your birthday or an anniversary date of some type. It is also common to get or feel stuck when you are in a slump and aren't feeling very good about yourself.

7. Expect to need the help of others and perhaps that of God or your higher power. While pride and possibly even a sense of shame or embarrassment (e.g., "How could I have been so stupid to stay with this person for so long?!" or "I can't believe that something this little is still bothering me!") may tempt you to isolate and go it alone, your chances of healing and happiness increase exponentially as you seek out the care and support of others (many believe that the divine works most powerfully through others).

8. Expect to need the help of professionals, such as a therapist or a competent, compassionate spiritual caregiver, if the magnitude of your hurts and their impact are such that you might benefit from their assistance. If you had a toothache, you would likely seek out a dentist. If you have an unremitting heartache and are hurting inside, even if you are still functioning reasonably well on the outside, you might be wise to

seek professional help. If you are depressed or thinking about hurting yourself or others, then you need to seek help *immediately*. Don't hesitate to call 911 or to present yourself at your local hospital's emergency room.

9. Expect to heal, not magically or instantly or without putting forth some effort, but truly expect to heal and recover. Adopt an attitude of "I *am* going to heal, move on, and be happy again, and *nothing* is going to stop me!"

10. Expect that as the frequency and duration of your painful thoughts and emotions gradually decrease, and as you learn to manage the intensity of your emotional pain with increasing skill and confidence, you will begin to notice, benefit from, and enjoy a gradual and corresponding increase in your:

   A. Ability to refocus in the present moment in a timely manner, make positive and effective choices on your own behalf, and experience a growing sense of peace and happiness.

   B. Energy level, so that you can fulfill your daily responsibilities, engage in self-care, take risks, and enjoy a sense of balance in your life.

   C. Capacity to live more fully in the present moment and be forward-oriented, rather than past-focused, so that you can be hopeful about your unfolding life, plans, and dreams.

We hope that some of the expectations above will prevent you from becoming overly discouraged when you feel stuck or when you encounter a bit of a slump on your recovery journey, for it is completely normal to suffer setbacks along the way. We also hope that a couple of the other expectations will help you to adopt an attitude in which you fully expect yourself to be able to heal, move on, and be happy again, because the very nature of life, of your life, is healing and regenerative. In the next section, we remind you of the importance of activating your seven intrapersonal allies, as they are powerful inner resources that can work together to help you heal your past and create a new beginning.

Your potential for healing is in direct correlation to how deeply you have been hurt. So if you have been hurt in a deep and serious manner, your potential to heal and be happy again, or for the very first time, is equally deep.

Activating Your Seven Intrapersonal Allies

In the West, for a variety of complex reasons, many of us have had a tendency to live too much in our head and approach life from an excessively intellectual standpoint. Instead of experiencing a unity of mind, body, and spirit, we "head-dwellers" are prone to feeling somewhat–or even profoundly–disconnected from our body and spirit and apart from all of creation. And despite the fact that so many of us do indeed spend an inordinate amount of time living in our head, as Buddhist teachers are prone to pointing out, Western minds are largely untrained. We are often swept away by a wide array of thoughts, and we seem to have little influence on, much less mastery over, the types of thoughts we are thinking.

We have resigned ourselves to going passively on this, at times, wild "thoughts ride," like passengers on a roller-coaster who have no say once the operator sends them down the track. Early in the morning, for example, we may be in an upbeat frame of mind, enjoying pleasant thoughts and emotions, only to have this shift on us abruptly and without our authorization, perhaps during our commute to work, as our mind latches on to something that is upsetting.

Back and forth and up and down we go, day after day, year after year. We always enjoy the pleasant thoughts, and corresponding enjoyable feelings, only wishing that they would last longer. And we definitely don't enjoy the painful ones, as we wonder why they invade our serenity and take over our consciousness when we neither asked nor wanted them to. What's worse, once they have taken over at any point in the day, we often feel powerless to expel them so that we can enjoy our peace of mind once again.

Though many of us might admit that we have not always protected and steered our "gift of thought" as well as we could have in times past, it is something we can begin to do today and re-begin whenever we catch ourselves thinking in a manner that is not serving us well. It is especially important to become a more skill-full thinker when you are striving to overcome your hurts.

Because you can think rationally and you make thousands of decisions each day that can be traced back to a thought, you can choose to put your mind, by which we mean your intellect, in charge of your healing and rebuilding process. Rather than being swept away by a memory of how you were hurt and all the emotional pain that comes with it, you can learn to activate your intellect to help manage the pain, replace the upsetting thoughts with less upsetting ones, and redirect your attention elsewhere. Instead of sitting there helplessly as wave after wave of disturbing thoughts results in you suffering more and more emotional pain, you can, with the help of your intellect, slow down or even stop these types of thoughts by redirecting your energy and focus elsewhere. For example, you might decide to do something quite mundane, such as load the dishwasher or go for a walk, or you might treat yourself to something special, such as having dinner at your favorite restaurant with a friend, spouse, or partner.

However, just as a restaurant manager needs help in order to run a restaurant, so too your internal manager, your intellect, needs some help in managing your emotional pain as well as your life in general. Below, we begin by saying a few words about how your intellect can help you to heal. Then we go on to offer a few insights regarding the roles that your other six "inner friends" have to play in your recovery process, but first, an analogy.

If you had a large task in front of you such as moving, you would be wise to use your intellect to plan this undertaking. Now even if you were physically unable to do any packing or cleaning or moving, suppose you had six willing, able-bodied, and trustworthy people at your beck and call. In such a case, it wouldn't make any sense to turn away these enthusiastic hard workers and try to do it all by yourself. When it comes to recovering from how you have been hurt, neither would it make any sense to turn down the assistance of your six other intrapersonal allies— attitude, action, spirituality, emotions, body, and heart—and try to rely solely upon your intellect. We start by offering a few comments regarding the critical role that your intellect has to play as the manager of the whole moving process, for you *are* moving, in this case from being trapped or dominated by how you were hurt, to being free to steer your life in a new and rewarding direction.

INTELLECT Your intellect is especially valuable in freeing yourself *from* emotional reasoning in which your emotions may be running and mismanaging the show of your life *to* using your ability to think clearly in order to manage your emotions and steer your life in a thought-full direction. With your intellect, you can think things through rather than remain stuck in emotional reasoning, which doesn't tend to be very reasonable when you are—or any of us is—feeling upset. Activating your intellect enables you to step back and gain a broader perspective. And because it is the manager of not only your hurt-healing process but of your entire life as you live it each day, you can use it to purposefully call upon any of your other six intrapersonal allies, such as your attitude, to help you break free. For example, with your intellect, you can assess whether black and white, all or nothing thinking is contributing to you feeling upset. If so, you can make an intellectual choice to strive for a broader perspective and a more hopeful attitude. Your intellect also allows you to stay in present time, which is invaluable when activating the alternative approaches to healing.

ATTITUDE Your attitude is the outlook with which you look out at and see the world, other people, and yourself. As children, some of us were accused of having "an attitude" from time to time, which usually meant something negative. Yet as adults, we can be intentional; we can choose to adopt and practice an attitude that works for us or one that works against us. Regarding your hurts, you can choose to begin fostering an attitude of "I *am* going to recover and move on with my life, and nothing is going to stop me!" or "I am now going to begin writing a new and better chapter despite how I was hurt in the past." You can also choose an attitude of "abundance" in which you see that the very nature of life is bountiful, and of "expectancy" in which you fully expect things to improve for yourself as you reclaim and activate your personal power to make little choices on your own behalf each day.

While some of us aren't inclined to have an overly positive outlook on life, taking just one small step toward the positive end of the negative-positive attitude continuum can be very liberating, especially when thoughts of negativity and helplessness/hopelessness have been battering you. As you choose a more hopeful or positive attitude, you will also be more inclined to engage in some type of positive action.

ACTION Taking action is critical to your recovery and healing process, for as the sayings go, "this is where the rubber hits the road" and "if nothing changes, nothing changes." Every little—even tiny and tentative—constructive or creative action-step you take moves you further down the road toward healing and happiness, while changing your life for the better. You can take action even when you don't feel like doing so, as evidenced by all of us who get up each morning and go to work when we'd rather sleep in another hour or two.

The types of actions you can take to help yourself recover, rebuild, and move on with your life are as limitless as your imagination. In fact, as you turn inward and access your innate wisdom to help you discern what specific steps you might take today, and as you seek the input of select others and perhaps God or your higher power as well if you are so inclined, you will know what to do to foster your wellbeing in the unique moments of each day. Of course, when a person is hurting, there is often a huge chasm "between the knowing and the doing," and when that is the case, calling upon your intrapersonal ally of spirituality can be especially helpful.

SPIRITUALITY Your spirituality is an "inner friend" capable of helping you on so many levels of life. While it would be both arrogant and presumptuous of us to try to suggest what the greatest benefit of spirituality is for you or anyone else, we do think that one of the main gifts your spirituality has to offer you is that of acceptance. So many people who have been hurt have a difficult time accepting themselves just as they are, especially when they are filled with a steady stream of painful emotions and vindictive thoughts toward their offender, or when they are struggling with "bad" or negative thoughts about themselves.

Because it is typical to get stuck, tired, or discouraged along the journey to healing and wholeness, maybe even to such a degree that you can't seem to take the smallest action on your own behalf, your spirituality and your spiritual practices can help you to accept yourself right where you are and exactly as you are: stuck, angry, hate-filled, bitter, discouraged, depressed, hopeless, or what have you. Many times, it is in accepting yourself where you are and how you are that you can then move forward once again. The alternative is to beat yourself up, which instead of helping you to move forward, tends to keep you stuck even longer. Acceptance of what is, and of yourself as you are, is apt to set you free sooner rather than later.

While what constitutes healthy spirituality is not easy—or even desirable—to pin down in a precise manner, we offer a few thoughts for your consideration:

Healthy spirituality...

- ↬ Comforts and nurtures you as you take tender care of yourself, and as you allow others, and perhaps God or your higher power, to be "tender caretakers" of you as well.

- ↬ Helps you to accept yourself just as you are at any given point in time (and oftentimes to accept others as they are, and life as it is, as well).

- ↬ Refreshes and renews your mind, body, and spirit.

- ↬ Fosters a sense of connection or reconnection with yourself, others, and life itself.

- ↬ Strengthens and inspires you at the very core of your being, again, in body, mind, and spirit.

- ✦ Engages you in life and stimulates a reawakened sense of wonder, appreciation, and gratitude.

- ✦ Enlivens and energizes you, while (re)awakening a sense of possibility, hope, and trust.

- ✦ Enhances your experiences in your religious tradition, whether it is one to which you have belonged all of your life, one you have recently returned to, or a brand new tradition.

So in essence, your spirituality and spiritual practices can be anything that is healthy and life-enhancing for you, which in turn will be healthy and life-enhancing for others in this interdependent, interconnected world of ours. Ways to refresh and renew your spirit can include reading a novel, reading scriptures, or "reading" nature. It can entail going out to dinner, going for a walk, or going on vacation. It can be as ordinary as playing with your children or grandchildren, playing a friendly game of cards, or going to a play. It might include prayer, meditation, or mindfulness. It might also entail gardening, golfing, or giving a helping hand or kind word to a neighbor – or to a stranger, for that matter. It is truly all-encompassing, present in every aspect of life, and as close to you and as simple as attuning to your next breath, which is a particularly helpful practice in managing painful emotions.

EMOTIONS Our capacity to experience a wide and rich range of emotions is what separates us from most other species, and is something that needs to be honored rather than ridiculed or discounted. When it comes to painful emotions, even though they are indeed painful, they can also be beneficial. They are part of life, and our capacity to feel sad, for example, tends to help us appreciate joy. Painful emotions, like pleasant ones, are often connected to some external event, as is the case when we feel anger after being hurt or mistreated, or happy when we receive a sincere compliment from an unlikely source.

One reason why painful emotions are so powerful is that many people tend to resist them or flee their presence, and "that which you resist persists." You can learn to abide with your painful emotions, at least to some extent, for they are but visitors on the move (the Latin root of "emotion" is "*emovere*," which means "to move out"). Running from your painful emotions, or shaming or scolding yourself for feeling a certain way, doesn't tend to work. It is much more effective to face them, perhaps with the assistance of a therapist, and gain some skills so they will become less overwhelming.

Emotions, even painful ones, can be like angels, messengers, who simply inform you of how you are feeling about something. In that sense, an emotion such as fear can serve as a protector, inviting you to proceed with caution. While you would be wise not to let your emotions run the show, you would be equally wise to listen to what they have to say to you. They may tell you, perhaps by a gut feeling, that a certain person is not safe, or because you feel so deeply hurt by someone, that the relationship you once had with this individual is not salvageable.

BODY At the beginning of this section, we advocated putting your intellect in charge of your healing and moving-forward process. Truth, however, does not just reside in your head; it is also at home in your body. As we mentioned when discussing emotions above, you can learn to listen to and trust your body. Your intuitive or gut sense about something is often accurate. While we would not advocate being led solely by your gut, linking your head and gut, your intellect with your intuitive sense, gives you a powerful combination with which to make decisions, both large and small.

Another way that your body can befriend your healing process is to live in it, attend to it, befriend it, and activate it. Just being physically active, to whatever degree you are able, increases the production of endorphins and provides you with a sense of wellbeing or better-being, which is helpful when dealing with depression. Releasing some of your anger through physical activity may be critical to your emotional management, for it could very well be that you have stored a ton of feelings in your body over the years. Perhaps pampering yourself via a luxurious bath or a massage is another way to foster your whole-person healing.

HEART Your heart, as an intrapersonal ally, represents the core of your being and serves as a reminder that your healing requires passion, something that you "want with all your heart" and something that you are willing to "give your heart to." You will likely heal to the same degree that you give your whole heart to the new life you are building in the present moment, rather than allowing your heart to remain a captive of those who have hurt you in the past.

Two particularly important characteristics that are associated with the intrapersonal ally heart are courage and mercy. It takes courage not to be a victim and to step out into the wider world again after being hurt, especially when you've been hurt in a serious manner. The Latin root of "courage" is "cor," or "heart," which is a common metaphor for inner strength, which both courage and mercy require. It takes a whole lot of inner strength to be merciful and gentle with yourself, especially during the difficult moments of your journey when you regress, or when you become temporarily overwhelmed by a host of upsetting thoughts and feelings.

As you go forth with your heart-traits of courage and mercy, and are willing to give your whole heart to your recovery process, accompanied by your other six "inner friends," you are well equipped to deal with the pain of the past, and to heal and move forward with your life into a renewed sense of peace and happiness.

INTELLECT

HEART

ATTITUDE

HEALING
&
HAPPINESS

BODY

ACTION

EMOTIONS

SPIRITUALITY

While our discussion of the seven intrapersonal allies has been, by necessity, brief, we hope that we have helped you to see that your healing process is a whole-person activity and not just something that takes place in your head. Your intrapersonal allies are there to serve and befriend you along the way. With their support, you will have the strength and balance to undertake the important task of doing a hurt-healing cost analysis or assessment, which is what we will explore next.

Regarding your hurts, you can choose to begin fostering
an attitude of "I *am* going to recover and move on with
my life, and nothing is going to stop me!" or "I am now
going to begin writing a new and better chapter
despite how I was hurt in the past."

Doing a Hurt-Healing Cost Analysis

One of the toughest aspects of reality each of us must deal with is the fact that the hurts we have suffered in the past, as well as the ones we have caused others to suffer (which we will address in Chapter Seven), cannot be changed or undone. How you were hurt at a certain point in time is part of your life history. In other words, what was, was. Unfortunately, "what was" may still be causing you pain and sorrow and unhappiness today, which is adversely affecting the quality of "what is." And as the pain of the past continues to cause you to suffer in the "what is" of each new day, day after day, and perhaps even year after year if not decade after decade, your "what will be," your future, becomes bound to and adversely affected by the unchangeable nature of the past as well.

In short, the pain of the past not only caused you to suffer at the time you were originally hurt, it may have caused you to suffer for quite some time since you were hurt. And unless something changes, it has the potential to cause you to suffer, perhaps needlessly, not only this day but for hundreds or thousands of future days to come, possibly even for the rest of your life. That is a very sobering reality – and a somewhat frightening one as well.

But because you are reading this book right now, it could very well be a sign, a powerful sign, that you are saying or acknowledging something like the following:

1. With all my heart, I want to heal, move on, and be happy again.

2. I have an irrepressible life-force within me that is trying to burst forth and help me live fully and freely again – or for the very first time.

3. I am ready to try something new in order to break free from the pain of the past, so that I can be happy and at peace.

Please don't misunderstand us. We are not implying that you haven't necessarily made all sorts of efforts in the past to deal with your hurts. Maybe you have done some significant work in therapy, or read a number of books, or sought out a support group. Or, you might be relatively new to the healing journey, and reading this book is among the first steps you are taking. In either case, it's a good time to remind you that this book is *not* "the answer book," nor is it a substitute for your possible need for professional help. Instead, *it's intended to set you free from "the forgiveness myth" so that you can discover your unique path to healing and happiness when you can't or won't forgive*, perhaps with the assistance of a therapist, religious or spiritual leader, or some type of support group.

A popular analogy calls to mind that it doesn't really matter whether it is a heavy rope or the slenderest of threads that is tied to a bird's leg, holding it captive, for in either case it is unable to fly. All of your past efforts to deal with how you were hurt, ranging from the intimate conversations you have had with friends, to doing some major work in therapy, to reading a number of excellent books, may have been analogous to undoing the multiple strands of a thick rope, one by one, that have been binding you to the past. Perhaps only a few strands remain, or maybe just one strand is keeping you attached to the pain of yesteryear. It could be that something in this book, such as the fact that you *can* move forward without forgiving, will enable you to break free from those final bindings, which might turn out to be as insubstantial as gossamer, so that you can take flight and soar again.

It's important for you to realize that many, many people never even get to the point where you are already. For example, a significant number of alcoholics never recover and get sober, not because treatment or AA or some alternative recovery method can't work for them, but because they *never even try to recover*. Millions never seek help and never try to change, and so they live – or exist – and die as active alcoholics.

But the fact that you are reading this book right now is a wonderful sign attesting to your desire, your *unstoppable* desire, and your willingness to do all that is within your power to break free from your hurts so that you can live fully and happily again. You might have access to the best therapist in the world, yet that person is but a minor player in comparison with the role that you play, because *you* are the star of *your* life. As the star, you have the most power as well as the most influence regarding how the rest of your life is going to unfold. Your supporting cast can pitch you the ball, but you need to be willing to pick up the bat and swing. And if you miss, you *get to try again*. There is no "three strikes and you're out" rule. You're only out when you stop swinging (i.e., trying), and even then, not permanently, because you can always decide to try again somewhere down the road, whether a day or a decade later.

Now if you're not athletic and this analogy is conjuring up painful grade school or middle school memories in which you were one of the last people selected for teams in gym class, imagine yourself today with a thick but light plastic bat in your hand. Now envision that your best and most trustworthy friend, or your therapist or some other supportive person, is pitching a beach ball to you. Trust us, you'll be able to hit it, and hit it solidly. What's more, this beach ball analogy applies to all of us, for we are each in need of having the equivalent of a beach ball pitched gently to us at various points in our life, so that we can taste success and gain confidence for life's tougher pitches and games.

Though recovering from your hurts will cost you, it will pay you back ten, a hundred, or even a thousand times over, many times in totally delightful and surprising ways. The cost of not trying to recover, or of expecting to heal without putting forth sufficient effort, will exact a price from you as well, and a very dear and severe price at that: your potential to be happy and at peace again. The epitaph on your tombstone can either say "ROUGH START, MISERABLE FINISH" or "ROUGH START, STRONG FINISH." Or it might read "I WAS HURT BADLY, SO I QUIT" or "I WAS HURT BADLY, BUT I BOUNCED BACK AND HAD A GOOD LIFE."

After being hurt, and once you are an adult, there is good and bad news. The bad news is: *You are totally responsible for the quality and direction of the rest of your life, which you can deny or refuse.* The good news is similar: *You are totally responsible for the quality of the rest of your life,* **and** *there are many resources, ranging from competent, compassionate people to excellent books, to help you rebuild so that you can have a high-quality rest-of-your-life.*

We are all going to die some day, and we each have the potential to die with bitterness, because we gave away our personal power and response-ability to rebuild after being hurt, or we can die with a sense of "betterness," because we seized and developed our personal power and responded to life's new opportunities. Our deepest hope for you is that you will recover from how you have been hurt and begin – or continue – to live fully and freely today. So we offer a few thoughts for your consideration regarding the cost of recovering from your hurts versus the cost of refusing to try to heal.

Basically, there are three aspects to a hurt-healing cost analysis or assessment:

1. What the **hurt** and its impact cost you at the time – and may be continuing to cost you today.

2. What **refusing** to take an active, central, responsible role in your healing process will cost you, both now and in the future.

3. What **choosing** to take an active, central, responsible role in your healing and recovery process will cost or require of you.

This hurt-healing cost analysis is something that can be done on a periodic basis, especially at critical junctures, rather than just once. One crucial point is at the beginning of your journey or from where you are restarting today. It is best to consider the three aspects of the cost analysis concurrently. You might assess the cost that a hurt is having on you, perhaps in a therapeutic setting or with a friend, and at the same time determine what taking action to recover, as well as not taking action, will cost you.

As a result of your analysis, let's say you come to realize that you are going to need some support in order to heal, which will require you to reach out and do some exploring. A short time later, you learn that there is a group for the separated and divorced that meets once a month in a church or community setting nearby, which is just what you need in light of your recent divorce. If you go, you might find some support; if you don't go, you won't. The latter choice might cost you a continued sense of feeling completely isolated and alone in your suffering, which is a painful price to pay. If you go, however, you will need to pay the price, the cost, of talking to some other people and opening up a bit—although at your own pace, of course.

WHAT THE ORIGINAL HURT COST ME
AT THE TIME — AS WELL AS WHAT IT
MIGHT BE COSTING ME TODAY

HEALING
&
HAPPINESS

WHAT REFUSING TO TAKE
AN ACTIVE, CENTRAL, AND
RESPONSIBLE ROLE IN MY
HEALING PROCESS WILL COST ME,
NOW AND IN THE FUTURE

WHAT CHOOSING TO TAKE
AN ACTIVE, CENTRAL,
RESPONSIBLE ROLE IN MY
HEALING PROCESS WILL
COST OR REQUIRE OF ME

Below, you will find some ideas to help you get started with your hurt-healing cost analysis. As always, this is not intended to be an exhaustive or complete list. Perhaps with the assistance of a friend, spiritual leader, or therapist, you will come up with some specific categories that are more relevant to the hurts from which you are seeking to recover.

1. What the Hurt and its Impact Cost Me

- Emotionally, physically, spiritually, and at the very core of my personhood.

- In terms of my health, self-esteem, or relationships.

- In terms of my career, my time and energy, my childhood, my adult life . . .

- Financially, my reputation, my broken dreams, my lost opportunities . . .

2. What Refusing to Take an Active, Central, Responsible Role in My Healing Process Will Cost Me

- My potential to enjoy peace and happiness again.

- Ongoing bitterness and negativity, which isn't very attractive to others.

- Essentially saying that my life ended with the person who hurt me.

- Depression, chronic sadness, anxiety, hopelessness, helplessness . . .

- My chances to enjoy new opportunities in life.

- A healthier relationship or friendship than the one that just ended.

- An increased risk for addiction, self-neglect, self-abuse . . .

- More likely to lash out at others in my own unhappiness.

3. What Choosing to Take an Active, Central, Responsible Role in My Healing Process Will Cost or Require of Me

- Coming face to face with the unpleasant reality that I discovered in number one and the severe price I will likely pay if I choose number two.

- The energy it will take to recover and rebuild.

- Relinquishing permanent victim status and the "blame game."

- Taking full responsibility for the quality and direction of the rest of my life, beginning with the next choice I make this day.

- The effort it may require to regain faith, hope, trust . . . in myself and others.

- Assessing what I lost, what's left, and what's possible.

- Patience and persistence, as my recovery is not going to happen overnight.

- Seeking and paying for professional help (at least the portion that insurance doesn't cover).

Reflecting upon these three categories can be a mixed experience: in turns sad, sobering, and exciting. Sad, because of how you were hurt and what you lost; sobering, because of the extreme price you will likely pay if you give your power away and don't take action on your own behalf; and exciting, because there is so much potential for healing and goodness in your life as you step up to the plate and swing the bat. As we said before, your potential for healing is as deep as your hurts. And you can't help but heal, especially as you set a firm intention to do so, which is the topic of the next and final section of this chapter.

The fact that you are reading this book right now
is a wonderful sign attesting to your desire,
your *unstoppable* desire, and your willingness
to do all that is within your power to break free
from your hurts so that you can
live fully and happily again.

Setting Your Intention to Heal and Move Forward with Your Life

When you have been hurt, especially in a prolonged or serious manner, but also when so-called "lesser hurts" are involved, you may feel like you are out at sea on a small raft, completely alone and without a paddle or sail. The relatively stable ground of your life as you once knew it is gone, and you have been set adrift against your will, confined to a precarious and lonely existence on a small and fragile vessel.

You long to get back on land (i.e., to heal and move forward with your life), but it may be all you can do to hang on to your raft as wave after wave of upsetting thoughts and feelings pound you. Sometimes the waves calm down for a while, but not for long, or at least not long enough, as a painful memory surfaces again, accompanied by another influx of powerful waves that threatens to capsize you.

You may feel totally defeated, with no sense of personal power, as you drift at sea. You know there's land out there somewhere; in fact, you may be able to see it from where you sit bobbing up and down on the water. Yet it might as well be the moon as far as you are concerned, for you have no means of getting to shore.

In contrast to literally being out at sea on a small raft without any way of heading toward land and safety, in actuality, there are many tools and resources you can access to help you "reach shore" and begin to rebuild. Returning to our raft analogy, imagine yourself lying down, totally defeated, perhaps even in tears, as you are carried along hopelessly and helplessly by your unremitting pain. Trailing your hand in the water, you accidentally notice something on the bottom edge of the raft. You pull on it, and a rudder that has been lying flat against the bottom of your "ship" pops into place. You now have the means to steer, but still no way to advance yourself toward the shore. However, energized by a taste of hope, you now go to the opposite side of the raft and feel around under the edge, but discover nothing. Your newfound hope is dampened by a powerful twinge of disappointment, but you decide to check the other two sides. Much to your surprise and delight, you find a paddle attached underneath one of these edges. In a matter of two minutes, you have gone from lying there hopelessly in a state of utter defeat, to being empowered by the discovery of first a rudder and then a paddle with which you can begin to head toward shore.

Setting your intention to heal and move forward with your life is like (re)discovering and activating your "internal rudder" to steer toward land, toward new life. And any step you take to move shoreward, toward healing, is analogous to paddling.

Because the pain you might suffer after being hurt can be so disempowering, it may feel like you are helplessly adrift at sea. Paradoxically, your pain can also motivate you to do something to reduce or eliminate it, so in that sense it also has the potential to be empowering. Sometimes you might have to grow tired of hurting before you become willing to take some steps to decrease your pain. Setting and resetting your intention to heal and move forward is a powerful way to reduce your pain and redirect your life toward new land, so to speak, and toward four wonder-full Ls that await you: **life, love, liberation, and laughter.**

In most cases, no matter how unaware any of us might be, we set an intention before doing something. For instance, you don't just find yourself with a toothbrush in your mouth and wonder how it got there, instead, you set an intention to brush your teeth, and then go off to the bathroom to do so.

Obviously, setting your intention to heal and move forward with your life after suffering some type of hurt is more challenging than setting an intention to brush your teeth. Yet, just as your teeth don't get brushed if you don't *intend* to brush them, your healing process doesn't tend to take place as fully as it might without first setting an intention. Doing so is a powerful way to take an active, central, and responsible role toward rebuilding your life, which we spoke of in the last section. Setting and resetting your intention time and again has many benefits:

1. **It helps you focus your power in the now moments of each new day,** so that you don't give away your power to the unchangeableness of a past hurt.

2. **It provides you with a sense of direction,** rather than just drifting aimlessly as painful thoughts and feelings wash over you time and again.

3. **It awakens your indomitable inner life-force**—which some call your true self, your spirit, or your soul—that desires to move toward more life, as opposed to feeling life-less as you focus endlessly on past hurts.

4. **It engages your capacity to be a mature and response-able adult,** which is a much more effective way of engaging life as a whole, and your hurts in particular, than does being impulsive or unresponsive.

5. **It inspires you to act upon your intention,** to take the tiniest initial steps, and not to give up after hitting a slump or getting stuck.

A handful of key synonyms for "intend," "intent," or "intention" include *determined, resolute, bound and determined, committed, decisive, eager, earnest,* and *enthusiastic.* Others are *firm, fixed, resolved, willing, dedicated,* and *purposeful.*

If you were to hire a person to remodel your home, you would likely contract with someone who was not only skilled but who intended to do the best job possible, as evidenced by some of the synonyms above, for instance, someone who was dedicated. As the "remodeler" of your life-after-being-hurt, setting and resetting an intention in an "enthusiastic" or "determined" or "resolute" manner is going to lay a wonderful foundation for the new home you are building for yourself in which the pain of the past will have less and less influence on the unfolding now moments of your life.

Intentions can be quite broad (e.g., I intend to recover and move forward with my life) and quite specific (e.g., I intend to seek out a therapist). Intentions can include what you are going to refrain from doing, such as seeking revenge in the first example below, and what you are going to try to do, such as picking up the pieces of your life in the third example. We offer a few sample intentions to help you get started in creating your own. As you read them, we invite you to try substituting a few of the synonyms from the previous page for "I intend" such as "I am committed . . ." or "I enthusiastically intend . . ." or "I am bound and determined . . ."

- ✐ I **intend** to forego taking revenge or making my offender's life miserable.

- ✐ I **intend** to fully feel and gradually release my painful thoughts and feelings about this person as best I can each day.

- ✐ I **intend** to pick up the pieces of my life and move on, not using this person's hurtful behavior as an excuse to be personally irresponsible or unhappy for the rest of my life.

- ✐ I **intend** to seek out a therapist and a support group, as I need some new people in my life.

- ✐ I **intend** to make a fresh start in my life and to keep the focus on me rather than on my offender.

- ✐ I **intend** to seek restitution in a firm but respectful manner and then move forward with my life.

- ✐ I **intend** to hold this person accountable, especially since it is within my power to do so, as a key step in my recovery process.

- ✐ I **intend** to take small, identifiable steps each day to rebuild my life and increase my chances of being happy and at peace again.

> ❧ **I intend** to release the pain of the past as many times as it takes each day, while simultaneously affirming my capacity to rebuild something new and better.
>
> ❧ **I intend** to be extraordinarily gentle with myself throughout my healing process, especially when I backslide, and to praise myself for the tiniest actions I take on my own behalf.

Setting an intention is a way to activate your passion, your "indomitable life-force within," which is critical to healing. If you don't feel passionate now, you can gradually reawaken and develop it, sometimes by setting a small intention.

Even if you are feeling depressed, you still have passion within you. It's just that your life-force is stymied and needs to be steered in another direction, perhaps with the help of medication, therapy, and a tiny willingness on your part to do something new. If you are feeling tons of hatred and anger toward the person who hurt you, you definitely have an abundance of passion at your disposal right now that can be steered in a new direction that will improve the quality of your life.

Dictionaries define "intention" as "the act or instance of determining mentally upon some action or result." In that sense, setting an intention involves your intellect, but it also includes your other six intrapersonal allies: attitude, action, spirituality, emotions, body, and heart. For instance, setting an intention to recover and heal is a positive and effective attitude, which will inspire you to take action, which activates your spirituality, and so on.

As you set and reset your intentions—renewing some, refining others, and replacing still others—you are setting yourself up to take consistent action on your own behalf. The next chapter is devoted entirely to helping you live out your intentions so that you can move forward into the new life that you are creating for yourself.

Setting and resetting your intention to heal and
move forward with your life is a powerful way to
reduce your pain and redirect your life toward new land,
so to speak, and toward four wonderful *L*s that await you:
life, love, liberation, and laughter.

$\sim$ 6 $\sim$

Healing, Moving On, and Being Happy Again

Whether a physician prescribes an antibiotic to treat an ailment such as strep throat, the likely goal, as well as the outcome, is to eliminate any signs and symptoms of the illness or infection so that a person can return to their normal self. In that sense, the antibiotic pretty much wipes out or destroys what was adversely impacting their health.

Nothing that we share with you in this chapter is meant to "wipe out or destroy" the effects of how you were hurt, much less your memories of being hurt, in a once-and-for-all manner. Instead, what follows is intended to help you make steady progress toward overcoming the impact that past hurts are having on your life today, so that you can, with ever-increasing effectiveness, heal, rebuild, and move forward with your life.

How you were hurt in the past is part of your life history, and some of your hurts, as mentioned before, are going to come to your conscious awareness on either a periodic or regular basis, perhaps even for the rest of your life. As we have tried to make clear, whenever a painful memory surfaces again, it is usually accompanied by some degree of upsetting thoughts and feelings. The healthy alternatives to forgiving, along with the specific suggestions and practices you choose to activate from the last chapter as well as this one, have three primary purposes:

1. To help you **accept** yourself and what you are thinking and feeling when a painful memory comes to your conscious awareness, rather than getting down on yourself or becoming overly discouraged because you are feeling upset again about a past hurt.

2. To help you **experience**—not simply believe in, but *experience*—a gradual reduction in the frequency and duration of these painful memories, while gaining the skills with which to better manage the intensity of your upsetting thoughts and feelings when they do arise.

3. To help you **refocus** your attention and energy *away* from dwelling upon how you were hurt in the past in a timely manner and *toward* something you can engage and positively impact in the present moment.

First of all, by timely, we mean in a shorter time frame than it has normally taken you in the past. So if a reawakened painful memory has typically resulted in you sinking and suffering internally for several days, or for a week or more, even though you may still be fulfilling your responsibilities on the outside, then a shorter time frame might mean just a couple of days, or even one day. Secondly, in our estimation, at some point down the road you could very well learn to manage your pain and redirect your energy in the present moment within hours or even minutes rather than days. That way the unchangeable hurt from the past does not continue affecting your life for an inordinate amount of time in the present.

If there is one word that conveys as well as any other what the healing journey is all about, it could very well be the verb "manage."

As adults, we each have the capacity to manage our lives with increasing effectiveness, even when we have been hurt. You can learn to take charge of your life in a skillful manner after being hurt, as you become willing to gain some tools with which to manage your upsetting thoughts and feelings so that you do not suffer needlessly. Additionally, you will be able to direct your daily-life's-energy in the present moments of each new day so that you can move forward with your life, even though you may still be in some degree of pain regarding the past.[16]

While most of this chapter is either directly or indirectly related to managing your past hurts and forward-oriented life's direction in the present moments of each new day, we thought it might be helpful to take a moment and list some synonyms for the verb "manage." However, for the sake of clarity, we will continue to use the word "manage" in the pages to come, though a different word or phrase might work better for you, perhaps one from the list below:

Take charge of	*Be in control of*	*Call the shots*
Command	*Conduct*	*Handle*
Operate	*Oversee*	*Influence*
Run the show	*Supervise*	*Take the helm of*

It seems obvious to us that you would *want* to manage, take charge of, conduct, run the show, or take the helm of your life from this day forward, rather than let those who have hurt you in the past dictate the direction and quality—or lack of direction and quality—of the rest of your life.

"Managing" might sound like a somewhat cold word, or even have business or work connotations for you. Yet recovering from how you have been hurt not only requires a passionate, whole-hearted commitment, it also calls for a dispassionate and analytical or business-like approach. As the manager of your life, you will need to make positive, business-like choices on your behalf even

---

16. One of the resources that inspired us to focus on managing as an effective approach to dealing with your hurts, as well as life itself, is the fine book *The Tao of Sobriety: Helping You to Recover from Alcohol and Drug Addiction* by David Gregson and Jay. S. Efran, Ph.D.

when you don't feel like doing so, because you are in the 24/7/365 "business" of healing and moving forward with your life. What's more, you probably don't want to allow past hurts to result in you mismanaging the "business" of the rest of your life as it unfolds today and tomorrow.

If you don't think you have the skills with which to manage your life in a successful manner, including the painful emotions that are associated with past hurts, you can easily acquire them. In fact, if you are willing to learn, experiment, and practice, it is likely that within a very short period of time you will become so skilled that you might be amazed at just how power-filled you have turned out to be. And we believe that the word "power," which is a noun, best states what it is you are trying to manage: *your personal power*. As you manage your personal power to make positive choices, you will improve your ability to manage the pain associated with past hurts, while moving forward with your life at the same time. As you manage your emotional pain, rather than let it dominate and mismanage you, you will gain an increased sense of personal power to move forward to the new opportunities that await you in life. The goal, as well as the path, is to **manage *your* personal power** in the present moments of each day, which, with regard to your hurts, means to:

MANAGE *your* **PAIN**
whenever memories of past hurts
resurface and trouble you

MANAGE *your* **DAILY-LIFE'S-ENERGY**
so that you can move forward
to new and better opportunities

Unfortunately, the very nature of being hurt, especially in a prolonged or serious manner, is a loss of personal power. In fact, it is not atypical to feel like you are completely devoid of power or powerless. However, the good news is that because you are alive, you still have an abundance of potential power available to you. Also, power that has been lost can be power that is regained and maintained. First, however, you must claim it. Then you need to learn how to access it.

You *can* transition from being power-less to being power-filled, so that you can manage your pain and move forward in your new life each day with increasing skill and happiness as you apply that which appeals to you from this chapter, as well as from earlier chapters. We begin by offering a few thoughts about what it means to heal, move on, and be happy again.

As the manager of your life, you will need to make positive, business-like choices on your behalf even when you don't feel like doing so, because you are in the 24/7/365 "business" of healing and moving forward with your life. What's more, you probably don't want to allow past hurts to result in you mismanaging the "business" of the rest of your life as it unfolds today and tomorrow.

What It Means to Heal, Move on, and Be Happy Again

Like most things in life, healing, moving on, and being happy again might best be portrayed by a continuum rather than in an either-or, all or nothing manner. This is true even when it comes to physical injuries or illnesses. For example, one person who has had knee problems and elects to have surgery might heal to such an extent that it is almost as if they never had any knee problems to begin with. Another person, however, could have the exact same problem and the exact same surgery by the same surgeon and their healing turns out to be partial. Their knee is much better than it was prior to having the surgery, but it still causes some periodic discomfort and may result in some lifelong limitations. Yet as this person makes a few adjustments to their lifestyle, they are still able to live in an active and satisfying manner, despite the fact that the healing they sought was not as complete as that of the first person.

When it comes to your interpersonal hurts, your healing might be partial or complete. In broad terms, it seems to make sense that the deeper and more serious the hurt, the more likely it is that you will experience partial rather than complete healing. Now you might be wondering if we are taking back the statement we made earlier about your potential for healing being as deep or as great as the hurts you have suffered. No, we still stand by this. We still believe that incredibly deep hurts have the capacity for incredibly deep healing—but not necessarily complete healing. There could still be some lingering effects, even some significant ones, which you might have to work around or reframe in a creative manner.

For example, if you suffered some type of serious mistreatment or abuse in your family of origin or in a former marriage that resulted in you having low self-esteem, you *can* overcome this hurt and develop a healthy esteem for yourself that allows you to be successful and happy at work and in your relationships. However, you might still wrestle with some low self-esteem from time to time, and a rather harsh inner voice that causes you to suffer—though not nearly as often as in times past. In this case, your healing has been deep and life-changing, but not necessarily complete or total. We trust that you will recognize the value of healing to whatever extent is possible, rather than insist upon complete healing when it might not be possible.

Regarding healing and moving on, we believe they are as interrelated as the cardiopulmonary system's heart and lungs. Just as the heart cannot continue to beat without the oxygen supplied by the lungs, neither can the lungs function without the blood supplied by the heart. Similarly, just as healing from being hurt by someone cannot take place if a person doesn't move on, moving on cannot take place without some measure of healing. Consequently, when you choose to employ a specific healing practice or suggestion, such as accepting yourself and what you are thinking and feeling even when you are upset, its purpose and effect is to help you move on. As you move on and engage the world around you more fully each day, you experience greater healing, as the memory of how you were hurt loses its ability to impact your life as much as it has in the past. Happiness, in contrast, is a byproduct or wonderful consequence of the dual and concurrent actions of healing and moving on, rather than something to seek or chase.

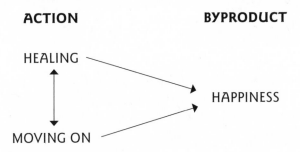

As we have said previously, healing and moving on basically means that you will experience an overall reduction in the **frequency** and **duration** of painful thoughts and feelings associated with past hurts, while being able to manage the **intensity** of your upsetting thoughts and feelings with increasing skill and confidence. For example, if you are thinking about your offender seven days per week and for a total of, say, two hours each day, suffering all sorts of painful thoughts and feelings as a result, an overall reduction might mean that you think of this person and get upset four days each week for a total of approximately one hour each day. To our way of thinking, that is deep healing, to go from fourteen hours of upsetting thoughts and feelings about your offender each week down to four hours. As you continue to heal and move on, the frequency and duration is likely to decrease much further.

When it comes to the intensity of your upsetting thoughts and feelings, on a scale of one to ten, they may feel like they are quite high, perhaps even an eight, nine, or ten. That's nothing to worry about as the intensity often does remain high when the memory of how you were hurt comes to mind again, even years or decades later. What has *changed*, however, and this is critically important, is you have acquired the skills to accept yourself and the intensity of your painful thoughts and feelings without overreacting. You no longer get down on yourself for having some painful thoughts and feelings, because you know that they are to be expected each time a hurt-laden memory comes to mind. Nor do you succumb to catastrophic or extreme thinking a la the frantic mantra of Chicken Little, "The sky is falling!," because although your emotional pain may be intense, you know from your own experience that *it is going to pass.* There's no need to do the drama dance, while clinging to and adding fuel to the fire of what is a temporary situation and inner state of being: upsetting thoughts and feelings. Again, they *will* pass.

But don't beat yourself up if you forget this truth, or if it doesn't even seem to ring true for you in the midst of feeling upset, as the intensity of your pain may be so all-encompassing at times that it might be all you can do to hang on. You *will* experience the passing of the intensity of your upsetting thoughts and feelings, even if you are unable to recall or believe in the axiom "This too shall pass" when you are hurting.

As the frequency and duration of your painful memories decrease and your skills with which to manage the intensity of your emotional upset increase, you will also notice – and enjoy – an increased ability to refocus in the present moment in a timely manner, so that you can make positive and effective choices on your own behalf. It is also likely that you will experience an increased energy level so that you can fulfill your daily responsibilities, engage in self-care, take risks, and enjoy a sense of balance in your life. Rather than remain past-bound, you will find yourself living more fully in the present moment, while being forward-oriented as you ponder new hopes, dreams, and possibilities in life. And the byproduct? Happiness.

Happiness can be described in many ways, but perhaps it includes some of the following: a sense of contentment, being at peace, being centered, and enjoying a balanced life. It might entail a sense of belonging, of oneness with all that is, of meaning and purpose. It could also include a sense of satisfaction, light-heartedness, wellbeing, reawakened wonder, and renewed appreciation for your life and the lives of others.

Once more, what's important for all of us to remember is that happiness is a wonderful consequence or byproduct rather than something to chase after. Each of us is floating on the sea of life, and none of us can control the sea (i.e., life). There will be rough waters and calm waters, stormy days and beautiful days. Each of our lives is like a boat with a cabin. When a painful memory is upsetting you on the sea of life, rather than staying on deck only to be pummeled by the elements, why not head into your safe and dry cabin? It can as big as you want it to be and decorated according to your tastes. In your cabin you can access your intrapersonal allies as well as your interpersonal allies, whether a friend, support group, faith community, spiritual or religious leader, or therapist.

As you come on in from the storm, you can also crank up the engines and then head to the sheltered helm of your boat to steer away from the rough weather. You have the personal power with which to *manage your experience of the storm*, at least to some extent, and perhaps to move away from it, rather than remain a passive and self-helpless victim of life's stormy moments, including memories of old or new hurts.

As the storm begins to break up, as storms always do, oftentimes accompanied by a rainbow, you can do your part to expedite the process by taking action and steering toward calmer waters, again, to whatever extent is possible. When the beautiful days return, it's time to get back on deck and enjoy your continued ability to heal and move forward with your life. New vistas and experiences await you, as does the byproduct of your rediscovered personal happiness.

As the frequency and duration of your painful memories decrease and your skills with which to manage the intensity of your emotional upset increase, you will also notice – and enjoy – an increased ability to refocus in the present moment in a timely manner, so that you can make positive and effective choices on your own behalf.

From "Why Me?" to "How Can I Begin to Heal and Move Forward?"

It is very common for many people to go through a period of time during which they ask "Why me?" in response to some of the hurts they have suffered, especially those that are most serious and upsetting. "Why was I hurt so badly?" "Why did my father sexually abuse me?" "Why does this person at work continue to single me out?" "Why was I passed up for the promotion when I was the most qualified candidate?" "Why did I get laid off after fifteen years when I had given them my best?" "Why did my spouse cheat on me?" "Why did I stay with him so long?" "Why wasn't I more careful before hiring this person?" "Why . . . ?"

Even some of the questions that don't begin with "Why" are really "Why" questions in disguise. "How could I have been so stupid?" "How could she have done this to me?" "How did I end up marrying the same kind of person twice? You would think that I would have learned my lesson the first time!" "How can this person sleep at night after what they did?" "Am I being punished?" "Is it my fault?" "Does God hate me?" "Did I somehow attract this person into my life?"

Raising these types of questions is usually part of the healing process, albeit a very painful part. Even though coming up with a satisfactory "answer" to the "Why" questions may be difficult, or even impossible, people who have been hurt often raise them for one or both of the following reasons:

1. Oftentimes asking "Why" is a way of crying out, a lament, an expression of outrage and grief, which might be directed toward a supreme or divine being (e.g., "Why, God, why?") or toward anyone or anything within earshot—even the empty void of the universe. In that sense, asking "Why" is somewhat rhetorical, because the person who is raising the question is really

173

expressing how unfair life—or another person—has been to them, while perhaps knowing in their heart that there is no answer that could satisfy their tormented mind, or fill the gaping hole in their soul or heart.

2. Many times asking why *is* in fact a demand for some type of reasonable explanation as to why this unreasonable hurt took place, even if the answer or explanation that is offered or discovered is not completely satisfactory. The demanding nature of "Why did this happen?" can be one in which some type of sensible response is desperately sought, because we human beings have a need to make some sense out of our lives, especially when things go woefully awry.

Unfortunately, many people are all too willing to offer *their* take on why *you* suffered what you did when you ask "Why?" in their presence, and sometimes even when you don't. People who have been hurt continue to hear a wide range of reasons from a variety of sources such as religion, cultural sayings, and pop or superficial spirituality or psychology. Included among the mix are such simplistic and oftentimes harmful "reasons" as:

- Everything happens for a reason.
- God has his purposes which remain a mystery to us.
- We are all here to learn certain lessons.
- God never gives you more than you can handle.
- No one said life would be easy or fair.
- God needed "Johnny" in heaven more than you did.
- It was God's will.

Others cite karma, the law of attraction, or arrogantly assert that we have all *chosen* every person who has ever been in our life and every experience we have had as the reasons for being hurt. Needless to say, "answers" such as these are not only unreasonable, they are also hurtful, if not heartless. How is a person who has suffered a hurt such as a serious crime or who was abused (which is also crime) supposed to respond to hearing, or perhaps reading somewhere, that "God never gives you more than you can handle" or that "It's all attributable to karma" or that "You chose or attracted the person who hurt you"?

While we do not presume to have any definitive or divinely inspired answers as to why people suffer the grievous hurts they do, we offer the following thoughts and guidelines for your consideration. Our purposes for doing so are twofold: first, to counter the simplistic and oftentimes harmful "answers" and "explanations" that are bandied about; second, maybe something that we propose will make a little more sense to you intellectually and intuitively than what you have heard elsewhere, especially if what you have heard *doesn't* make sense, or has even compounded your suffering.

We invite you to take or tweak what we suggest below, and leave the rest. Maybe a unique insight of your own will come to you that will help you find a measure of peace regarding why you suffered what you did as you consider the validity or helpfulness of the following comments:

1. Although there may be no perfectly satisfying answers or explanations to the "Why" questions, some suggestions or responses are more satisfying and sensible, both to heart and mind, than others. You may need to discover what works for and speaks to you, rather than trust any outside authority, especially those who offer simplistic solutions to something as complex as to why you or a loved one were hurt in a serious manner.

2. Oftentimes the hurt you suffered had nothing to do with you whatsoever. While it's difficult *not* to take hurts personally, in truth, it might not have been about you at all. It could have been completely about the other person and their personal issues, and not about

you or your personhood in any way, shape, or form. This is especially true when abuse, crime, betrayal, and other types of serious hurts are involved, but also true of less serious, yet painful, offenses such as being bullied or gossiped about at work or rejected or ostracized in a social or family setting.

3. In some cases, you may have had a part to play in the hurts you suffered. For instance, in a prior marriage, both you and your "Ex" may have been at fault, though your "Ex" may have had a larger role to play. Each of us is a growing, evolving person, and we all make mistakes and poor choices, some of which we learn from only at great cost and in hindsight. You didn't set out to have a lousy marriage or a feud with a neighbor or a conflict with a coworker or a falling-out with a friend or sibling, but perhaps the skills and maturity and wisdom that you have now were simply not available to you back then. Most of us know more in our forties, fifties, sixties, and beyond because of what we experienced earlier in our lives. The steepest learning curve for the overwhelming majority of us occurs in our twenties and thirties, when we simply lack life experience.

4. However you choose to wrestle with the "Why" questions, we hope that you will not waste too much time blaming yourself, even if you had some part to play in the hurt, and not blame yourself at all if you didn't have any role to play. Regarding the former, it is much more effective to look upon yourself in a detached behavioral manner in which you see yourself doing the best you could at the time with the skills you had at the time. You can now learn from your experience, especially since much of life is a trial and error undertaking, and make choices as to what you would like to do

differently from this day forward, rather than condemn yourself globally for not knowing then what you know now. You wouldn't be hard on a kindergartner for not knowing what a twelfth grader knows; nor does it make sense to get down on yourself for learning things in "the school of life" at a later age and stage that you didn't know earlier.

5. If you believe in God or a higher power, we would suggest that the divine intimately companions and supports you in life but does not—perhaps even cannot—protect you from all potential hurts, just as involved and concerned parents cannot always protect their children, no matter how great their desire to do so. Certainly, it was not God's will that you were hurt.

6. Striving for an understanding of the divine who cares about all of us, but who sets each of us free in a world that can—and does—both wound and wonder us, may enable you, as it has both of us, to give up childish notions of a God who will spare you and your loved ones from the dangers of living in a risk-laden world while not sparing others. Adult faith, perhaps reluctantly, seems to recognize that there is no ultimate protection or security, for built into the uncertain nature of life is the potential to be hurt. But that doesn't mean there isn't a loving and protecting Spirit or God who is powerfully present, intimately involved, and extremely eager to help you heal and move on in life, while interfacing with the other powers that be, including human beings who can and do hurt each other quite seriously.

7. Over time, you can learn to set down the "Why" questions so that you can pick up the "How" questions, primarily, "How can I begin to heal and move forward?"

You can always return to the "Why" questions, but in order to begin to heal and move on, it may be necessary to set them down, at least for a little while. For if, metaphorically speaking, it takes both hands to continuously hold your "Why" questions about the past, it will be nearly impossible to reach out for and receive the tangible healing and good things in life that can come in the present – and future – as a result of asking "How can I begin to heal and move forward?" You may have to empty your hands (i.e., your heart and mind) of the former in order to live into and receive the latter.

8. It may very well be that as you begin to heal and move forward with your life as best you can, the "Why" questions will lose some of their power. The nature of life, of human life, is resilient and regenerative. The fact that you are hanging in there, perhaps after being hurt in a devastating manner, is testimony to your resiliency, to your ability to recover, as well as to the regenerative or re-creative life-force within. And that's what you are invited to do by life itself, as well as by loved ones and perhaps by God or your higher power as well: recover and recreate your life, maybe even completely anew out of the ashes of a painful past.

We close this section by gently urging you to consider what many, including both of us, have discovered through personal experience when we have transitioned from "Why" to "How." And that is, when you ask, "How can I begin to heal and move forward?" you free yourself to take initial action steps that will help you to rebuild and move on with your life, whereas focusing exclusively on "Why me?" for too long a period of time is prone to keeping you stuck in unremitting pain. The "How" questions can be broken down into the smallest action steps, which are much more doable than coming up with a satisfactory "answer" to "Why" when there simply might not be one.

The "Why" questions may be unanswerable, at least in a precise "This-is-the-reason-why" manner, and dwelling upon them excessively can become disempowering and depressing. Nonetheless, we want to reassure you that asking them *is* part of the healing process. You need to raise them, either rhetorically as an expression of grief or outrage, or because you really want some kind of explanation as to why you had to suffer what you did, for as long as *you* deem necessary. It is not our place or anyone else's to tell you when–or even if–you should let them go. But if or when you are ready to set them aside–at least for a short period of time initially rather than permanently–we hope that something we have suggested in this section will help you take the "leap of faith" as you ask "How can I begin to heal?" For we believe that you *will* be able to rediscover and reclaim your personal power to move forward with your life and rebuild, even after suffering serious hurts you neither caused nor deserved.

Although there may be no perfectly satisfying answers
or explanations to the "Why" questions,
some suggestions or responses are more satisfying and
sensible, both to heart and mind, than others.
You may need to discover what works for and
speaks to you, rather than trust any outside authority,
especially those who offer simplistic solutions to
something as complex as to why you or a loved one
were hurt in a serious manner.

Accessing and Activating
Your Healthy Adult Power

In recent decades much has been written about the "inner child." Millions have been intrigued by this concept, especially those who grew up in alcoholic or otherwise chaotic, abusive, or dysfunctional families.[17] Because at one time both the literature and cultural awareness of the inner child became so commonplace, even to the point of over-saturation in some circles, comedians, as they are prone to doing, provided a necessary correction or counterbalance by poking some fun at the whole inner child phenomenon. More than a few evoked some self-conscious laughter among those of us who caught glimpses of ourselves in their stereotypical caricatures, especially of the excessively fragile inner child—in an adult body, no less—whose need for around-the-clock affirmation and constant coddling knew no bounds.

While the inner child movement often focused on re-parenting yourself if your childhood was extraordinarily painful, for no small number it turned out to be more of an appealing concept than a doable practice. Many longed to re-parent themselves in a kinder and more respectful manner, while hoping to provide nurturance to the wounded child within. But because this child existed only in memory, it was oftentimes an elusive, if not impossible, practice. Thousands found it difficult to parent the child they once were, at least on any kind of consistent basis, in part because this child no longer existed. It was like trying to parent a ghost, even though some of the unhealthy coping methods, reactionary behaviors, and approaches to life that originated in childhood were far from ghostlike. In fact, they were often negatively impacting significant life arenas such as relationships and work, while frequently contributing to various addictions and compulsive behaviors. In

---

17. We are both supportive of the twelve-step program Adult Children of Alcoholics (ACOA). Learning the thirteen characteristics of adult children as well as the steps and "solutions" are effective ways for many to begin to overcome the legacy of a painful childhood.

other words, the wounded child was gone, but the legacy of the wounded child was alive and well: unhealthy and ineffective behaviors and approaches to life that made the longed-for success, happiness, and inner peace virtually unattainable. Another reason why it was difficult for many to re-parent themselves with any kind of success was due to the daily demands of adult life; thus, would-be "re-parenters," quite understandably, would tend to lose sight of their inner child for extended periods of time, which made for some rather inconsistent re-parenting at best, nonexistent at worst.

The gift of the inner child concept or movement, in our opinion, was not so much the re-parenting angle as it was the way it invited the many millions who grew up in hurtful and dysfunctional family systems to take a conscious look at how their childhood experiences, particularly the coping methods and overall approaches to life they acquired, may be adversely affecting their lives today, including their ability to deal with their hurts. In fact, we think that in many if not most cases, rather than trying to re-parent a child who no longer exists (just as a forty-year-old doesn't tend to try to maintain an ongoing relationship with the "inner thirty-year-old"), it may be more beneficial to write a symbolic letter of goodbye to the child you once were. In such a letter, you can send the child of yesteryear off to an imaginary yet visionary place in which he or she can be with, and play with, other boys and girls who have been wounded, and they are legion.

Why write such a letter? Because adult life, including the consistent efforts it takes to heal from both childhood and adult wounds, is an *adult undertaking*. Your "inner child," especially if the wounds you suffered as a child are adversely impacting how you deal with life as an adult today, has nothing to offer you; he or she has no adult skills or perspective, much less wisdom, with which to do the adult work that healing requires. In fact, your inner child – or, if you don't subscribe to this whole inner child notion, the counterproductive ways of dealing with and mismanaging life's hurts that may have their origins in childhood – could be getting in the way of your potential healing and happiness today. How? Because you may still be engaging life, including how you are reacting to being hurt, from the standpoint of a wounded child, and that simply doesn't tend to be very effective in an adult world.

Instead of trying to re-parent that which doesn't exist anymore – the child you once were – why not send your child away, so to speak, so that you can continue on your way to a new and better adult life. As you clear out the space occupied by the wounded child of yesteryear, as well as any deeply entrenched pain-driven habits and reactions that originated in childhood, you can gradually fill the void with effective adult skills so that you can manage your pain, both that which is associated with your childhood as well as with your adult life, while moving forward to new and better opportunities. Maybe one of you has to go, and since you are the only one who really exists in the here and now, it might make sense to say goodbye to the child you once were.

Lest this sounds a bit cold or callous, it may very well be the warmest and most sensitive thing you could do – even for the child you once were, and especially for the adult you are today. If your inner child could speak to you right now, from a place of hard-won insight rather than blinding pain, he or she might say to you:

"Say goodbye to me and send me away. If you don't, I will continue to stay and get in your way. I want you to be happy. I can't change the past, and neither can you. But you can heal and move on, especially if you send me away. I had my day, and even though it wasn't the best, there were still some good times. Now it's your turn, and you can have a better life as an adult, because that's what you are today and always will be until the day you die: an adult. In fact, some of the most wonderful traits or characteristics attributed to children can be yours as a result of letting me go: playfulness, curiosity, wonder, laughter, spontaneity, presence, trust, openness, and joy. Where I am going, you can't come anyway, as it's for children only. And where you want to go in life – toward greater healing and happiness – I can't come either, because it's for adults only. Let's

part for now. We can always hook up again after this life is over. For now, go for it! Heal and be happy. As for me, I've got a lot of playing to do with all the other kids. The best thing you can do for me—and especially for yourself—is to send me away and move on. But I need you to initiate this action, because it requires the discipline and strength of your healthy adult self."

With the hurting inner child sent away, or again, as you decide to let go of the survival or coping mechanisms you may have learned in childhood—ranging from a helpless victim stance to retaliation to the blame game—you can fill the void with healthy adult skills and power.

Accessing and activating your healthy adult power in a proactive manner has so much more to offer you than does approaching your hurts from a reactionary, unhealthy position, which, again, may have its roots in childhood. When any of us has been hurt, especially in a prolonged or serious manner, but even when mid-sized or so-called "small hurts" are involved, it's amazing how quickly our unhealthy—and even childish—urges and coping methods can return. Even when getting cut off in traffic, for example, many of us struggle to refrain from reacting in a retaliatory manner, sometimes successfully and sometimes not. So please do not misinterpret what we are saying. We are *not* saying that you are childish or unhealthy; rather, we are saying that how any of us responds to being hurt can either be healthy and adult-like or unhealthy and childish. And most people, including both of us, do some of both.

Our point is that you can respond better to being hurt and enjoy a more complete measure of healing and happiness as you approach your hurts from the standpoint of your healthy adult power. It's simply a matter of which is more effective: continuing to cling to whatever unhealthy reactions you may have picked up along the way as a child, or replacing them with healthy adult skills and responses that will work better for you. Being hurt requires that you access and activate the latter, so that you can heal, move on, and be happy again to the fullest extent possible.

Below we contrast examples of unhealthy and counterproductive childish reactions with healthy and productive adult responses. As always, this is not meant to be a comprehensive list; instead, it is intended to show you that more possibilities result when you choose to access and activate your healthy adult power.

UNHEALTHY REACTIONS TO BEING HURT, WHICH MAY HAVE ORIGINATED IN CHILDHOOD, AND WHICH CAN GET IN THE WAY OF HEALING AND HAPPINESS.	HEALTHY RESPONSES TO BEING HURT, WHICH YOU CAN LEARN BY ACCESSING AND ACTIVATING YOUR HEALTHY ADULT POWER TO FACILITATE HEALING AND HAPPINESS.
Claims permanent victim status.	Victimized, but refuses the victim identity.
Gives in to vindictive and retaliatory urges and tries to repay pain with pain.	Makes efforts to refrain from vengeance, as it takes a huge toll on the soul.
Gives power away to their offender, and to the past, resulting in powerlessness.	Claims and activates personal power in order to rebuild, heal, and move on.
Seduced by endless self-pity.	Recognizes self-pity as a form of grief, but becomes willing to set some limits to it.
Loses perspective and is reluctant to strive for a "big picture" point of view.	Aims for a broader perspective with which to place hurts in context and reduce pain.
Engages in thinking that is characterized by helplessness and hopelessness, while succumbing to chronic negativity.	Seeks help if needed, helps self, and fosters hope by adopting a more positive mindset.

Bound by painful emotions and "emotional reasoning."	Develops skills to manage emotional pain by activating intellect and other inner allies.
Fantasy- and illusion-based, characterized by "I wish that . . . " and "If only he/she/I . . ."	Reality-based in dealing with what was and is, visionary-based in fostering what can be.
I can't . . .	I will try, and if what I am trying doesn't work, I will try something else.
Lacks patience and desires quick healing or is prone to giving up prematurely.	Practices patience and recalls that healing is a process and that happiness is a byproduct.
Clings to excuses as a way to stay "little" and avoid responsibility.	Releases excuses time and again, and seeks ways to be "big" (adult) and response-able.
Feels overwhelmed by it all and is prone to becoming immobilized.	Mobilizes self to take action by breaking down overwhelming tasks into mini-steps.
Clings to pain, in part, because staying hurt and unhappy is familiar and safe.	Repeatedly releases pain and acts even when hurting, so as to risk – and reap – happiness.

Again, the above are just a few examples of the unhealthy reactions that tempt and trap many of us, and healthier responses that can empower and liberate us. It is likely that you will find yourself either believing in or acting out of your unhealthy patterns from time to time. If so, you are but human like the rest of us. However, at some point, perhaps even now if you are so inclined, you might want to identify just exactly what some of these unhealthy reactions and patterns are, especially the ones that you may have mastered in the past and that could be getting in the way of your healing and happiness today. Then, for each one, you might write down a new and more effective replacement behavior pattern or approach to the situation that you can begin to implement.[18] For instance, if you have mastered self-pity and tend to blame yourself for getting hurt by others, you might replace this unhealthy reactionary pattern with something like the following:

> "I choose to see self-pity as a form of grief, but with my healthy adult power I am willing to set some limits to it, because daily self-pity parties simply will not result in me being happy again. Besides, no one tends to show up but me. I am also willing to release my tendency to blame myself, as that only keeps me small and makes me feel like a victim. Instead, I will place responsibility where it belongs, so that I can let go of a victim identity and claim my healthy adult power, which is only going to grow stronger and stronger."

We close this section by saying that being adult and accessing and activating healthy adult power is not always easy, but it's almost always rewarding. The payoffs, of course, are not always immediate, though many times they are, because activating your adult power, even when you have to–or get to–wait a while to reap the benefits, is worth it in and of itself. This is because you are choosing to take charge of your life in the now, rather than remaining helplessly bound to a past you cannot change.

---

18. We walk you through this process in our workbook, which is available at www.theforgivenessmyth.com

Accessing and activating your healthy adult power
in a proactive manner has so much more to offer you
than does approaching your hurts
from a reactionary, unhealthy position, which . . .
may have its roots in childhood.

Accepting Yourself – Especially When Feeling Upset

If there is one single adult skill that may serve you better than any other on your journey to healing and happiness, it is learning to accept yourself as you are, especially during those times when it is most difficult to accept yourself. Self-acceptance isn't really an issue or struggle for most of us when:

- ⏀ We are feeling pretty good about ourselves and the direction of our life.

- ⏀ We are feeling pretty good physically and are not wrestling with serious health issues or chronic pain.

- ⏀ We are performing well and our behavior at home, at work, and in other arenas is pretty much in line with our values (a few bumps here and there but nothing major).

- ⏀ We are having mostly positive, warm, and kind thoughts about ourselves and others.

- ⏀ We are experiencing and enjoying mostly pleasant and gratifying emotions such as peace, joy, contentment, and gratitude.

- ⏀ We are feeling centered, serene, and balanced, connected with our innermost self, others, and life itself—and perhaps with God or our higher power as well.

However, many of us have discovered through personal experience that if we are struggling in just one of the above areas, much less two, three, or more, self-acceptance can be pretty much absent.

In short, when we are thinking, feeling, and acting in certain ways—positive thoughts, pleasant emotions, acting within our value system—self-acceptance is rather easy. But when we are thinking, feeling, and acting in certain *other* ways—negative thoughts, unpleasant emotions, acting outside our value system—then, accepting ourselves can be among the most difficult tasks.

While an entire book could be written on the challenges and pathways to greater self-acceptance, we will limit our discussion in this section to the struggles many of us have in accepting ourselves when we are experiencing a host of upsetting thoughts and feelings regarding someone who has hurt us. In other words, when we are having thoughts and feelings that are of a vindictive, punitive, hateful, angry, and bitter nature.

No small number of us who have struggled with forgiving, both with our inability as well as our unwillingness to forgive certain individuals, suffer a huge sense of guilt or shame as a result. As we come face to face with not only our *lack* of forgiveness, but also with our *excess* of hate-filled and condemning thoughts, we tend to slide into the lonely abyss of heartless self-rejection:

- ↷ Wow! I am *really* a hateful person. If other people knew I thought and felt this way, they would . . . (go away, not want to be my friend, look down on me . . .).

- ↷ What's *wrong* with me?! Why do I continue to rip this person apart in my mind, especially when it's been more than twenty years since I've seen her? Why can't I just let it—and her—go?

- ↷ This is really bad. I shouldn't be thinking and feeling this way, especially since I . . . (am in a twelve-step program, go to church/temple/mosque, practice mindfulness . . .). I feel so ashamed.

Those most influenced by the Christian tradition are especially prone to feeling massive amounts of guilt or subterranean shame for their forgiveness failings. And many others, though perhaps not members of a particular religious tradition, may try to use certain spiritual practices such as meditation or loving-kindness to keep "unloving" thoughts and feelings away, or at least somewhat at bay. When these upsetting thoughts and feelings sneak or barge in anyway, they, too, may suffer guilt or shame.

You, like millions of people, may be prone to rejecting yourself for what you are thinking and feeling, especially when you are upset about how you were hurt, even if the hurt took place decades ago. If you have a long history of rejecting yourself in the midst of feeling anger, hatred, vindictiveness, rage, bitterness, and the like, you could qualify to be a member in good standing of the "Self-Rejection Club." But scolding and rejecting yourself for thinking and feeling these completely normal—albeit highly upsetting—thoughts and feelings doesn't tend to set you free from their grip. In fact, getting down on yourself for having such thoughts and feelings only serves to increase their power over you.

Paradoxically, accepting yourself and your upsetting thoughts and feelings is one of the quickest ways to make their intensity more manageable. Doing so reduces their binding and blinding power over you in the present, thus freeing you to see some options so that you can redirect your energy elsewhere (i.e., away from thinking about your offender and toward something else). Rejecting yourself for feeling upset is like banging your head against a wall to get rid of a headache—not too likely to work; in fact, it will probably make your headache worse. Practicing acceptance is like taking some Tylenol or aspirin: it's simply a remarkable, and oftentimes fast-acting, emotional pain reliever.

Jarrod is prone to coming down very hard on himself whenever he experiences upsetting thoughts and feelings toward his father, who mistreated and disrespected him throughout his childhood years. Now in his mid-forties, Jarrod still finds himself feeling very upset from time to time about ancient hurts he suffered at the hands of his father. Here's a summary of one of his journal entries: .

I read a quote the other day by Bill W. [one of the cofounders of Alcoholics Anonymous] in which he said something like "love the best in your enemy and never fear their worst." I don't think my father has a best, and whatever his best might be, it's not good enough. He's such a jerk, completely self-centered, unaccountable, and unremorseful. I really hate him. I will never forgive him. Yet my therapist says that I've got to get him out of my head. But to be perfectly honest, I don't think I want to. Or maybe I can't. He's never apologized or tried to make amends. Besides, it's way too late for that now.

After Jarrod vented some more, he then shifted the focus to himself, and proceeded to reject and shame himself for having these types of thoughts and feelings:

What's **wrong** with me?! Why do I continue to think about my dad and what he did to me? When am I ever going to let it go? Why can't I forgive him? Something is definitely wrong with me. I've been sober for sixteen years now, and I'm still bitter. What a loser I am! I can't – actually, I WON'T – do what Bill W. suggests: look for and focus on the good in my father. If that means I'm a horrible person, so be it. But if other people knew that I am still struggling with this after all these years, they probably wouldn't want to be with me.

Countless times over the years, Jarrod has suffered from this proverbial one-two knockout punch: his upsetting thoughts and feelings about his father, which is painful enough, and then his self-condemning thoughts and subsequent sense of shame for getting angry and upset again. Jarrod is especially prone to rejecting himself because he takes his sobriety and recovery seriously. He has incorporated the twelve-step program into his daily life and has worked diligently with a therapist on many issues, including forgiving his father. Because he often goes for months without feeling any anger or resentment toward his father, it is especially hard on him when upsetting thoughts and feelings return, even without any triggering event such as the holiday season.

Yet there is a way out for Jarrod. When he experiences upsetting thoughts and feelings toward his father, as expressed in his first paragraph above, he can cut short this experience, say, within a couple minutes, rather than letting it go on for ten or twenty minutes, by saying aloud, writing down, or both, a statement of self-acceptance.

Right now, I am having terrible thoughts and feelings about my father again. I accept myself completely as I am, and I wholeheartedly accept the bitter, angry, and hate-filled thoughts I am having at this moment. I now choose to . . .

Jarrod basically has two choices. He can return to thinking about his father and feeling upset about him, in which case, he would say aloud or write:

I now choose to spend a little more time thinking about how my father hurt me, fully realizing that I will continue to feel upset, but I'm willing to pay that price, because right now I don't want to stop. I will strive to accept myself as I am, and accept what I am thinking and feeling without passing any judgment on myself.

Or, because he has interrupted his bitter and resentful thoughts and subsequent painful emotions with a statement of self-acceptance and acceptance of what he is thinking and feeling, Jarrod might say aloud or write:

I now choose to stop thinking about my father, because I know that continuing to do so will result in me feeling more and more upset. And I don't want to continue heading down this nowhere path into the past. Instead, I am going to turn on the radio and clean up the kitchen.

Of course, it's not quite as easy to stop a stream of upsetting thoughts and feelings as it is to flip off a light switch, especially after they have gained some momentum, so even as Jarrod begins to clean the kitchen, he may still be feeling very bitter about his father. However, a statement of acceptance can prevent the second punch from coming, that of beating himself up for getting swept away by painful memories and subsequent upsetting thoughts and feelings. Or at the very least, it can reduce the impact of this second punch, for he may still get down on himself, because it is a deeply ingrained habit. But perhaps he can learn to become a little less ruthless and self-punitive each time he remembers to say aloud or write down that he accepts himself and what he is thinking and feeling. Then, as he continues to clean the kitchen, perhaps singing along with a song on the radio, the thoughts of his father fade entirely, replaced by something he feels positive or excited about. As a result, he is able to distract himself away from thinking about his father, which allows him to move forward with *his own life* once again.

Making a statement of self-acceptance and acceptance of what you are thinking and feeling is like slowing down your car, your mind, which may already be racing seventy miles per hour with upsetting thoughts and feelings toward and about your offender. Rather than add to the speed and potential "emotional crash" that is likely to occur as you beat yourself up and reject yourself for feeling upset in the first place, you make a statement of acceptance, which, again, is like slowing down your car. Then, as you take in your own self-accepting words, especially your acceptance of what you are thinking and feeling in that moment, you can turn your car, your mind, around and head in a different direction. Or if you're not done focusing on your offender, you can resume speed and pick up where you left off. Maybe in another five or ten minutes you will have had enough, in which case you can, once again, make a statement of self-acceptance, and then turn around and head in a more peaceful direction.

Because accepting yourself, as we said at the beginning, is as powerful and effective as any other single skill or practice, we will say more about it in the next section. For now, we invite you to practice by saying the following, aloud if possible:

I accept myself completely just as I am.
I wholeheartedly accept what I am thinking and feeling, even when I am having angry, bitter, resentful, and hate-filled thoughts and feelings toward and about (name).

Accepting yourself and your upsetting thoughts and feelings is one of the quickest ways to make their intensity more manageable. Doing so reduces their binding and blinding power over you in the present, thus freeing you to see some options so that you can redirect your energy elsewhere (i.e., away from thinking about your offender and toward something else).

More on the Healing and Liberating Power of Acceptance

While acceptance can mean to receive something or someone with approval, as in the case of accepting with approval a contractor's bid for a home project, although you may wish it was lower, or a new leader for a faith community, though you might prefer that this individual was ten years older or younger, accepting doesn't always entail approval. For example, after every election, the supporters of losing candidates eventually need to accept the fact that their candidates lost while also accepting, even though not necessarily agreeing with or approving of, the candidates who won.

So when Jarrod, in the previous section, practices accepting himself and the upsetting thoughts and feelings he is having about his father at any point in time, he is not necessarily approving of what he is thinking or feeling; rather, he is accepting himself *as he is*, as well as the upsetting thoughts and emotions he is having at the time. Basically, he is accepting his current reality, rather than fighting and resisting it, and rejecting and shaming himself for what he is experiencing. *I completely accept myself as I am in this particular moment, and I wholeheartedly accept the upsetting thoughts and feelings I am presently experiencing.*

One very effective way to address whatever your reality might be at any point in your life, including after being hurt, is to make statements of acceptance. And because accepting is such a paradoxical and, for many of us, unaccustomed response, it can be helpful to include such superlatives as "completely," "wholeheartedly," "unconditionally," and the like: I *completely* accept . . . , I *wholeheartedly* accept . . . , I *unconditionally* accept . . . ," as a way to strengthen the power of practicing active acceptance of yourself and what is. In fact, the more you struggle with and resist accepting yourself, your current reality, and the upsetting thoughts and feelings you may be experiencing, the more potentially effective it can be to use extreme words, even to the point of excess, in your statements of acceptance. You don't have to believe them, and it's not likely that you will when you first employ them. But with practice, you may find that this new effective adult skill of radical, unconditional acceptance is gradually replacing the old ineffective practice of resistance and rejection.

While some may argue that we never see reality as it really is, just our interpretation of it, for our purposes, the reality (e.g., my spouse cheated on me) and a person's interpretation of it (e.g., my life is ruined; no one wants somebody who has three kids . . .) are not necessarily at odds with each other. There's really not much room for interpretation if your spouse or partner really did cheat on you, as that seems to be a cold, hard, unasked-for reality. The interpretation, "my life is ruined . . . ," is what can be modified to a greater or lesser extent by accepting the reality of being cheated on and by accepting "my life is ruined" types of thoughts. Denying, resisting, or rejecting the reality that you were cheated on, though oftentimes an initial response to being shocked, will not serve you in the long run. It will not allow you to heal, move on, and be happy again. Neither will fighting and resisting upsetting thoughts, such as "my life is ruined," and feelings, such as bitterness, resentment, anger, self-pity, and so on.

Accepting yourself as you are, your reality as it is, and yourself for what you are thinking and feeling—even when it is not what you would *like* to be thinking and feeling—frees you to spend your finite daily-life's-energy dealing with and managing your emotional and mental pain so that you can move forward again, sooner rather than later. Fighting what you are thinking and feeling, coupled with scolding and shaming yourself for having these types of thoughts and feelings, simply tends to be ineffective and draining. It results in a great loss of energy, akin to stepping harder on the gas pedal when you are stuck in mud or snow: you do a lot of spinning in place, while burning gas (your daily-life's-energy) and going nowhere.

We once heard about a Buddhist nun who lost all her family in a war and was placed in solitary confinement for six years. She did a meditation in which she walked back and forth in her cell while saying over and over again: "I feel angry. I feel angry. I feel angry. I accept my anger. I accept my anger. I accept my anger." This helped her to forgive as she understood forgiving. In your case, doing so may set you free to move on with your life and rediscover happiness, even if you don't want anything to do with forgiving. Adapting her practice, we have found it helpful to silently say in our mind what we are feeling on the inhale, and to accept what we are feeling on the exhale, in a repetitive manner—even for just a minute or two—as in the examples below:

INHALE	EXHALE
I feel angry	I accept my anger
I feel bitter	I accept my bitterness
I feel petty	I accept my pettiness
I feel vindictive	I accept my vindictiveness
I feel sorry for myself	I accept my feelings of self-sorrow
I feel self-loathing	I accept my feelings of self-loathing

If you stop and think about it, all of us have a deep and inexhaustible longing for acceptance. Much of our pain in life is due to the rejection, real or perceived, that we experience from others, as well as the way we often reject ourselves. We crave and need acceptance more than ever precisely during those times when we have deemed ourselves to be unacceptable, basically, when we are experiencing the opposite of the bulleted comments on the first page of the previous section.

We are not suggesting that making a statement of acceptance in and of itself is instantly liberating, freeing you from all of your present moment pain. Yet it *can* be a critical first step toward slowing down and eventually replacing the upsetting thoughts and feelings you are having about your offender and the self-rejecting thoughts and feelings you may be having toward yourself because you are experiencing bitter thoughts and feelings. In that sense it is like taking an ice cube, which represents your upsetting and self-rejecting thoughts and feelings, out of the freezer, so that the hardness of what you are experiencing and your frosty self-rejection can begin to melt. Of course, melting isn't instantaneous, but if left in the freezer, it won't happen at all.

If you don't take the ice cube out of the freezer, then your upsetting thoughts and feelings about your offender and toward yourself remain ice-hard, while depriving you of the peace, happiness, and self-acceptance you desire.

**UPSETTING THOUGHTS & FEELINGS
ABOUT YOUR OFFENDER**

**SELF-REJECTING THOUGHTS AND FEELINGS
FOR BEING UPSET ABOUT YOUR OFFENDER**

Among the many definitions of "accept" and "acceptance," two in particular are especially relevant to our discussion:

1. to regard as normal, suitable, or usual

2. to allow into a group.

First, the upsetting thoughts and feelings that any of us may have with regard to a person who has hurt us are "normal, suitable, or usual." But because these take place within the privacy of our heart and mind, we tend to think they are *ab*normal, *un*suitable (inappropriate, unfitting, unbecoming), and *un*usual (unique to us rather than universally common). Yet our ability to heal, move on, and be happy again may call for each of us to accept our emotional upset as par for the course, nothing more and nothing less. We were hurt, and now we are having perfectly "normal, suitable, or usual" upsetting thoughts and feelings about the person who hurt us. And it matters not whether any of us is feeling upset days or decades after the original hurt took place.

Second, while many of us are amused by Groucho Marx's quip, "I would never belong to a club [or group] that would have me for a member," a profound degree of healing and inner peace can be ours as we begin to allow all the thoughts and feelings that we have learned to reject over the years (i.e., anger, bitterness, rage, vindictiveness, resentment, etc.) entrance into "the club" or "membership" of what it means to be human. As human beings, we can have the loftiest and most pleasant and peaceful thoughts and feelings imaginable, and we can have – and do have – their polar opposites, as well as everything in-between. Of course, experiencing the likes of hatred, bitterness, and anger is upsetting, but they are a part of us that can be better managed by, first of all, accepting them. Then, because we have accepted rather than rejected them as part of our present moment reality, we can take steps to release them, thus clearing the space for thoughts and feelings of a more peaceful and enjoyable nature to return.

Accepting yourself as you are, your reality as it is,
and yourself for what you are thinking and feeling –
even when it is not what you would *like* to be
thinking and feeling – frees you to spend your finite
daily-life's-energy dealing with and managing your
emotional and mental pain so that you can
move forward again, sooner rather than later.

Refuting Powerlessness, Relinquishing Pain, Reclaiming Possibilities

Practicing acceptance of yourself and acceptance of the thoughts and feelings you are having whenever a painful memory troubles you can serve as a lifeline of sorts, especially when the inner intensity of your emotional upset threatens to sweep you downriver toward increasingly rough rapids. The ultimate purpose of a lifeline thrown to a person who is truly in danger is to keep them from going under, and to pull them safely toward shore or back on the boat. Perhaps the fundamental objective of employing a statement of self-acceptance is to keep you from "going under" in the midst of the upsetting thoughts and feelings you may be having at any point in time about your offender, yourself, or both, so that you can get back onto land or into the safety of your boat. But once you are back on solid ground again, or in your boat – if the river is seen as a metaphor for life itself – then more is needed. You need to "walk" or "steer" away *from* the reawakened painful memories and subsequent upsetting thoughts and feelings that have just threatened to take you under and overpower you, and move (or steer) *toward* something that is more freeing and satisfying.

It simply wouldn't be very effective for any of us to sit passively along the river bank or in our boat while repeating over and over, "I accept myself and the upsetting thoughts and feelings I am having at this time," while staring at, and perhaps drifting toward, the dangerous rapids, all the while hoping that we don't fall in again. Remember, a statement of acceptance is but a first step toward slowing down or even stopping the momentum of painful thoughts and feelings that accompany a reawakened hurtful memory. In that sense it is very much like the first step of Alcoholics Anonymous, in which alcoholics admit and *accept* their powerlessness over alcohol and the unmanageability of their lives when they are under the influence.[19]

---

19. The first step of Alcoholics Anonymous reads as follows: "We admitted we were powerless over alcohol – that our lives had become unmanageable."

In effect, a statement of acceptance is a powerful practice in which you acknowledge *temporary* powerlessness and life-unmanageability when a past hurt has come to conscious awareness and resulted in you feeling upset again.

*I **accept** that I am feeling (powerlessly) upset right now and that I can't seem to stop the resentful thoughts and bitter feelings I am having (unmanageability). I also **accept** that I am feeling bad about myself for thinking and feeling the way I am, because I believe that I should be over this by now, especially since I am . . . (in the program, in therapy, a spiritual person, a Christian, a Jew, a Muslim, a Buddhist, etc.).*

The acknowledgement and acceptance of powerlessness by people in various twelve-step programs is but a stepping stone toward recovering authentic power in the subsequent eleven steps, so that they can manage their lives with increasing effectiveness. So, too, the practice or "first step" of accepting yourself in the midst of feeling powerlessly or helplessly upset about a past hurt is just a beginning. To move (or steer) away from the rapids in an increasingly power-filled manner, three additional steps or practices are needed:

- ⊷ Refuting powerlessness
- ⊷ Relinquishing pain
- ⊷ Reclaiming possibilities.

While many of us might *perceive* that we are powerless when the memory of a past hurt is dominating our consciousness, in actuality, we often have more power at our disposal than we realize. One of the ways to access our personal power again is by refuting powerlessness over the situation in which we find ourselves, in this case, over the upsetting thoughts and feelings we are presently having about someone who has hurt us in the recent or distant past.

By refuting powerlessness you are:

1. Countering any notion you may have that you cannot handle the upsetting thoughts and feelings you are currently experiencing.

2. Taking a strong stand against any beliefs you may have that you are helpless to engage in some type of action to break free from being upset in order to regain a measure of inner peace.

Refuting powerlessness—as is true of practicing statements of acceptance—is primarily about changing the messages you give yourself. Instead of saying to yourself, or believing at a subconscious level, something like, "I can't handle how upset I feel right now and there's absolutely nothing I can do to regain my inner peace," you consciously and deliberately refute this belief and replace it with something along the lines of the following:

*I **can** handle the upsetting thoughts and feelings I am currently having toward and about this person who hurt me. Though I feel very angry right now, this isn't going to kill me—it just feels like it is. And I absolutely **refute** the notion I've held most of my life that there's nothing I can do to take the edge off of how upset I feel. I do have some tools that I can use to help me recover my inner peace.*

Changing your self-talk from "I can't handle it" and "I can't do anything to change what I am thinking and feeling" to "I *can* handle it" and "I *can* take some action to reduce the intensity of how upset I feel" makes a huge difference. Even when you are feeling most powerfully upset, you can reclaim a measure of personal power by simply *refuting your **ultimate** powerlessness or self-helplessness regarding the pain you are experiencing in that particular moment.*

The next step is to relinquish the upsetting thoughts and feelings you are having at the time, in other words, to give up your pain. The odd thing is that when an upsetting memory comes to mind and the painful thoughts and feelings get on a good downhill roll, some of us may be quite ambivalent about stopping our descent. On the one hand, we probably don't like the fact that we are feeling upset again, but on the other hand we don't necessarily want to stop our indignant preoccupation with our offender's faults and failings. In effect we are saying, "I want to stop hurting now, but I don't want to stop focusing on how terribly this person treated me" or, more bluntly, "I want to stop hurting now, but I don't want to stop hurting now."

However, one of the most liberating aspects of the whole alternatives to forgiveness approach is that you can relinquish or set aside your resentful or otherwise upsetting thoughts and feelings about your offender for the time being, and pick them up again later if you would like. Unlike with forgiveness, there is no expectation that you have to let go of the hurt or your hurt feelings on a once-and-for-all or final basis. But having said that, if you are feeling upset *now* and you want to enjoy a little bit of peace in the *near future*, perhaps in as little as fifteen minutes, then you do need to relinquish the types of thoughts and feelings that are contributing to your suffering.

I choose to relinquish (give up) the upsetting thoughts and feelings that I have been having for the last twenty minutes or so. I make this choice for myself and not for the person who hurt me. I simply don't want the rest of this day to be ruined, so in order to give myself a chance to enjoy at least a little bit of peace and happiness, I let go of my emotional and mental pain for now.

Continuing to hang on to the pain, though completely understandable, tends to result in passivity. Unremitting pain can lead to inertia and immobility in which you might feel that there is little or nothing you can do to help yourself. That is why making a conscious, intentional choice to relinquish the pain – at least for the time being – can be so liberating. It frees you to take some type of action, however small, to be your own liberator.

Once again, an analogy might be helpful. Let's say that a memory of how you were hurt comes to mind, putting you in a jail cell of inner misery in which painful thoughts and feelings are tormenting you. Accepting that you are imprisoned by this memory and the upsetting thoughts and feelings you are having about your offender – and maybe about yourself as well – is like unlocking and opening your cell door. But because you have grown a little bit accustomed to your cell, to feeling upset about how you were hurt, you may be a bit reluctant to leave your confines. However, in order to step out of your cell and out of the jail completely, you need to relinquish or let go of the painful thoughts and feelings that have captured you, at least for the time being, and risk freedom.

In this case, it really is an either-or choice: either you walk out of your cell or you stay in it; either you continue to hang on to and feed these types of thoughts and feelings and reap the consequence of staying upset, or you let them go for now and give yourself a chance to regain some peace and happiness in the very near future.

Accepting your current reality of feeling upset about a hurt or person who hurt you, refuting your powerlessness to help yourself become less upset, and relinquishing the pain you are currently suffering because you have been fixating on your offender, brings you to the next step: reclaiming possibilities. Reclaiming what is possible, especially that which is imminently doable or attainable, but also that which will require more time (e.g., the development of a new relationship), is energizing and mobilizing. Hope stirs again within, and inspires you to get up and do something, almost anything – right now – to help you move away from your pain and toward something that is potentially satisfying.

I'm going to get up and take a shower. Then I will throw in a load of laundry and call my friend Sue to see if she wants to have lunch and walk around the mall.

As you get involved in something else in the present moment, and focus on what you are doing in that moment (e.g., showering, doing laundry, savoring your food while enjoying "Sue's" company, and taking in the sights and sounds of the mall), your pain will decrease, allowing you to see what might be possible further down the road of your unfolding, open-ended life journey.

To summarize, as we suggested in the last two sections and also mentioned briefly at the beginning of this section, it all begins with **accepting yourself** and the upsetting thoughts and feelings you are having at the time. Because you have accepted yourself and what you are thinking and feeling–in other words, your current reality *as it is*–you are able to deal with it by **refuting your ultimate powerlessness** over the pain you are experiencing. Because you have claimed your personal power, you can make the power-filled choice to **relinquish the pain,** to let go of it for the time being. Then you are free to redirect your attention and energy elsewhere, toward something that you can engage and perhaps even enjoy, as you **reclaim the possibilities** available to you in that moment. We also explain this sequence in our workbook, which is available online at www.theforgivenessmyth.com.

While many of us might *perceive* that we are powerless when the memory of a past hurt is dominating our consciousness, in actuality, we often have more power at our disposal than we realize.

A New Reference Point from Which to Reorient and Recreate Your Life

It is not at all uncommon for many of us who have been hurt to reference or revolve our life around our offender. Like a show-horse in a circus that walks around the circumference of a circle because it is tethered by either rope or command to the trainer at the center, you may find yourself "walking" in endless circles around someone who has hurt you. You could be spending way too much time and energy talking about, thinking about, and perhaps even dreaming about this person, which, of course, is likely to upset you and inhibit your ability to move forward and be happy again.

What's particularly sad is the fact that the person who hurt you may no longer be in your life, or no longer have any real power over you if they are. Yet you might feel as powerless to stop referencing or revolving your life around this person – or persons, if there are more than one – as a show-horse is to break free from its trainer, walk out of the circus, and find a verdant pasture on its own.

At times, though you certainly don't want to be doing so, you may be referencing your life around your offender by referring to them and how they hurt you in your conversations with others and in the privacy of your own thoughts, even though there is no real rope or verbal command connecting you to them. Unlike a show-horse who has no power to break free, you may be unintentionally giving away your freedom-power to this person, who in reality may be but a phantom of the past. Perhaps you are spending an inordinate amount of time and energy, at least on some days, thinking and talking and feeling upset about this individual, yet you, on the other hand, aren't even on *their* radar screen at all. You stay stuck in your internal circus of sorts by rehashing the past and by citing this person's faults and failings over and over again. Therefore, around and around you go, even when the exit signs are clearly visible and there's a wide world of new opportunities and an abundance of potential peace and happiness waiting for you.

Lest you feel embarrassed – and we certainly hope that you don't feel any shame – if you recognize yourself in the above scenario, we have both been like captive and passive show-horses at times, as we have given our power away to certain individuals who have hurt us in the past, and orbited our lives around them. The purpose of this section, and indeed this entire book, is to help all of us break free from making those who have hurt us the reference point of the rest of our lives. We will say more about that in a moment, but first we invite you to do a quick assessment.

The questions below are simply meant to help you gauge how tightly you are bound to someone, or several "someones," who have hurt you in the past. Please do not judge or condemn yourself if you are hooked by these individuals, for it is entirely normal after being hurt or wronged. And as we have said so many times before, it makes no difference if the person you are orbiting around is someone who hurt you decades ago, for our desire is that you begin – or continue – to break free as much as possible today.[20]

1. How often do you refer to those who have hurt you in your conversations?

2. How often do you think about them when you are alone?

3. How often do you have upsetting dreams about them while sleeping?

4. How often do you engage in imaginary arguments in which you are telling them off or envisioning scenes of retribution?

5. When you start to think or talk about someone who has hurt you, how hard is it for you to stop? Do you find yourself not even *wanting* to stop?

---

20. This section was written on the fourth of July, Independence Day in the United States of America, and any day of the year can be *your* Independence Day, as you break free from referencing or revolving your life around someone who has hurt you so that you can enjoy a new beginning.

6. How difficult is it for you to talk about yourself and keep the focus on your life today, and on what you would like to accomplish or enjoy, as opposed to talking about and focusing on someone who has hurt you?

7. How upset do you become when you are talking or thinking about your offender?

8. Are you able to retain your personal power as you talk or think about this person or does it tend to trickle – or even gush – away?

9. Do you feel energized to move forward with your life and be happy again when you talk or think about how you were hurt, and your offender's faults and failings?

10. Do you feel depressed or happy? Angry or at peace? Bitter or excited about life?

11. What steps to help you be happier, including taking prudent risks and seizing new opportunities, are you avoiding because you are orbiting around and around this other person?

12. How do you tend to feel, and how would you assess your energy level and degree of inner peace and happiness, when you are *not* focusing on them?

Now please do not misunderstand what we are saying. If you have been hurt by another individual, it makes perfect sense that you refer to, talk about, or think of this person quite a bit. That's part of the process. So if you are in therapy to help you recover from a serious hurt, you absolutely *need* to talk about the person who hurt you as much and as often as you see fit. Or if you are in a recovery or some other type of support group, you likely need to spend some of your time talking about this person. The point we are making is that those who have hurt you no longer have to be your reference point, even if you have a need to talk or think about them on a regular, periodic, or occasional basis.

In the wilderness, prior to GPS, campers and adventuresome lovers of the outdoors tended to rely on a compass to help them find their destination and not get lost. This ancient instrument helped them to find their bearings–their reference point–so that they could then proceed in any direction of their choosing, either deeper into the woods or back toward civilization. The reference point of compasses, as you probably already know, is north. Your "north," from which you can orient yourself and then move forward in any direction you so choose, needs to be *you and who you are at this point in your life–<u>not</u> the person who hurt you, how they hurt you, or their faults and failings*. However, this is easier said than done, so first we want to say a little bit more about the powerful hold that your offender may very well have on you.

The primary image we would like to use to portray the power that someone who has hurt you in the past can have over you in the present is a vortex. Below is how one dictionary defines "vortex." We have highlighted certain words that we will comment on.

1. a **whirling** mass of water, especially one in which a force of **suction** operates, as a whirlpool

2. a whirling mass of air, especially one in the form of a visible column or spiral, as a **tornado**

3. a whirling mass of **fire**, flame, etc.

4. a state of affairs likened to a whirlpool for violent activity, **irresistible force**, etc.

5. something regarded as **drawing into its powerful current** everything that surrounds it: *the vortex of war*.[21]

---

21. *Webster's New Universal Unabridged Dictionary.* New York: Barnes and Noble, 2003

So when you allow someone who has hurt you to continue being your reference point, around whom your life revolves in the present moment, you are not necessarily doing so out of choice; more likely, you want to break free, but might not know how to go about it. The power this person has had on you – and may still have on you – can have these characteristics:

- ✎ Their power over you can be **whirling** in its effect as you continue to think and speak about this person excessively, making it difficult for you to move forward with your life (remember how hard it was to walk after whirling around as a child?).

- ✎ Their power can be like a **suction** and suck you back into the pain of the past as you focus on them, even though they may no longer be in your life.

- ✎ Their power, when you allow them to be your reference point, can be compared to an internal **tornado** or to a **whirling mass of fire**, which destroys your ability to be happy in the present and possibly in the future as well.

- ✎ They seem to have an **irresistible force, drawing you into [their] powerful current** as you, time and again, go to **war** with this person in your thoughts, words, and perhaps even in your dreams.

The good news is there are a number of ways that you can break free from those who have hurt you and the power they may have over you today. One key way is to *no longer reference or define yourself in terms of this person and how they hurt you.* You don't have to allow them to be the reference point on your internal compass from which you get your bearings. Instead of having their name appear as "north" on your compass because of the power they can still have over you, you can move forward with your life as you become your own "north," your own reference or starting point from which you can reorient and recreate your life today. The magnetic hold they have on you will become a thing of the past as you discover and claim your own personal power to steer or chart your life in a direction of your own choosing.

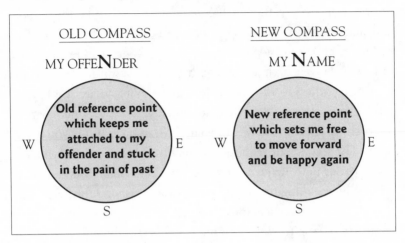

While those who have hurt you may visit you from time to time in your thoughts, your words, and even your dreams, you do not have to allow them to continue living "rent-free" in your head and heart, at great personal cost to you. You can kick them out, get them off your compass, and walk toward the exit of the internal circus in which you have been revolving around them, so that you can reorient and recreate your life anew. In the final three sections of this chapter, we show you how.

When you allow someone who has hurt you to continue
being your reference point, around whom your life
revolves in the present moment, you are not necessarily
doing so out of choice; more likely, you want to break
free, but might not know how to go about it.

Stopping the Orbit around Your Offender and Starting One Anew around You

In order to become your own reference point from which you can re-orient and re-create your life anew, you need to be intentional and active in two concurrent processes. The first one involves making a choice to *stop* revolving around your offender—and not just once but each time you catch yourself spinning around this person. In others words, when you realize that you are thinking or talking or obsessing about this individual when it isn't necessary to do so, there's nothing to be gained from it, or it is causing you to feel upset. The second one requires you to *start* revolving around yourself, around your new life and what you can do to make it better, more enjoyable, meaning-filled, and personally satisfying in the present moments of that particular day, and each subsequent day.

To try to stop the self-harming habit of dwelling obsessively on your offender, focusing excessively upon their faults and failings, and endlessly rehashing how they hurt you without replacing this deeply ingrained tendency with a new one can be next to impossible. It would be like someone trying to stop their habit of eating too many donuts and pastries, yet who continues going to the bakery every day "just to look." Obviously it would make more sense not to go to the bakery at all, and to replace this routine with something new and different (e.g., going for a walk, or going elsewhere to buy something to eat that is both flavorful and nutritious).

So it is with those who have hurt you. You will find it much easier to *stop* thinking about and orbiting around them as incessantly as the earth orbits around the sun, as you *start* redirecting your time and energy toward orbiting around yourself and the new life you are creating.

Stopping this old life-less orbit around your offender and starting a happiness-enhancing orbit around yourself takes practice. Yet each time you activate your personal power and take the *smallest* action step to do something different, you create a slight and initially imperceptible, yet critically important, groove in the orbit around the new life you are creating. What starts out as a slight and inconspicuous groove soon becomes a bit more noticeable and established, eventually superseding the old one. You become increasingly at home in your new life, and have no time or energy, and most importantly *no inclination*, to focus on and orbit around your offender any longer. Life's simply too short, and there's way too much new living to be done.

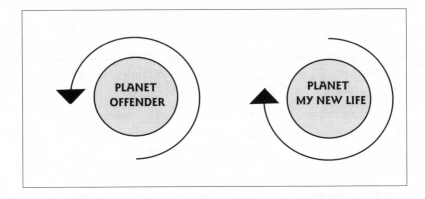

Initially, you can expect to go back and forth between these two "planets" in a figure-eight-like manner.

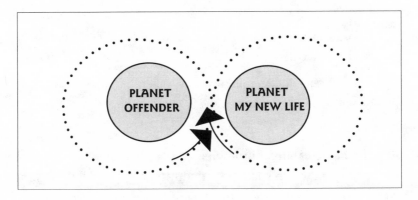

Sometimes, out of habit, you will make several painful mental orbits around your offender before you even realize that you are doing so. However, when you do become aware of what is going on within, you simply *stop* focusing on your offender and *start* focusing once again on yourself and the new life you are creating. You don't judge and condemn yourself; instead, you dispassionately acknowledge that you got temporarily sidetracked or "side-orbited" from where you belong. Then you simply come home–to yourself. With patience, practice, persistence, and the passage of time–four powerful Ps–you will find yourself spending more and more time on "Planet My New Life," while visiting "Planet Offender" less frequently and for shorter periods of time. What follows is a detailed description of a powerful practice to help you begin to break the old orbital pattern so that you can establish a new one.

When thinking or talking about your offender, simply refer to them by their given name rather than engaging in name-calling, putdowns, and fault-finding, and instead of referring to them in terms of the role or relationship they once had with you. This practice is especially effective if you were hurt by someone who was once a major figure in your life (e.g., a former spouse, partner, significant other, or friend) or if you were hurt by someone who also had a lot of power over you (e.g., a parent or former boss). It involves three tasks–two stops and one start:

1. Stop the name-calling, putdowns, and fault-finding.

2. Stop referring to them in terms of the role or relationship they once had with you.

3. Start referring to them by their given name when you have a need to think or speak about them.

Stop the name-calling, putdowns, and fault-finding. If you were in a marriage in which you were seriously hurt by your "Ex," or hurt over a prolonged period of time, you may be so angry, so hurt, so bitter . . . that you find yourself calling this person various names in your head or in your conversations with others (e.g., "idiot," "jerk," "loser," and worse). You might also have gotten into the habit of putting them down in your thoughts or words and focusing on their many faults.

While doing so is certainly a normal yet painful part of the healing process after being hurt, at some point, whether it is weeks or months or years or decades down the road, you need to stop—unless you want your life to stop with how this person hurt you. Instead of enabling you to move on and be happy again, continuing this self-harming practice keeps you spinning more deeply in the already deep rut you have unwittingly established around the person who hurt you. If you want to break free and be happy again, you need to make a commitment to eliminate, or at least reduce, the name-calling and hostile, contemptuous, or sarcastic language about this person, both in your head while alone and in your conversations with others. At some point, stating or thinking something you have said or thought a million times before serves no purpose other than to keep you spinning miserably around "Planet Offender" (e.g., My "Ex" is an absolute jerk. I've never met anyone more selfish in my entire life! He is completely self-centered. He never thinks of anyone except himself. He doesn't even really care about the kids; he just wants custody so that he can hurt me . . . ").

Stop referring to this person in terms of the role or relationship they once had in your life but no longer do. In the case of your "Ex," you need to stop referring to this individual as "my Ex" or "the Ex." Now you might argue that this person *is* your "Ex." And while that's true, continuing to refer to this individual *as* your "Ex" tends to keep the hurts you suffered in your past relationship with this person alive and well in your heart and mind in the present. The reason being is that whenever you reference your "Ex," you are referring to and raising to conscious awareness in the present moment your marital relationship and the hurts associated with it, which is now over. It is likely that you want to get over this relationship and move beyond this person, but using "Ex" language may inadvertently be keeping you trapped in it. Also, "Ex" language is often loaded, as it's so easy to say "my Ex" or "the Ex" with varying degrees of dehumanizing and wound-opening contempt, hostility, or sarcasm. However, the person who is being dehumanized and wounded is you. You probably don't refer to your fourth grade teacher as "my *ex* fourth grade teacher" or "*the ex* fourth grade teacher." Similarly, it may be freeing to no longer refer to your former spouse as "the Ex."

Start referring to this person by their given name. It's not likely that you have forgotten the name of your "Ex," or of someone else who has grievously hurt you. We have found that when people refer to the person with whom they once had a significant relationship or who played a key role in their life by their given name, they don't get emotionally hooked as easily or for as long a period of time as they did in the past. Because they are less easily hooked, they are freer to focus on their own lives. And the more they focus on and enjoy their own lives in the present, the less inclined they are to return to "Planet Offender." In fact, starting to refer to their offender by their given name is oftentimes the critical orbit-breaking step that frees them to begin a new orbit around their own life (see number three in the diagram below).

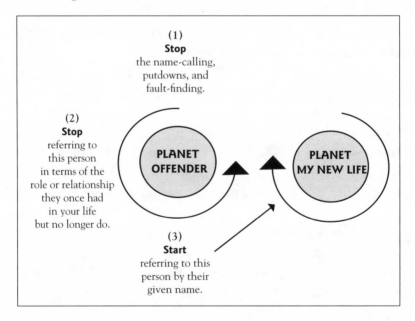

Notice in the diagram on the previous page that when you are orbiting around your offender you are going counterclockwise, which is symbolic of going backward in time or in reverse, as you revisit old, tired, lifeless terrain, which doesn't exist anymore—except in your head. But when you get to the point where you can refer to them by name in a somewhat dispassionate manner, you are breaking free from this past-bound orbit so that you can begin to orbit around yourself and the new life you are creating in the present moment. This is symbolized by the clockwise rotation around "Planet My New Life" in which you are moving forward.

Some who are unable to forgive one or both of their parents, and who are struggling with painful memories whenever they refer to their parents as "my parents" or as "Mom" and/or "Dad," may be able to finally break free by referencing one or both of them in their thoughts, and in their speech with others, by their given name instead. This isn't done out of disrespect or to punish their parents, but so that the hurt person can move beyond the painful memories that continue to surface when "Mom" or "Dad" or "parent" language is used.

We know of one person, Brian, who has chosen to refer to his father by his first name in his thoughts and in his speech with others. Continuing to speak or think of him as "Dad" tends to elicit all sorts of father wounds, launching Brian back in time as he takes yet another costly orbit around his father and the hurts he suffered so many years ago. By referencing—referring to—his father by his given name, George, in his mind and in his conversations with others, Brian is able to retain his personal power as an adult in the present.

He has been delighted by the fact that as he remembers to use "George" rather than "Dad" or "my dad" or "my father" when he thinks or speaks of him, he has been thinking and speaking about him much less often than in times past. Consequently, he is able to focus on his own life in the present, and no longer relinquishes his power to the role and power his father once had over him as a child. Brian is now "Brian the adult" and not "Brian the little boy" who needed fathering. And Dad is now simply George, an older man who Brian can engage in a more detached and effective way.

If, like Brian, you are unable to forgive someone who was once a major part of your life, and who may or may not continue to be in your life in some capacity today, you might find it helpful to refer to this person by their given name, rather than by the role or relationship they once had with you. This is true no matter what the role or relationship may have been, whether the person who hurt you was a former boss, a former business associate, or a former spouse with whom you still need to have some regular contact because of your co-parenting responsibilities.

For sure, refraining from—or at least reducing—name-calling, putdowns, and fault-finding is an essential practice at some point in your healing journey. It tends to keep the memories of past hurts from having an unnecessary detrimental impact upon you and your new life in the present. It may also be very self-liberating to call your offender by their given name when you have a need to speak or think about them. Doing so helps you to recognize that you are no longer bound by or connected to this person in the same way that you were in the past. The relationship or role they once had in your life is either over or it has changed dramatically, so there's no need to use old relationship or role language.

Using your offender's given name helps you stay in present time where your new life is unfolding and being recreated today. In the next section, we explore several additional practices to help you stay in present time, for that is where all your power is. The more you choose to activate your power to stay present and actively engaged in the now, as opposed to surrendering your power by re-living what took place in the past, the more freely and happily you will be able to live your life from here on out.

Each time you activate your personal power
and take the smallest action step to do something
different, you create a slight and initially imperceptible,
yet critically important, groove in the orbit around the
new life you are creating.

Staying in Present Time and Living Fully and Freely Today

It seems logical that most of us would want to focus on and repeatedly call to mind our happiest experiences in life, yet oftentimes just the opposite seems to be the case: we tend to spend far more time and energy rehashing past hurts. And it's not because any of us is masochistically choosing to dwell upon a painful memory instead of a pleasant one. More likely, it doesn't feel like we have a choice at all, as time and again recollections of past hurts appear to rise up on their own, re-upsetting us in the present moment.

As we have been exploring throughout this book, painful memories may come to mind and upset you again for any number of reasons, one being that it is difficult to stop thinking about how someone hurt you if you were not offered a sincere and timely apology, adequate amends, or an appropriate measure of accountability and justice. Even if you were, the effects of how you were hurt might not be lessened, much less eliminated, as a result. Another reason is that most of us have been living our entire life under the influence of the forgiveness myth, believing in something that isn't any more accurate or true than the once widely accepted pre-Copernicus and pre-Galileo myth that the sun revolved around the earth. So when forgiving was either undoable or undesirable, we may have been unaware of any other options available to us with which to manage our feelings of anger toward our offender or to mitigate our sense of guilt for not forgiving.

Though memories of past hurts *seem* to have a life of their own over which you have no control, the fact is *you* **do** *have a life of your own* over which you can begin or continue to exercise a great deal of control today. One critical skill with which to manage and control the pain of the past so that you can live fully and freely is to practice staying in present time. As you stay in the here and now, present to and in the present, journeying backward in time to revisit painful experiences will become something you can avoid, or at least reduce, with increasing skill and success.

How you were hurt is in the past, and the only *real* life you have is taking place in present time at this very moment. Yes, you were once hurt in a way that never should have happened to you. But, unfortunately, it did. No, you didn't ask for it or deserve it. Yet, regrettably, it is a part of your life history. Of course, all of history, including the personal history of each one of us, cannot be changed or erased. It was what it was. You can't get rid of your history of hurts, even if certain parts of it are still adversely affecting your life today, but you *can* reframe what you have suffered and approach it from a wider angle, broader perspective, or higher viewpoint. Most importantly, you can either choose to emphasize it and give it great power, perhaps even ultimate power over the rest of your life, by continuing to focus on your hurts, or you can choose to de-emphasize it, defuse its power over you, and refocus on living fully and freely in the present time of today.

While acknowledging that your past hurts cannot be changed or undone may be painful, the good news is that admitting this truth comes with two huge payoffs:

1. You set yourself free to become wholeheartedly engaged in and focused on the present moments of today, rather than keeping half of your heart – and half of your energy and focus – in the past.

2. You are better able to adapt to what was, and make the necessary adjustments and changes so that you can move forward and be happy again, because you are no longer straddling the fence and keeping one foot solidly in the past and one foot tentatively in the present.

The alternative to living fully and freely in the now is to continue straddling the fence with most of your weight (i.e., focus and energy) on the "past side," while wishing over and over again until the day you die that the hurts you suffered didn't happen, resisting the reality that they did, and insisting that they be undone before you move on. While wishing, resisting, and insisting are part of the process, completely human and totally understandable, they don't change what was. Someone once said that even God cannot change the past.

Many of us have revisited and relived some of our past hurts to such an extent that we have developed a deeply ingrained habit of doing so. Strangely enough, we continue this pattern despite the unchanging result: feeling upset each and every time. Again, we aren't usually *choosing* to suffer; instead, we might not know how to stay in present time, or we fear losing something if we "climb the fence" and move on fully into the present. The truth is, we *will* lose something, but it is something we need to lose in order to heal and be happy again—the power that the past continues to have over us as we continue to focus on it.

Fortunately, there are specific practices you can activate to help you stay in present time—or return to present time should you periodically go back over the fence to revisit the pain of the past—so that you can live fully and freely today. We invite you to think of staying in present time as an *active practice* that you will become better at as you practice.

Earlier in this chapter, we encouraged you to refute ultimate powerlessness over the pain of the past. Now we urge you to refute any sense of powerlessness you may have regarding your ability to take action in order to stay in present time, or quickly return to the present after revisiting past hurts. Again, present time is the only thing that is real, which is why it is so powerful. Plus, it's where ALL of your power lies: in the here and now.

What follows are five practices to help you focus on staying in present time. The first two are especially effective when a past hurt, or an amalgamation of all of your hurts, is causing you so much pain that you feel overwhelmed, perhaps to such an extent that you doubt whether you can bear it. The remaining three can be used in times of intense emotional pain as well, but they are also intended to help you ward off painful memories before they gain too much of a foothold, analogous to taking some type of pain reliever at the earliest signs of a headache. Additionally, they can help you to live more fully and freely in the present even when past hurts are not bothering you at all.

1. Focus on short timeframes

In this practice you are trying to stay in the thinking part of your experience as a way to manage painful emotions that have become particularly intense. Sometimes your emotional pain might be so intense that you need to focus on a short, measurable timeframe. One reason for this is that it can be very frightening and overwhelming to imagine living with this much pain for the rest of your life, which is what your emotions may have you *mistakenly* believe when you are hurting or feeling most upset. But by activating your intrapersonal ally of your intellect and focusing on shorter timeframes, as opposed to "the rest of my life," you are making the pain you are suffering more manageable.

The spiritual teacher Eckhart Tolle offers this reassurance: "You can always cope with the now, but you can never cope with the future—nor do you have to. The answer, the strength, the right action, or the resource will be there when you need it, not before, not after."[22] Though the pain you are suffering in the now may feel like it is absolutely unbearable, one way to cope with it until the intensity reduces, which it always does, is to practice staying present in short, focused, manageable timeframes. These timeframes might be one day, one hour, or fifteen minutes—even one minute, if necessary. As a result, you will be more able to make constructive choices in the midst of your emotional pain when you focus on a shorter period of time: "Okay, what can I do during the next fifteen minutes to help me get through this?" As you get through that particular timeframe, you gain a little more confidence to get

---

22. We highly recommend Eckhart Tolle's fine book *The Power of Now*, and *The Power of Now 52 Inspiration Cards*, which serve as excellent reminders of key points in his book, as he has some wonderful suggestions and practices for staying in present time.

through the next one. Then, as the intensity of your emotional pain begins to lift, which it will, you can lengthen the timeframe, or perhaps set this practice aside until you need it again.

2. Focus intensely in the present moment and on your immediate surroundings

This practice is especially effective for those who have suffered some type of trauma, whether it occurred recently or long ago. For example, it is not uncommon for sexual abuse victims as well as victims of other types of violence to feel overwhelmed by various types and degrees of pain–emotional, physical, mental, or spiritual–even long after the original assault took place. Some who have suffered such serious hurts might feel like they cannot survive when the pain they are experiencing is at its most intense. Common symptoms include shortness of breath, a racing heart, nausea, anxiety, and body-pain memories. Oftentimes there is a time distortion as well; either time seems to move incredibly fast or very slowly, even to the point of stopping altogether.

The way this practice works is that you begin describing to yourself where you are, the date and time, what you are wearing, and your immediate surroundings in great detail. You include the colors, shapes, and textures of various objects as well as what you hear and smell. Doing so helps you stay in present time and regain control of the intensely painful emotions you are currently suffering. Here's an example:

"I am in my apartment sitting at the kitchen table. The day is Friday, April 5th and it is 4:17 p.m. I am wearing a pair of somewhat faded blue jeans and a navy blue sweatshirt. There is a bowl of fruit on the table with three bananas and two apples in it. Two of the bananas appear to be good for eating, mostly yellow with just a bit of green coloring toward both ends; the other one looks like it is overly ripe and has several bruises on it. The apples are both shiny and red. There are four chairs at the table. I am sitting on one of them. The refrigerator is humming. Other than that, I don't hear anything. No, I hear a plane passing by overhead. . . . "

As with the previous practice, focusing intensely in the present moment will help you move into the thinking part of yourself, so that you don't react, or overreact, to the trauma—or the memory of the trauma—that is causing you to suffer right now. You meet the *intensity* of your emotional pain that is associated with past hurts or trauma with the *intensity* of focusing on and describing your surroundings with your intellect. Again, you state the date and time, your location, and describe what you are wearing and your immediate surroundings in great detail. Regarding how long to continue this practice, we suggest that you keep it up until the physical symptoms (i.e., racing heart, anxiety, etc.) begin to pass, which they will.

3. Focus on your breathing
in an attentive, mindful manner

Sometimes in the midst of feeling very upset, you may forget to breathe. Of course, you still *are* breathing, but you might be doing so in a way that is adding to, rather than decreasing, the intensity of your emotional pain (e.g., holding your breath, hyperventilating, or gasping). Concentrating on your breath and each inhalation and exhalation not only provides you with a focus point for your attention, for your mind, it also restores a measure of calm, sometimes within a minute or two. Your body befriends you as you regain a sense of peace, perhaps because focusing on the natural rhythm of each breath for a period of time is inherently self-soothing.

Because there are so many different teachings on how to breathe (e.g., counting as you inhale or counting as you exhale, or both, or not counting at all, etc.), and because we do not have the expertise to recommend any one particular approach or technique over another, we refrain from doing so.[23] However, much of Buddhist teaching on breathing, according to our understanding, seems to suggest that you simply breathe naturally. There's no need to try to breathe especially deeply; instead, just let your breath flow freely

---

23. There are many articles and teachings on various breathing practices available online or in bookstores, particularly if you look under Eastern or Buddhist spirituality. If you prefer CDs, you might consider one of the products produced by Sounds True, located in Boulder, Colorado. See www.soundstrue.com.

without trying to force anything special to happen. The practice is simply to focus on your breathing, as you direct your attention to its rhythmic risings and fallings. As you do, and again oftentimes in just a manner of minutes, you will find that the edge has been taken off of your emotional pain and upsetting thoughts, which will allow you to refocus on your life in the present moment.

One breathing exercise we have both found to be helpful is that of visualizing the pain associated with a painful memory or the memory itself dissipating or losing its power with each exhalation, and strength, power, and clarity growing stronger with each inhalation. You might consider experimenting with this technique to see if it helps you keep, or restore, your power in the present moment when you have been feeling upset.

4. Focus fully on what you are doing in an attentive, mindful manner

This practice is helpful when you are having one upsetting thought after another about someone who has hurt you, and you feel powerless to stop it. It is a way to regain a degree of calm and composure as you redirect your full attention to what you are doing, or are about to do, in the present. As you give your full attention to what you are doing, the upsetting thoughts and feelings that were pulling you powerfully backward in time just a few minutes ago tend to lose their power and dissipate rather quickly.

For example, if you have been sitting on your couch journeying backward in time by obsessing about how someone hurt you, you purposefully get up to do something in order to break the trance-like effect that these types of painful thoughts have been having on you. Let's say that you decide to get up and go to the bathroom to simply rinse your hands and splash some water on your face. You pay the utmost attention to the various movements you make as you prepare to get up from the couch including the positioning of your feet. As you push up from the couch, you concentrate on every detail of that process as if experiencing it for the first time: how it feels in your thighs, your calves, your feet, your hands and arms. . . . Then, before taking your first step, you notice how it feels throughout your body to stand up and to have your weight equally distributed. As you begin to walk, you pay attention to every detail: lifting and pushing off with each foot, the heel to toe rhythm, the slight movement of your arms, etc. In the bathroom, you concentrate on turning on the water—though it really requires no concentration at all because you have done it countless times before. You listen to and observe the water pouring out of the faucet, and notice everything about it much like a fascinated small child would. Then you attend to how the water, including the temperature of it, feels on your hands as you begin to rinse them, and so on.

This practice links two intrapersonal allies that many of us have found to be somewhat disconnected from each other more often than not: your intellect and your body. Together, more powerfully than either one alone, your intellect and your body can help you stay fully in the present moment as you pay full attention to the smallest, most nuanced details of something you—and most of us—normally do with very little awareness because our minds are elsewhere: getting up from the couch, walking, and rinsing your hands and face with water.

When your mind is prone to taking you back in time to revisit old hurts that no longer need further visiting, this practice can bring you quickly back into the present moment where you can once again live fully and freely in the now. Also, the more awareness you bring to the normal and so-called mundane activities of each day, the less likely it is that the pull of the past will be able to recapture you for any significant period of time, because you are focusing on living fully, attentively, and mindfully in the now.[24]

---

24. Mindfulness is a Buddhist meditation practice in which you observe your thoughts without judgment or censure. However, you can practice paying full attention to the details of all that you do, from getting into your car to working in your garden to walking down the hall at work, in an attentive, mindful manner, even if you do not practice formal mindfulness meditation. If you would like to learn more about mindfulness, both the meditation practice and how to be mindful (fully attentive) to the normal activities of each day, visit your local bookstore or simply type in "mindfulness" on your Internet search engine. It is an ancient yet timeless practice that can help you stay in present time and experience life to the full. What's more, you don't have to be Buddhist to benefit from it.

5. Focus on catching and stopping needless thoughts about your offender and redirecting your thoughts and energy in a positive direction

Most of us know by now that when we continually – and perhaps needlessly – go backward in time to think about how we were hurt by someone, the first thought we have about that person quickly leads to another, and then to another. In a matter of moments, we may easily find ourselves on a rapidly accelerating descent into the lifeless land of past hurts. One powerful antidote is to practice catching and stopping these unnecessary thoughts as soon as possible so that you don't suffer unnecessarily. Then you simply redirect your thoughts and energy in a positive direction. Of course, if you don't catch your pain-producing thoughts until after you have gone on a twenty-minute or two-hour or two-day descent, then, you simply make a choice *at that time* to stop, so that you can redirect your thoughts and energy elsewhere. With practice, you will catch the needless thoughts about your offender earlier and earlier, be able to stop them, and quickly redirect your attention elsewhere.

To begin building a habit of monitoring your thoughts, you might decide to check in with yourself five times each day – at 9:00 a.m., noon, 3:00 p.m., 6:00 p.m., and 9:00 p.m. – and ask yourself questions such as these:

- What kind of thoughts have I been having during these past three hours?
- Have my thoughts been primarily positive and peaceful or negative and upsetting?
- Who have I been thinking about?
- What have I been thinking about?

You can also do this on an hourly basis if you are feeling especially at-risk to fall into the trap of thinking needlessly about your offender, which often results in you feeling needlessly upset again. At-risk times might include anniversary dates or various holidays such as

Christmas or Valentines Day. Certain situations or events such as parties or family gatherings – even funerals – may also be times when you feel vulnerable to the power of past hurts. Regardless of when you are most susceptible to being swept away by memories of past hurts, raising the aforementioned questions and monitoring your thoughts can help you stand your ground, and keep your ground, as well as your heart and mind, firmly in present time.

Whether it is during one of your check-ins or not, as soon as you **catch** yourself thinking about someone who hurt you in the past when nothing can be gained from it, you make a firm, disciplined choice to **STOP**. You might even say to yourself, aloud or in the silence of your mind, "STOP! I am *not* going to think about this person any longer and how I was hurt by them." Then you **redirect** your thoughts toward something else, preferably towards someone or something that you feel good or positive about. It might be someone you care about very much. If so, think about what it is that you like, love, or admire about this person. Perhaps you will dwell upon some of your favorite memories, or focus on what you plan to do together in the near future. Or you might choose to think about your favorite TV show, movie, book, sports team, or CD and why you like it so much. You might also purposefully think about a favorite hobby or pastime, whether it is fishing, reading, knitting, or gardening. Virtually anything that normally interests or appeals to you, or that you feel passionate about when you aren't in pain, is something you could focus on when a painful memory that doesn't need any additional "air time" arises, so that you can live fully and freely in present time.

If the painful thoughts you have been having refuse to leave, despite your best efforts to direct your thoughts elsewhere, then you need to *do* something in an attentive, mindful manner. Sometimes you can think your way into a better frame of mind and consequent emotional state; at other times, the upsetting thoughts and feelings you have been having about your offender will dissipate only as you engage in some type of activity or as you get up and change your location. Even moving from one room of your house or apartment to another is often all it takes to begin loosening the grip they have been having on you. Then, especially if you do something in that new setting and give your full attention to it, their grip loosens even more. Soon, you are completely engaged in something else, and the painful thoughts that had been upsetting you a short time ago have dissolved and scattered like clouds on a windy day.

Many of us have revisited and relived some of our past hurts to such an extent that we have developed a deeply ingrained habit of doing so. Strangely enough, we continue this pattern despite the unchanging result: feeling upset each and every time.

Safeguarding Your Inner Peace and Happiness

It is typical for mothers and fathers to try to do everything within their power to keep their children safe, healthy, and reasonably happy. Regarding safety, they take necessary precautions, especially in potentially dangerous situations such as when crossing a busy street. And they don't leave their children with strangers, or even relatives, who might harm them. In fact, most parents would do anything and everything within their power, even to the point of sacrificing their own lives, in order to protect their children from harm and to ensure their wellbeing.

Whether you are a parent or not, we urge you to protect or safeguard your inner peace and happiness, your emotional and mental health, and your physical and spiritual wellbeing with the same passion and dedication of a caring parent. This is especially important if you did not receive this kind of parenting when you were growing up.

Many who were mistreated or abused as children don't think they deserve to be treated with kindness and respect as adults. Others who have been beaten down by various hurts during their adult years, perhaps in abusive relationships, might lack the assertiveness and inner strength to insist upon being treated with basic kindness, respect, and human dignity, though deep inside they crave it with all their heart. Regardless of when the hurts you are trying to recover from took place, whether during your childhood or as an adult or both, you deserve to *feel* safe and to *be* safe emotionally, physically, mentally, and spiritually.

As a child, your safety and overall wellbeing, whether it was consistently ensured or grievously violated, was in the hands of your parents or other caretakers. It was *their* responsibility. Now as an adult, you are your own primary caretaker and self-care giver, and you need to take care of, and give care to, yourself. It is now *your* responsibility to protect yourself, to safeguard your priceless inner peace and happiness. This doesn't mean that you withdraw from the world and from life because you are excessively afraid of being hurt again, and of hurting others, for both are inevitable due to the inherent imperfection that comes with being human. *What it does mean is that you do everything within your power to avoid being hurt* **unnecessarily**.

Basically there are two types of hurts that you don't need to suffer any longer:

1. Re-living painful memories and focusing on those who have hurt you in the past to such an extent that you are unable to live as fully and freely in present time as you otherwise might.

2. Being hurt by people with whom you don't feel safe, or who have hurt you in the past and are likely to hurt you again in unacceptable ways.

The first is self-inflicted. You already suffered the particular hurt that is troubling you once during your life history, which was bad enough. Reliving and suffering it again and again and again, when doing so is no longer a part of the grieving/anger/healing process most of us go through, creates needless pain. It reaches a point where it becomes a self-harmful habit that will only continue to harm you unnecessarily—and at great cost—unless you make a passionate and dedicated effort to replace it with a commitment to focus on your life and safeguard your peace and happiness in present time. And you, like all of us, need to decide, and will probably know intuitively, when your tendency to focus on your offender is because you are still hurting, and when it has become something that you have become accustomed to doing out of habit, despite the fact that it causes you needless suffering.

There's absolutely no judgment or condemnation if or when it's the latter case because many people, including both of us, have realized at times that we have been focusing on our offender when it is no longer healing or helpful to do so, and we don't necessarily want to stop. In fact, because we have developed a habit of fixating on this person, it is far easier to continue to do so than it is to stop and refocus on ourselves, for the simple fact that a lot of backward momentum has been generated. Yet none of us needs to continue shooting ourselves in the foot–or in the heart–by focusing on the past and revolving around "Planet Offender" when there's absolutely nothing to be gained. Occasional orbits are inevitable and to be expected, for example, during the holidays, on anniversary dates, and at other vulnerable times, otherwise unnecessary spins are quite costly: we end up sabotaging our potential to enjoy inner peace and happiness again because we do not ground ourselves in the present and focus on ourselves.

The second type of unnecessary hurt is other-inflicted. It's not something you cause, but it is something you can take steps to prevent, for there may be certain individuals in your life who are unsafe, untrustworthy, and likely to hurt you again in unacceptable ways. If so, it makes no sense to put yourself in their line of fire and to let *them* shoot you in the foot, or worse, in the heart. Consequently, you might need to make some very tough choices on your own behalf that others may not approve of. This could entail setting and resetting boundaries that ensure your wellbeing. Or it could even mean that you cut certain people out of your life on either a temporary or permanent basis, much like a person who chooses to separate from their spouse because the relationship is no longer safe enough to work on the issues that need addressing, or who chooses to divorce because trust has been irrevocably broken. These certain people may be one or both parents, a sibling, a friend, or a colleague who may have been significant in the past, or who are still a part of your life today.

Denise was verbally abused throughout her childhood by her mother. She suffered putdown after putdown and was constantly criticized; nothing she did was ever good enough. She left her parents' home at eighteen, and quite understandably found herself–actually, lost her *true* self–in one abusive relationship after another. Now a single parent in her late thirties, she has begun to heal as a result of her work in therapy and participation in a twelve-step group. But because her mother continues to zing her with blatantly hurtful comments, as well as passive-aggressive putdowns whenever Denise sees her or talks with her on the phone, Denise has chosen to cut off all contact with her. She simply can't afford to suffer one more hurt from her mother.

She would like to be in some type of relationship with her dad, but because he is not strong enough to stand up *to* her mother and *for* Denise, and because he and her mom seem to come as a "package deal," she has made the tough choice not to see him either. Plus, he does not approve of her decision to stop seeing and talking to her mother. Denise is beginning to wonder why he didn't stick up for her and protect her when she was a child, and why he won't support her now. Perhaps he isn't as innocent or helpless as she once believed him to be in regards to the abuse she suffered.

Denise has also chosen to "divorce" her siblings, who believe that she should forgive and "honor your father and mother." And she has decided not to see anyone in her extended family of origin, as she has no real relationship with any of them. Besides, seeing them reawakens old wounds, resulting in Denise feeling anxious and at-risk for losing her hard-won capacity to stay in present time. She no longer attends any family functions including funerals, weddings, family reunions, and holiday gatherings.

When Denise first decided to cut these people out of her life, she second-guessed herself time and again.

Am I making too big of a deal out of this? Am I being overly sensitive? Am I bad for not seeing my parents? Will I regret this after they die, especially when my dad dies? Should I just forgive my mother and put up with my siblings? Will God punish me? I wonder what the other relatives think of me when I don't show up for funerals.

However, with the support of her therapist and her "new family" of safe, trustworthy, and supportive friends, she has stood her ground. It hurts her to make this choice, and it didn't come without a price to pay, including the need to grieve what was and what will never be. Yet it would have hurt her and cost her so much more to continue trying to be in relationship with her family of origin, especially when they are not capable of understanding, accepting, or respecting her for who she is today.

Life is simply too short and precious, and your peace, happiness, and wellbeing are far too important to needlessly put yourself in harm's way. This is true whether the "shots" come in the form of alleged jokes (e.g., "I see that you're not missing any meals"), sarcasm (e.g., "I suppose that's not good enough for *you*"), verbal putdowns ("I told you not to marry him"), or by passive-aggressive behavior including silent – but obvious – disapproval.

Questions to ask yourself as you evaluate the safeness, trustworthiness, and respectful nature – or lack thereof – of certain people in your life, especially those who have failed to be accountable in the past and whose track record leads you to conclude that they will hurt you again in unacceptable ways include:

- Do I feel comfortable being around them? Do I feel safe with them? Do I trust them?

- Can I authentically be myself, or do I have to pretend to be something or someone I am not?

- Does my time with them feel natural and real, or forced and artificial? Do I have to keep my guard up, or can I relax and be myself?

- Is where I am at in my life and how I am choosing to live it something they can understand, and if they can't understand it, can they accept and respect it?

- Do they seem balanced and healthy? Am I able to retain my inner balance and preserve my mental, spiritual, physical, and emotional health when in their presence?

- What can I possibly gain from being with them? What is the risk/reward ratio?

- Do I feel adult when I am with them? Am I able to stay in present time? Do I feel like I can keep my personal power? Am I respected as an adult, or do they see me as a child or as someone who is lacking in some way?

- Am I trying to stay in relationship with them in order to get some type of approval or blessing or praise that they are not capable of giving?

- Do I look forward to being with them, or do I worry about it or even dread it?

- Am I in relationship with other people who think and believe and act in this way? If not, does it make sense for me to try to be in relationship with (name) when we hold virtually nothing in common?

- Am I feeling like I should act in a certain way, do something I don't want to do, or try to be in a relationship that no longer feels right for me because my religious or personal belief systems tell me I must?

Depending upon your responses to some of the questions above, or to others you may raise that are more applicable to your situation, you can then decide to set some boundaries, separate yourself for a period of time until the various issues involved can be worked out, or divorce yourself completely from those who have not been accountable in the past and with whom you do not feel safe or comfortable in the present. As you make your decision, it may be helpful for you to know that you can have:

- Love for someone without being in relationship with them.

- A respectful relationship with someone without having love for them.

- Both love for someone and a respectful relationship.

- Neither love nor a relationship.

Many who have chosen to divorce or completely separate themselves from their family of origin, for instance, still have love for them, at least at some level, but they can no longer afford to be in a relationship with them due to the risks involved. Others have discovered that both love and the relationship died long ago, and it's no longer worth it to get together or talk by phone, even on an occasional basis.

Relationships tend to change, even in families, and your "inner circle" may change several times during your life. You may have shared a close and intimate walk with certain individuals during an earlier phase of your adult journey, even for many years, and then for whatever reason—a geographic move, a change in religious beliefs, the children grew up, or a conflict—resulted in a parting of paths. Since being in relationship with people for part of your life's journey, rather than all of it, is the norm, it might not make sense to try to be in relationship with certain individuals in your family of origin if they are not safe or respectful or are likely to harm you again in needless ways.

One more point: virtually everything in life is made up. For instance, shaking hands is common when meeting someone in the United States. Why? Why don't we gently step on each other's toes instead as we introduce ourselves or are being introduced? Because somewhere along the line a custom of shaking hands became the norm. Going to funerals, weddings, holiday gatherings, or family reunions are customs that you can reexamine, so that if you choose to participate, you are doing so because you *want* to be there and it is a *healthy* place for you to be, and not out of a sense of obligation or people-pleasing. Because you are now your own primary self-protector, it doesn't make sense to go to any event or gathering if doing so is likely to pull you out of present time into the hurts of the past, causing you to suffer yet again. Nor does it make sense to go and try to "make the best of it," because some people expect you to be there, when it is likely that you will be hurt again.

As an adult with a huge amount of personal power in present time, you get to make up your own rules, your own norms, which may be different than what is expected of you or different from how you have lived in the past. Here are four thoughts for you to consider as you decide what is going to be normal for you from this day forward:

1. You don't have to be in relationship with anyone you don't want to be in relationship with.

2. "To thine own self be true," in other words, trust your gut when it comes to your relationships with others and do what is best for you.

3. You need to protect yourself and safeguard your inner peace and happiness, especially from those who have hurt you in the past and who are prone to hurting you again in unacceptable ways.

4. You can and will heal and be happy again as you keep the focus on yourself and stay in present time.

Perhaps you won't have to cut anyone out of your life when all that may be needed is for you to set and articulate your boundaries in a clear, firm manner. That way others know what you expect from them. If they continue to cross the line, then you might find it necessary to separate or divorce yourself from them, for it simply doesn't make sense to put yourself in situations where you will be hurt unnecessarily.

Of course, we have all hurt others too, individuals whose inner peace and happiness is as precious and precarious as our own, and many of us have an even harder time forgiving ourselves than we do forgiving others. So in the next and final chapter, we explore why forgiving ourselves can be so difficult, and what we can do to make peace with the past when self-forgiveness eludes us.

As an adult with a huge amount of
personal power in present time,
you get to make up your own rules, your own norms,
which may be different than what is expected of you or
different from you how you lived in the past.

~ 7 ~

Making Peace with the Past When You Can't – or Won't – Forgive Yourself

When we shifted the focus at one of our presentations from how others have hurt us to how we have hurt others, an elderly woman quietly remarked to those in attendance, "I did everything wrong." Perhaps because she lacked the words to explain or elaborate upon this overwhelming sense of having done "everything wrong" when she was raising her family, or because it would have been uncomfortable for her to say anything more about her deepest, most private heartache in the presence of strangers, these words hung in the air, affecting everyone in the room.

While we hope that you don't feel like you did "everything wrong," like millions of others, you may be struggling to forgive yourself for *some* of the things you did do "wrong" in the past. Or, perhaps you struggle to forgive yourself because of what you didn't do "right" but wished you had, such as being more actively involved in your children's lives, or returning to school when you had an opportunity to do so, or simply being more patient with someone who seemed to bring out the worst in you.

One of the toughest realities in life is that none of us gets any retakes like photographers do, multiple takes as actors and movie directors do, or mulligans like golfers do. Instead, we have to go with whatever happens as it happens – and with the consequences of whatever happens as well. Sometimes things turn out pretty well, and sometimes they don't; we make good choices that benefit others and ourselves, and we make poor choices that hurt others and ourselves.

For example, if we asked all those parents who made some mistakes and poor choices with their oldest child that their next child didn't have to suffer to line up, it would be a very long line indeed, and would include both of us. Probably just as many parents would line up if we asked them how many had finally figured out how to do this parenting thing by about the time their youngest child headed out the door to find his or her way in the world. We would both likely find ourselves in that line too.

This is not to say that those of us who are parents were, or are, horribly incompetent; rather, it simply illustrates that life doesn't come with a "how-to" manual, and competency is often acquired as a result of learning from two of the best teachers around: "Experience" and "Mistakes." A learning curve usually accompanies every new endeavor, whether it is parenting, marriage, being a manager or boss, serving in one of the helping professions, or coaching or teaching kids.

Reading about swimming helps to a certain point, but only by jumping in and experiencing the water and learning from trial and error will you be able to swim. Most of us are not naturals at anything, and reaching a level of proficiency is a process which entails progress, setbacks, and comebacks. Even masters of various types of martial arts never claim to have perfected the most elementary technique, as there is always something more for them to learn or relearn.

While you might feel very bad about what you have done or

said, or failed to do or say, that hurt another vulnerable human being, feeling bad doesn't undo the harm that was done. This is true whether you feel bad for how you hurt your own children or some other person such as a spouse, coworker, employee, neighbor, or stranger. What happened is in the past. Even when we are the ones who did the hurting, feeling bad about it doesn't change what took place.

In previous chapters we have stressed that you can learn to manage the upsetting thoughts and feelings that are associated with memories of how you were hurt whenever they surface. Doing so allows you to move on with your life, even when some degree of anger and bitterness is present on any given day. The same is true regarding the upsetting thoughts and feelings you may be having about yourself for hurting others. You *can* move on with your life and make a contribution in the here and now, even on those days when the memory of how you hurt another human being comes to mind again, causing you to feel some reawakened remorse or regret.

In this chapter, we make a strong case for letting go of shame and replacing it with remorse, for the latter allows you to address and correct your behavior, which then enables you to heal, whether by forgiving yourself or by calling upon one of the healthy alternatives from Chapter Four (e.g., "making a fresh start right where I am").[25] The very nature of shame, on the other hand, does not allow you to address and correct your behavior; consequently, it is immobilizing. In essence, shame says that *you* are bad, defective, and what you have done – or didn't do but *should* have done – is beyond any possible healing.

When any of us tries to forgive ourselves, or to make peace with the past without necessarily forgiving ourselves but with the help

---

25. A synonym for "remorse" is "guilt." However, we have elected to use the word "remorse" because the culture as a whole seems to view the emotions of guilt and shame as being one and the same, despite the fact that they are radically different. Also, for many people, the word "guilt," much like the word "forgiveness," has so many negative connotations associated with it, and is accompanied by so much religious and personal baggage, it is virtually ruined. Using the word "remorse" seems to be relatively free of negative connotations and unnecessary baggage.

of one of the healthy alternatives, we are never excusing what we did to hurt another human being. Just as we don't want others to soften what they did to hurt us (e.g., when the abuser claims to have been "strict" rather than abusive), we will find no true freedom in trying to euphemize or soften what we did to hurt others. The truth itself will set you free, rather than couching your hurtful behavior in the most delicate terms possible so as to ease your conscience, or magnifying what you did to such an extent that you deem yourself to be among the worst human beings to have ever walked the earth.

So while the objective is not to excuse ourselves, we can certainly explore the reasons why we did what we did, examine the various factors that may be contributing to our inability or unwillingness to forgive ourselves, and most importantly, consider some ways to heal, move on, and be happy again. At the end of the day, it comes down to one of two fundamental choices that we must each make, not just once, but several times:

1. We either choose to punish ourselves day after day for the rest of our life because of our wrong and hurtful behavior earlier in our life, which is what shame would have us do, and which will not allow us to make peace with the past, move on, and make a contribution in present time.

or

2. We choose to address our wrong or hurtful behavior and learn from it, which is what healthy remorse would have us do, so that we can make peace with the past, move on, and make a contribution once again.

Feeling sorry or remorseful can be quite painful, make no mistake about it. Yet even when we are feeling the deepest possible remorse for what we did, it doesn't undo the consequences of our behavior. Sometimes these consequences can even result in a serious loss, as is true for some parents who were active alcoholics or who made hurtful choices they regret when their children were growing up that have impacted the quality of the relationship they have with their adult children today. In some cases, their grown children might want little or nothing to do with them.

Yet as painful as the consequences can be, accepting them is freeing because it allows you to grieve, learn from your mistakes and poor choices, and move on. Choosing to punish and beat yourself up endlessly, on the other hand, does not allow for grieving, learning, and moving forward with your life, because it is rooted in the quagmire of shame. And shame says *you* are bad and must be punished forever, rather than your behavior was wrong or hurtful. Remorse says: (1) my behavior was wrong or hurtful, (2) I need to address it, and (3) yes, the consequences of my behavior may be quite painful, but I can learn from the past, move on, and strive to make a contribution in the here and now, *because I am still a valuable human being who has much to offer.*

As you move on and make a contribution in present time, you will feel bad about the past less often (frequency) and for shorter periods of time (duration) while learning how to manage the pain (intensity) so that it doesn't stop you from contributing, which, in turn, contributes to your growing sense of peace and happiness.

In this chapter, we make a strong case for letting go of shame and replacing it with remorse, for the latter allows you to address and correct your behavior, which then enables you to heal, whether by forgiving yourself or by calling upon one of the healthy alternatives.

Why Did I Do What I Did?

Sally had her first child in her late teens, and by the time she was twenty-five she felt trapped by all the responsibilities that came with parenting three kids under the age of seven. One night when she was out with a couple of her girlfriends, she met Dan, a guy who thought that she was funny and attractive. He was fun and unattached, while Sally's husband was anything but fun because he worked all the time. She felt like she was in a rut that would never change. Shortly after meeting Dan, Sally left her husband and children, giving her husband full custody. About a year later, she found out that Dan had several other girlfriends, and that she wasn't "the one and only." She also learned that her "Ex" was now in a serious relationship with another woman whom the children were calling "Mom." Sally feels that she can never forgive herself for what she did.

Bruce was a raging alcoholic when his son and daughter were growing up. He finally went in for treatment after his oldest, John, had enlisted in the army, and his daughter Julie was entering ninth grade. Bruce made a 180-degree turnaround with his life, and Julie enjoyed her high school years during which she had a sane, sober, and caring father who did everything within his power to make amends to her. For John, however, it was too late.

After a stint in the service, John found a good job, got married, and settled down to have kids, but he wanted nothing to do with his father, who repeatedly tried to apologize and make amends for his "terrible behavior" when John was growing up. Now Bruce is desperate to have a relationship with his grandchildren, but John is so hurt and so angry that he doesn't allow his dad to see them. Bruce is struggling to forgive himself, and can't accept the consequence of being denied access to his grandchildren. He also doesn't understand why his son won't try to have a relationship with him now, especially since he is a completely different person than when he was drinking.

Mary and Joe had been lifelong friends with Jim and Grace.

246

They got together for dinner on a weekly basis and also went on vacations together. Their children had known each other since they were born. One night while vacationing in Mexico, Joe and Grace had too much to drink. Their spouses had already gone to bed, and after another drink, they had sex. The next day they were beside themselves with regret. Although their spouses never found out, it ruined the friendship and neither could forgive themselves for what they had done to their faithful spouses and to the friendship.

Like Sally, Bruce, Joe, and Grace, each of us has made choices that have hurt others, ourselves, or both. What you are struggling to forgive yourself for might seem to be more serious or less serious than the examples above. Regardless of what you have done, or failed to do, that has harmed another person or yourself, the first question that needs addressing, is "Why did I do what I did?", because having some kind of an understanding, even if it is not necessarily perfect or complete, is critical to your healing process. In fact, it is our hope that something we suggest in the following pages will help you to be gentle with yourself so that this daunting and haunting question will lose some of its stinging power. For at some point, with or without a perfectly satisfying answer, each of us who is struggling to forgive ourselves – or to make peace with the past without forgiving ourselves but with the help of the healthy alternatives – needs to set aside "Why did I do what I did?" in order to heal, move on, and be happy again.

We begin by reminding you that our purpose for exploring why any of us did what we did to hurt another human being is *not* to excuse ourselves for our harmful behavior, nor are we looking for a loophole through which we can escape being accountable and responsible. Instead, we are seeking some kind of *understanding* that will appeal to both head and heart so that we can move forward and make a contribution in present time. For with a measure of understanding comes mercy, and with mercy comes healing, and with healing comes an opportunity to make a fresh start right where we are and just as we are, no matter how wrong or hurtful our behavior was in the past.

247

As psychology has taught for quite some time, we are all products of a combination of nature (our genetics) and nurture (our environment). A quick look around will remind you of the diversity of "cards" that were dealt. Some, at least based on outward appearance, were dealt a great hand, while others appear to have received a very poor hand. Yet people with a great hand can and do make very poor choices in life that hurt others and themselves, while people who were dealt a lousy hand can and do make wonderful choices in life that benefit others and themselves. Most of us were dealt a mixed hand, neither a royal flush nor a complete bust. With your mixed hand, you have made both positive and negative choices that have had an effect on others.

To make a long and complex story short, you were shaped by your genetics, your environment, and your experiences in that environment. At the age of eighteen or twenty-one, society deemed you an adult, fully responsible for *all* of your actions, even though you might not have been very well prepared for adult life. And like so many young people, you may have made some choices that weren't the best.

As a young person, you had limited exposure to, and opportunities to learn from, the two master teachers in the adult school of life that we mentioned previously: "Experience" and "Mistakes." So guess what? You gained some experience and made some mistakes, in part, at the expense of hurting others and yourself.

Now maybe some of the things for which you are struggling to forgive yourself happened when you were older, perhaps in your thirties, forties, fifties, sixties, or beyond, rather than in your twenties. Well, learning from experience and making mistakes is not something we all wrap up in our twenties; in fact, we have just begun. Yes, it's true that the learning curve is often steepest and most costly when we are young and inexperienced, but it can also be steep and costly at other ages as well. The reason is simple: we are flawed, imperfect people who have unique issues, problems, and weaknesses that accompany us throughout life, which are present and active in, *especially in*, our relationships and interactions with others. Fortunately, we have unique strengths, gifts, and talents – as well as the capacity to learn – which we bring to the relational arena as well. However, we don't just bring the latter; we bring both: the good and the bad, our best and our worst, our strengths and our weaknesses, our magnanimity and our pettiness.

When it comes to hurting others, many of us would painfully admit that, no matter what age we were at the time, we knew that what we were doing or saying would end up hurting another person. We knew that the hurtful comment or behavior would really hurt this other person, yet we still said it or did it. As mentioned before, there is often a wide gap between knowing better and doing better, and many of us, despite knowing better, did not do better.

The tough news is that regardless of the background we each came from, and no matter what our unique genetic makeup may be, *each of us is completely responsible for everything we did once we became an adult.* What's more, that's the way it has to be, otherwise everyone, to a greater or lesser degree, can claim that they were responsibility-disabled and pass the buck, which we see a lot of today.

The truth of the matter is that each of us has hurt others due to one or more of the following three reasons:

1. We purposefully intended to hurt the other person and ended up doing so, despite knowing better.

2. We didn't purposefully intend to hurt the other person, but we ended up doing so because we were acting out of a state of being wounded or hurt ourselves (e.g., angry, frustrated, impatient, impulsive, rageful, shame-based, bitter, immature, needy, reactionary, chemically dependent, overwhelmed, compulsive, out-of-balance, etc.), or because we got some of our needs and wants met in an unhealthy manner at their expense.

3. We didn't intend to hurt the other person, but we ended up doing so because we acted out of ignorance, which means we lacked knowledge, learning, or information (e.g., making a joke that hurt another person though that wasn't our intent; shaming another person without even realizing that we were doing so; or teaching religious "truths" about sex that we may have believed at the time, which we learned later were not so healthy or true, etc.).[26]

Obviously, it's a great deal easier to forgive ourselves for what we did out of ignorance because we didn't know any better at the time, than it is to forgive ourselves when we purposefully, deliberately, chose to hurt another human being. However, we would submit that *the majority of hurts we fallible human beings have inflicted upon each other are due to the second reason: we were in pain or hurting in some way ourselves and took out our pain or hurt on another person, or we got some of our needs and wants met in an unhealthy manner at their expense.* Even if you think your hurtful behavior is due to the first reason cited above, it may really be due to the second reason, or, at the very least, to some combination of the first and second reasons. Our rationale is based upon a number of factors.

First of all, the fact that you are reading this chapter is a strong sign that you have a good heart, a good conscience, and a highly developed value system and sense of right and wrong. Second, you are probably reading this chapter because you truly regret and feel sorry for what you have done to hurt others – and possibly yourself as well – and have struggled mightily, perhaps in vain, to forgive yourself. Third, because you have a good heart and conscience, you most likely did *not* wake up on the morning that you hurt another person and said to yourself, "I feel like hurting someone today,"

---

26. There are also pathological issues that cause some people to hurt or do great damage to others, which we will not be addressing, as doing so is beyond the scope of this book.

and then set out to do so. In most cases, you hurt others without planning to do so.

Now that doesn't excuse you, or any of us, for hurting another human being. But, once again, what it is intended to do is to help you gain a measure of *understanding* as to why you did what you did. For as we mentioned earlier, with a measure of understanding comes mercy – self-mercy – and with mercy comes healing, and with healing comes the ability to move forward again in life and make a contribution.

Our purpose for exploring why any of us did what we did to hurt another human being is *not* to excuse ourselves for our harmful behavior, nor are we looking for a loophole through which we can escape being accountable and responsible. Instead, we are seeking some kind of *understanding* that will appeal to both head and heart so that we can move forward and make a contribution in present time.

Common Reasons Why So Many of Us Can't Seem to Forgive Ourselves

Besides the fact that many of us haven't been able to forgive ourselves because we feel very bad about hurting someone else–whether we did so intentionally, or because we reacted poorly, or out of ignorance–there are several other reasons why self-forgiveness can seem so difficult, if not impossible, at times. Some of these reasons also impact our ability–or inability–to forgive certain individuals who have hurt us, while others are uniquely problematic when trying to forgive ourselves for hurting others. We begin our discussion with the former and then turn our attention to the latter.

In Chapter One we addressed ten common obstacles that can make forgiving others a difficult or futile undertaking, four of which can also impede self-forgiveness.

1. **There is no clear, universally accepted definition of forgiving.** Just as we are not always clear what we mean by the word "forgive" when we say "I can't seem to forgive so-and-so," we may not be sure what forgiveness means when we say "I wish I could forgive myself but I just can't." Does self-forgiveness mean that we will never feel bad again about we did, or that we will forget about the incident, or that the relationship with the other person will resume as if the hurt didn't happen? Or does it mean something else?

2. **The head-heart dilemma.** We may know intellectually that we are not trying to excuse our hurtful behavior, yet in our heart if we were to forgive ourselves, as is true when forgiving certain others, we might feel like we *would* be excusing our behavior. And we don't want anything to do with excusing ourselves for our hurtful behavior, because it was wrong then and it's still wrong now. Therefore, we might not be able to forgive

ourselves, because what we hold to be true in our head and what we really believe in our heart are at odds with each other.

3. **Impossible litmus tests of "true" forgiveness.** We may believe – or hope – that if we forgive ourselves we will experience one or more of the following:

- We will forget about how we hurt the other person.

- We will no longer have any painful thoughts and feelings about how we hurt them, even if the memory just pops into our head on its own.

- We will be able to think and feel warmly and positively about ourselves, or at the very least neutrally, even when the memory of how we hurt this other person comes to mind again.

Yet these litmus tests can be as unobtainable for self-forgiveness as they often are when forgiving others, because:

- Forgiving ourselves doesn't mean that we will forget about how we hurt the other person.

- When a memory of how we hurt someone else comes to mind – as is true of when a memory of how we were hurt by someone else resurfaces – some degree of painful thoughts and feelings is to be expected.

- It is hard to feel warm or neutral about ourselves when recalling how we acted in ways that were not only *not* warm or neutral, but were truly harmful to another human being.

4. **What about justice and accountability?** Many times when we have hurt someone else we do not have the opportunity to be accountable to them and to make things right or just. In some cases, we didn't have the maturity or awareness at the time to be accountable and to make amends. In other cases, we may have hurt a stranger whom we will never see again. And in still other cases, we didn't become aware of just how hurtful our actions were until years later, perhaps long after losing contact with this person. Or so much time may have passed since we hurt them, that to offer amends at this late date could stir up their pain, pain that they may have put behind them without us being accountable and offering justice.[27] Nonetheless, because we want to make things right—or at least better—but we can't, we may struggle to forgive ourselves.

Then there are certain challenges and difficulties that are totally unique in our attempts to forgive ourselves, including these four:

1. **We must continue to live with ourselves while knowing that we hurt another person who wants all the basic things in life that we do: respect, happiness, love, kindness, opportunities, etc.** While we can walk away from just about anybody who hurts us if we so choose, we can't walk away from ourselves. Yes, we can punish, abuse, and neglect ourselves for what we have done in the past, but we can't ever escape ourselves. Part of living with ourselves means that we must live with our entire history as it is, including our history of hurting others.

---

27. The Twelve Steps of Alcoholics Anonymous speaks to this dilemma in step eight, "Made a list of all persons we had harmed, and became willing to make amends to them all," and especially step nine, "Made direct amends to such people whenever possible, *except when to do so would injure them or others*" (emphasis added).

2. **We may feel that it is wrong to forgive ourselves, while knowing that the person we hurt has not forgiven us.** Interestingly enough, a relatively small number of inmates who have developed a high degree of morality during their extended incarceration are among the most un-self-forgiving. They feel that they cannot forgive themselves – indeed, have no right to forgive themselves – because their victim or victim's family hasn't forgiven them. Many of us who have hurt others in non-criminal ways may also feel that it would be wrong to forgive ourselves if those we have hurt haven't been able to forgive us, or have chosen not to.

3. **We may feel like a hypocrite if we were to forgive ourselves for hurting another person, while at the same time not forgiving certain others who have hurt us.** People who struggle to forgive themselves tend to hold themselves to a very high standard. They often want to be consistent in their approach to life, and so if they are not going to forgive some people who have hurt them, then they may feel that they have no right to forgive themselves, at least for some of the hurts they have caused others to suffer.

4. **We don't know how to forgive ourselves, or how to make peace with our past if we decide that we can't forgive ourselves.** Many who can't forgive themselves don't have the slightest idea how to go about it. If you stop and think about it, most of us have received even less training in how to forgive ourselves than in how to forgive others. We have often been encouraged to do both, but in many cases, shown how to do neither. As is true for those who aren't aware of other ways to heal and move on when they can't forgive certain individuals who have hurt them, many who struggle with self-

forgiveness are unaware of any alternative ways to make peace with the past when they have done the hurting.

Finally, we would contend that *the number one reason why so many people can't seem to forgive themselves is because they are viewing and interpreting their wrong and hurtful behavior through the highly distorting lens of* **shame**. And shame, by its very nature, does not allow for self-forgiveness. Two manifestations of shame that quite a few disabled or unable self-forgivers have learned—even mastered to the highest degree possible—that make forgiving themselves virtually impossible are perfectionism and over-responsibility.

Perfectionism is simply a case of high standards, dedication, and integrity left to run wild without any restraints or limits. This world sorely needs more people to have high standards, dedication, and integrity, but if no limits are set, then, as is true of almost anything else that is potentially positive yet taken to an extreme, it becomes harmful. Yes, other people can pay a price when living with, working with, or otherwise interacting with perfectionists, but they don't come close to paying the constant and exorbitant price that perfectionists themselves pay.

Because perfectionists are intolerant of their own mistakes and poor choices, they have no room in their heart for self-mercy or self-forgiveness. While they may be reluctant to accept that others make mistakes and poor choices, they are absolutely unwilling to accept that they themselves make mistakes and poor choices, including ones that hurt others. And when they do fall short of perfection and hurt another person, they are totally unwilling to forgive themselves. Even though their heart is crying out for a bit of self-gentleness, their heads respond with yet another blow from the ever-present hammer: "How could you have been so heartless, so stupid?!" "You should have known better!" "You *did* know better, yet you still made a very selfish and harmful choice!" (The use of the second person "you" in their internal self-talk is indicative of the common origins of perfectionism: parental and other adult voices from childhood.)

Regarding **over-responsibility**, both men and women can be overly responsible, but women, especially, have been culturally conditioned to assume responsibility for much of what is simply not their fault. Countless wives and mothers struggle to forgive themselves for the poor choices their husbands and children have made. They also tend to feel bad when things simply go wrong – even in other parts of the world! – and wonder what they could have done to prevent it. Or they are plagued by troubling thoughts and feelings when someone or something didn't turn out as well as they, or others, had hoped. They often second-guess themselves, berate themselves, and struggle to forgive themselves for all sorts of things that they either had no ability to influence one way or the other, or in which they did their very best but other factors affected the outcome. Again, when a spouse or child fails, falls short, or makes a poor choice, many of these women who have learned to be overly responsible can't seem to forgive themselves, even though they weren't the ones who failed, fell short, or made the poor choice. In a way, their inability to forgive themselves for what someone else did, even when it is a loved one, makes perfect sense, as they, like all of us, can only try to forgive themselves for what *they* did.

Many men also feel overly responsible and struggle to forgive themselves, especially when a girlfriend, spouse, or child is seriously hurt. And if the hurt was caused by a criminal, self-forgiveness can be very hard to come by, even though it was the criminal and not themselves who did the hurting. They often feel like they failed in their role as "protector," despite the fact that there was absolutely nothing they could have done to protect their loved one from suffering what they did. Fathers, especially, struggle with overpowering feelings of remorse when their children get hurt, whether emotionally, mentally, or physically, in a world that is beyond their ability to control.

Whatever barriers are blocking your ability to be self-forgiving or self-merciful, whether it is a manifestation of shame such as perfectionism or feeling overly responsible, or the fact that you desperately want to apologize and make amends to the person you hurt but you don't know how to contact them, we now turn our attention to differentiating between shame and remorse.

Many who can't forgive themselves don't have the
slightest idea how to go about it. If you stop and think
about it, most of us have received even less training in
how to forgive ourselves than in how to forgive others.
We have often been encouraged to do both, but in
many cases, shown how to do neither.

Distinguishing Between
Shame and Remorse

Returning to our nature-nurture discussion that we began in the section "Why Did I Do What I Did?," as a child, you were in effect a brand new visitor to this planet, in a similar situation to the science fiction alien who is totally clueless as to what is deemed appropriate here on Earth. New to this world, others began to "write" the rules and what was expected of you on a blank chalkboard, which represented your new and unmarked life. Your chalkboard began to fill as you absorbed their rules and expectations, while learning from your own budding life experiences and from the direct and indirect teachings and examples of others. Early on, your most powerful teachers, rule-givers, and expectation-holders – as well as judges and determiners of right and wrong – were your parents or caregivers and other significant adults such as school teachers and religious leaders. As you moved into adolescence, your peers and siblings took on increasing power as the ones who deemed you fit and acceptable or not. Also, beginning in adolescence, you began to take the chalk and eraser from others and write out new rules and expectations while erasing some of the old.

In healthy family, educational, and religious systems, the mistakes and poor choices that inexperienced children make are corrected in ways that leave the child's sense of inherent goodness intact. Children are taught that their *behavior* was "bad" or wrong or unacceptable, but that *they* are good, right, and acceptable – even when acting "badly." Hence, children learn that their mistakes and poor choices, even ones that hurt others, are not fatal, and that there is something they can do to feel better about themselves again. In short, children learn to have healthy remorse, which enables them to address their behavior, accept the consequences, learn from the experience, and try again, all of which helps to bring closure to the incident itself and to their feelings of remorse. We call this concept **discipline**, in which parents and other adults teach

259

and correct children's misbehavior in a gentle and respectful, yet when necessary, firm, no-nonsense manner.[28]

In dysfunctional family, educational, and religious systems, mistakes and poor choices that inexperienced children make are not corrected in ways that leave their inherent sense of goodness intact. In fact, children are frequently shamed for what they did, scolded or punished for not knowing better—even when no one took the time to teach them, or when what was expected of them was beyond their developmental capabilities at the time. In short, they were taught shame at an early age (the onset of shame takes place between the ages of two and four), so that when remorse was developmentally available to them (around the age of five or six), shame had already laid the foundation for dealing with life's mistakes, poor choices, and wrong or hurtful behavior.[29] Shame became the *distorting lens* through which mistakes and poor choices, including behavior that hurt others, was viewed and interpreted (e.g., "I am bad" rather than "my *behavior* was bad"). And we call this concept **punishment**, which is largely about inflicting pain, laying blame, and instilling fear, as a way to get children to do what is expected of them.

Many who struggle to forgive themselves, perhaps including you, interpret what they have done wrong through the distorting lens of shame, rather than through the corrective lens of remorse. Shame does not allow you to be human, and its inhumane messages include:

1. **There is no point in addressing your wrong or hurtful behavior** because you and your behavior are one and the same: BAD.

---

28. If you see "discipline" and "punishment" as being one and the same, it may be helpful for you to know that "discipline" comes from the Latin word "disciplina," which means "instruction given to a disciple," who is a student. Punishment, on the other hand, is about blame, pain, and fear. Being disciplined can also be painful, but its intent is to correct and teach so that a person can move forward and try again.

29. We are indebted to Gershen Kaufman and John Bradshaw, as much of what we share with you on shame in this chapter has been shaped by the invaluable insights they have articulated in their excellent books.

2. **You should have known better** or done better, as mistakes and poor choices are unacceptable (i.e., be perfect and do it perfectly every time).

3. **No amends is good enough,** and your behavior is beyond correcting or improving.

4. **The consequences** of your wrong or hurtful behavior include **feeling "bad" forever and being punished – or punishing yourself – forever,** which means you can never move on and you have nothing to contribute in present time.

5. **You are inherently flawed** as a human being, damaged goods, fundamentally bad, and always will be.

6. **There is no closure available to you through** forgiveness, not from others, and especially not from yourself, so, of course, you can't try again.

Remorse, on the other hand, allows or permits you to be human, which is all you or any of us can be, while factoring in the following humane allowances:

1. It allows you to **address your wrong or hurtful behavior,** because you are *not* your behavior, although you are responsible for it.

2. It allows you to **learn** from what you did wrong, as it recognizes that mistakes and poor choices are part and parcel of the human condition.

3. It allows you to make **amends** to the person you harmed – including to yourself when you are the one you ended up hurting – and **correct** and **improve** your behavior.

261

4. It allows you to accept the **consequences of your wrong and hurtful behavior,** but these consequences DO NOT INCLUDE FEELING BAD OR GUILTY **FOREVER,** AND THEY DO NOT INCLUDE BEING PUNISHED OR PUNISHING YOURSELF **FOREVER,** which means you can move on and make a contribution again.

5. It allows you to retain, or reclaim, **your inherent goodness and value** as a human being, in a manner that recognizes this unalterable truth: *I am still—and always have been and always will be—a good and worthwhile person, even when my behavior is bad or wrong, harmful or unacceptable.*

6. It, most importantly, **allows you to bring closure to the incident and to your feelings of remorse or regret** because you addressed it, which allows you to heal by being forgiven by the person you harmed, or by yourself, or both, so that you can try again.[30]

What we want to emphasize is that the key to healing, moving on, and being happy again, so that you can make a contribution in present time, is to move from an unhealthy shame-based punishment system to one that is based on healthy remorse and corrective discipline. Healthy remorse is one of the antidotes to toxic shame, which will allow you to move on again in life, whether you forgive yourself or not.

Adults who struggle to forgive themselves often come from shame-based systems. Being aware of this is not intended as an excuse for wrong and hurtful behavior. Instead, we are simply looking

---

30. Just as we have the right to move on without forgiving those who have hurt us if we so choose, others also have the right to move on without forgiving us. This is true even when we have apologized, been accountable, made amends, and corrected our behavior. But even if some we have harmed cannot—or will not—forgive us, we can choose to forgive ourselves or make peace with the past with the help of one of the healthy alternatives to forgiving.

at the organic causes as to why so many of us struggle to forgive ourselves, which can help us gain a better understanding of what we are up against. What's more, we aren't seeking to blame your or our parents, caretakers, teachers, or preachers, because they didn't invent shame; they simply passed along the shame that they learned. They often used it as a means of controlling behavior, limiting or eliminating that which they had been taught was harmful or sinful. But for those of us who were recipients of shame, there is little wonder as to why so many of us are so relentless – and ruthless – in our self-punishment when we have hurt others or ourselves.

To help you assess whether your difficulty, or even your inability, to forgive yourself has its roots in a shame-based punitive system, we offer the following questions for your reflection. By exploring questions such as these, perhaps in your journal or with a support group or therapist, it may become painfully obvious to you where you learned to be so harshly un-self-forgiving.

- What do I remember learning about life and about making mistakes as a child, both from what I was overtly taught and from what I observed?

- When I made mistakes and poor choices, was I gently and respectfully corrected, helped to understand, and taught a better way, or was I scolded, shamed, hit or shaken, threatened, or otherwise punished?

- Was I expected to know things before I was taught how to do them, or before I was developmentally capable of doing them?

- Was I expected to be perfect rather than simply human, simply a child?

- Was I taught healthy remorse or was I immersed in toxic shame?

> ❧ Were the consequences of my misbehavior appropriate or excessive?
>
> ❧ Did the love and acceptance of the key adults in my life, primarily my parents or caregivers, come across as being unconditional, or conditional based upon whether my behavior was "good" or not?
>
> ❧ What connection do I see between my earliest experiences as a child who made mistakes and poor choices and how I have treated myself as an adult when I have hurt others or myself?

If you were raised in a shame-based environment in which punishment was used as a way to control your behavior, and which left you with a legacy of feeling unceasingly bad about yourself whenever you hurt or failed others as an adult, you can make three powerful choices with which to make peace with the past. We have found that these choices, like so many others, are most effective when you make a commitment to employing them regularly as opposed to just once.

1. Make a conscious, deliberate choice to replace unhealthy shame with **healthy remorse.**

2. Make a conscious, deliberate choice to replace ruthless self-punishment with extraordinary **self-gentleness.**

3. Make a conscious, deliberate choice to replace feeling bad about what you have done in the past that hurt others or yourself, which is fostered by continuing to interpret these painful memories through the distorting lens of shame, with **behavior in which you make a contribution in present time.**

In the next section we will explain why it is impossible for any of us to make peace with the past if we are immersed or rooted in shame, for not only is shame about unending punishment, its "rules" are inherently unfair. And when the rules aren't fair in *any* game, it is nearly impossible to win. In the case of the shame game, what we can't ever win is our freedom from feeling bad about what we have done in the past so that we can move on, try again, and make a contribution in the present.

Adults who struggle to forgive themselves
often come from shame-based systems.
Being aware of this is not intended as an excuse
for wrong and hurtful behavior. Instead, we are simply
looking at the organic causes as to why so many of us
struggle to forgive ourselves, which can help us gain a
better understanding of what we are up against.

The Can't-Win Shame Game

When it comes to how we can respond to our wrong or hurtful behavior, there are three possible affect (emotional response) systems or bases available to us: (1) remorse (2) shame or (3) none. We certainly don't want the third choice, as that is the base of narcissists and sociopaths. For those of us who have been based or rooted in the second one, though none of us would choose this of our own volition, we will expand upon the explanations we offered in the previous section as to why shame does not allow us to make peace with the past. And in the next section, we will show you why remorse is the best choice. We will also suggest a few practices to help you break free from being shame-based, so that you can activate healthy remorse as a way to heal and feel good about yourself again. First, however, we want to convince you to stop playing the shame game, because it is set up in such a way that you can't possibly win – ever.

Of the more than thirty meanings of the word "base," three in particular are relevant to our discussion:

1. a fundamental principle or groundwork; **foundation** [of a person]

2. the **principal ingredient** or element of anything [or of a person]

3. a **starting point** or point of departure.[31]

This means that the very "foundation" on which the lives of many people who cannot seem to forgive themselves has been built, often beginning at a very young age, and on which their lives now stand as adults, is shame. It also means that the "principal ingredient" of many of these dis-abled self-forgivers is shame, which leaves them feeling very bad about themselves when they have harmed others, whether intentionally or because they acted out of their own

---

31. *Webster's New Universal Unabridged Dictionary.* New York: Barnes and Noble, 2003 (emphases added).

sense of being wounded – which all shame-based people are – or out of ignorance (unknowing). Therefore, shame is the "starting point" from which many of us who can't forgive ourselves must begin our healing journey, even though none of us chose it.

We would like to "start" by expanding upon what we have said about shame thus far:

- Because the onset of shame takes place between the ages of two and four, and remorse is not developmentally available until age five or six, in shame-based systems you learn to interpret your life, your very being, and *your behavior*, including your wrong or hurtful behavior, through the highly distorting lens of shame.[32]

- Shame occurs when others, usually parents and other authority figures, put their values and value system on you (e.g., go to church/synagogue/mosque, don't get angry, don't hit, be good, etc.).

- Many of these values are not necessarily bad or wrong in and of themselves, but in a shame-based system, *you* are deemed bad or wrong when you don't live up to them (e.g., "Shame on you for hitting your sister!" or "When are you *ever* going to learn?" or "Why can't you be good for once?").

- You learn to feel bad about yourself *as a person* when you don't meet the values and expectations of these powerful others.

---

32. You might envision this lens as being like contact lenses or eyeglasses that were put on you without your awareness or consent. However, instead of helping you to see yourself as valuable and your misbehavior as something you can address and learn from, this lens resulted in you seeing yourself as valueless, and your behavior as something that warranted punishment, especially when you did not live up to the values and expectations of important and powerful others. You may have lived with this distorting lens of shame for so long that it seems to be a normal, unchangeable part of you, yet it can be discarded.

- When you hurt someone else, you tend to feel bad at the core or center of your being because you are unable to distinguish between your inherent and unchanging worth as a person and your wrong or hurtful behavior.

- Instead of feeling healthy remorse when you hurt someone else, or when you make a poor choice that ends up hurting yourself, you feel hopelessly bad about yourself.

- The worse you feel about yourself as a person, the more unable you are to address your wrong or hurtful behavior and then let it go, which makes you feel worse about yourself as a person and leaves you more unable to address your wrong or hurtful behavior and then let it go . . . and so on.

- Shame does not allow for forgiveness from others or from yourself, as it basically expects you to do it perfectly every time.

Shame is not only a game that you can't ever win, you don't have to play it either. Here's how the shame-based system works regarding our wrong or hurtful behavior:

1. We do something that is wrong or hurtful.

2. We feel attacked, judged, condemned, punished, and exposed by *external* shaming voices for violating *their* values that have been put on us. The shaming message we "hear" may have actually been said to us in the past, perhaps by a parent (e.g., "How could you have *done* such a thing?!"), which we hear again now. Or someone important such as our boss says it to us now, or we can imagine our boss or someone else easily making a shaming comment such as this, even if they don't.

3. The shaming external attack becomes one that we continue by attacking and punishing ourselves, because we have learned to *internalize* shame and see ourselves through the distorting lens of shame.

4. We feel completely *overwhelmed and immobilized* by our shameful thoughts and feelings because . . .

   a) We never should have done what was wrong or hurtful in the first place, as shame does not allow for mistakes or poor choices and subsequent learning.

   b) We cannot address our wrong or hurtful behavior, make sufficient amends, or bring closure to this incident because the shame game is about unending punishment rather than corrective discipline.

   c) We rediscover how bad and defective we are as evidenced by our recent wrong or hurtful behavior.

After doing something that is wrong or hurtful, any sense of healthy remorse is as impossible to access as a breath of fresh air when swimming under water. This is because in a shame-based system the external voices of shame are always with us, eager to pounce on and punish us for our failings, both real and imagined. These voices leave us with a sense of being totally exposed, as if everyone, or at least those whose opinion of us matters, is aware of what we did and can see just exactly how terribly different and irreparably defective we are at the very core of our being. We can even feel this sense of exposure and defectiveness in those cases when *we* are the only ones who know what our wrong or hurtful behavior was, as inside our head and heart the eyes of our "shamers" are still on us, their voices still with us attacking and judging us.

Having long since internalized these external voices, we are tormented by the shame we have been immersed in, which is always especially acute and intense when we have done something wrong or hurt someone else or ourselves. Consequently, we are left to suffer intense self-shaming thoughts and feelings. We may even feel like we are all alone on a distant planet and that we don't belong here on Earth, such is the power of shame. There is no way that we can ever bring closure to the shameful feelings we have about our wrong or hurtful behavior. Eventually, the intensity of our shameful thoughts and feelings will quiet down, but *only* until the next time that our behavior falls short. Then they will rise up again in all their overpowering and immobilizing intensity as we, once again, try to play, and get thoroughly trounced by, the can't-win shame game.

To illustrate the above, we will use an example in which a cashier mistakenly gives us twenty extra dollars in change, which we are aware of immediately. At first, we are happy to have come upon a little extra cash, rationalizing that it's a big company that makes millions of dollars each year, and besides they charge way too much, and they'll never miss the twenty bucks.

Not too long after leaving the store, we start to feel shameful. We recall a time when we stole some candy from a drugstore when we were a kid, and how we were shamed and humiliated by our parents when they found out. Perhaps they made a big scene when they marched us back to pay for the candy. "I did *not* raise a thief!" we remember them saying in a loud and indignant voice. "You pay them back right now!" The eyes and judgmental thoughts of the other customers seemed to pierce our very souls, leaving us feeling more exposed and naked than if we were indeed literally naked.

We also recall other times when we experienced shame and humiliation for our misbehavior. Regarding the extra twenty dollars in change from the cashier, these external voices now come to the forefront and begin to shame us for keeping the money. Even if we quickly return it, say, within an hour, we still feel overwhelmed and immobilized by shame. So we remain immersed in feelings of shame, unable to forgive ourselves and unable to try again, because we are being tormented and punished by external judges from the past or present—even if they are only in our head—as well as by our own internalized self-shaming voice. We are bombarded by these voices-not-our-own, but which *seem* like our own voice because we took over the shaming role of our original "shamers" long ago:

➤ "What is *wrong* with you?!"

➤ "What kind of person keeps an extra twenty dollars in change anyway?!"

➤ "You haven't changed at all since you stole that candy from the drugstore when you were ten."

➤ "If your boss/pastor/spouse . . . knew, they would be shocked."

You might try to counter with the fact that you returned the money an hour later, to which the external voice of shame says with an indignant huff:

➤ "WELL, you never should have kept it in the *first* place!"

➤ "Why did it take you a *whole hour* to return it, especially since you knew right away that the cashier had given you too much change?"

➤ "Besides, returning the money doesn't undo what you did."

➤ "Do you think your brother would have ever done something like that? He could be starving to death, and *he* wouldn't do *that!*"

With shame, our tendency is to hide what we did because we fear abandonment. So even though we return the twenty dollars, we keep the whole incident to ourselves because we feel embarrassed and fear that others will look down on us, judge us, laugh at us, or abandon us in some other way (abandonment doesn't always mean literally leaving someone).

Even though the store manager thanks us for returning the money and says she wishes more people were like us, her words fall on deaf fall on deaf ears because the *external* judging and attacking voices of shame, which we have internalized, are so noisy, ruthless, and relentless in their condemnation – not only regarding this incident, but all the other unclosed cases from the past in which we were unable to resolve our shameful feelings after making a wrong or hurtful choice. The cumulative effect is a wholesale condemnation of our personhood, as we are judged and denounced once again: DEFECTIVE, DAMAGED, IRREPARABLE, NO GOOD.

The above is an illustration of how shame is an absolute can't-win game. In fact the only way that you *can* win is not to play it. Now you might be wondering why returning the twenty dollars did not free us from our remorse. The answer is that *remorse is not really available to us when we are immersed in a shame-based system*, just as remorse is not developmentally available to very young children because the frontal lobe of their brain has not yet developed sufficiently to truly understand cause and effect, and like a breath of fresh air is not available to us when swimming underwater. Our remorse over keeping the twenty dollars, even though we only kept it for an hour, gets completely drowned out by the shame messages from the past.

Yes, stealing twenty dollars – or keeping twenty dollars that is not ours when we are given too much change, if you'd prefer – is wrong and perhaps harmful to the cashier who may face some kind of consequence for coming up short at the end of their shift. But from a shame-based perspective, we can't bring closure to this incident by returning the money, because the external shame messages that we received long ago are interfering with our "remorse signal."

We hope that we have convinced you of the futility of playing the can't-win shame game. In the next section we will show you some ways to break free from shame so that healthy remorse can become available to you. When you make a remorse-based system your behavioral foundation, you will be able to break free from feeling remorseful about past *behaviors* so that you can try again and feel good about yourself *as a person*, rather than remain stuck in shameful feelings.

In a shame-based system the external voices of shame
are always with us, eager to pounce on and punish us for
any failing, both real and imagined. These voices leave us
with a sense of being totally exposed, as if everyone, or
at least those individuals whose opinion of us matters,
is aware of what we did and can see just exactly how
terribly different and irreparably defective we are at the
very core of our being.

From Debilitating Shame to Healing Remorse

One of the key points from the previous section is that we acquire shame as a result of the values others put on us, and how we are treated when we fail to live up to them (i.e., attacked, judged, condemned, punished, and exposed). Shame is not something we are born with; rather, it is taught to us and put on us without our awareness or consent. It is like a faulty lens, much like prescription eyeglasses or contact lenses or reading glasses that make our ability to see or read a hundred times more difficult. The lens of shame distorts our entire worldview, especially our view of ourselves when we act in a wrong or hurtful manner. In fact, the primary debilitating thought pattern of shame-based people, even if it isn't articulated in these exact words, is, in effect:

> If you (think of one or several people whose opinion of you matters) knew who I **really** was, what I have done, and what I have contemplated doing, you would be so shocked and disgusted that you would go away and tell everybody else to go away. And I can't let that happen, so I've **got** to keep you away from that which I feel shameful about.

The subsequent fear that is aroused by this shame-based thought pattern can be summed up in one word: **abandonment**. And we would propose that the fear of abandonment, which is based in part upon the times we have each suffered some type of abandonment—relationally, socially, physically, emotionally, and so on—is humanity's primary wound, both individually and collectively. We believe that most other wounds have at least some origin in, or relationship to, the fear or experience of abandonment.

So fearing the external exposure, judgment, condemnation, attack, and punishment of others—and some type of abandonment such as withholding love is among the cruelest of all punishments—we learn to hide what we did that was wrong or hurtful from these

274

potential "shamers." However, what is completely nonsensical about being shame-based, and why we can't ever win when playing the shame game, is that we then proceed to launch an all-out attack on ourselves that is far more harsh and relentless than anything our worst real-life "shamers" ever did, or even would if they could. We hide from others so that *they* won't punish and beat us up, and then *we* take the equivalent of a baseball bat and punish and beat ourselves up, sometimes for decades.

Unfortunately, no one can stop you from beating yourself up, as it's completely legal, and in some systems (e.g., certain families and religions) it is encouraged and expected – even admired. But when it comes to making peace with the past it is no more effective than the analogy we have used before: banging your head against a wall in order to get rid of a headache. A far better way is to replace the distorting, even *self-disfiguring*, lens of shame with the corrective lens of healthy remorse, which will then allow you to make a fresh start.

A key step in making this foundational shift from being shame-based to remorse-based is to identify and claim *your own* values, including your behavioral values, which basically covers two main areas:

1. How you would like to value and treat yourself.

2. How you would like to value and treat others.

A good place for each of us to start in redefining or recommitting ourselves to our *own* behavioral values might be with one of the many variations of the Golden Rule, "Do to others as you would have them do to you," but with a key emphasis *on doing to **yourself** that which you would like to do to or for others.*[33] For how we treat others and how we treat ourselves are intrinsically related. When

---

33. If you are interested in learning how different religious and spiritual traditions express the equivalent of the Golden Rule, you might look it up online. We particularly like Judaism's emphasis on not doing to others what you wouldn't want done to yourself, for as it applies to self-forgiveness or otherwise making peace with the past, it seems to suggest that we not harm or punish ourselves.

we are gentle and respectful with ourselves, we will be more gentle and respectful with others; when we are gentle and respectful with others, we will find it easier and more natural to treat ourselves in a gentle and respectful manner.

Basically, it comes down to what works better: punishing and beating yourself up in the harshest manner possible or easing up on and being gentle with yourself. We are betting that you have already mastered self-punishment and can do it far better than anyone else. So since you've mastered it, and since it hasn't enabled you to make peace with your past, perhaps it's time to try something new.

Returning to our discussion of values, one of the great liberties and joys of being an adult is that we can choose our own values. Though it hurts *us* when we act contrary to our values in a way that causes harm to someone else, it is a necessary pain that motivates us to address our behavior, learn from it, and try to do it differently in the future. Furthermore, it makes sense that the further we stray from our own core values, the more painful our feelings of remorse will be for those of us who have a good heart and a well-developed conscience.

Obviously, when we act just slightly outside of our values, as evidenced by the level one ring in the diagram on the next page, or even when we do something that is a bit more serious as signified by the level two ring, it is a whole lot easier to address our behavior, apologize, make amends, forgive ourselves, and make a relatively quick fresh start than when we do something that is much more serious and hurtful, as represented by the level three and four rings.

But even when we have violated our own values and hurt someone else in a very serious manner, addressing our wrong or hurtful behavior from the perspective of a remorse-based system can help us to move on and make a contribution once again, whereas shame essentially says your life is over. *When a remorse-based system is your behavioral foundation, there is always a way to make it back to the center of your being, to the core of your personhood, which is good, even when your behavior has been very poor or hurtful.* In a shame-based system, you can never make it home again, and you can never truly feel good about yourself or be at home with and within yourself, because you and your behavior are foundationally, and permanently, bad.

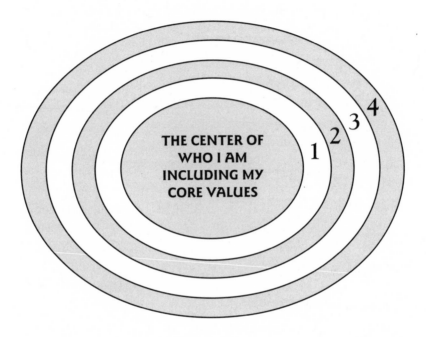

Keep in mind that a level four offense does not necessarily mean murder or robbing a bank; more accurately, it represents what *you* would deem to be an extremely serious violation of *your* values. Since each person's value system is unique, cheating on a spouse or partner might be a level four violation for one person, while losing their temper and using profanity with a loved one might constitute a level four violation for another person. In both cases, self-forgiveness, or making peace with the past via one of the healthy alternatives, is going to be more difficult than if they had each committed a level one violation. We suspect that you are reading this chapter because it is something of a more serious nature that has resulted in you feeling very bad about yourself, and for which you haven't been able to forgive yourself or otherwise make peace with the past.

Here's how a remorse-based system works, and unlike shame, it works *for* us, rather than against us:

1. We do something that is wrong or hurtful.

2. We feel the painful feeling of remorse (also known as regret or feeling sorry) because we have acted outside of *our own* value system and caused harm to another human being (and sometimes to ourselves).

3. We accept that feeling remorseful is one of the necessary and inevitable consequences for our wrong or hurtful behavior; there may be others as well (e.g., loss of a relationship or job, loss of trust, etc.).

4. We address our behavior, what we did that was wrong or hurtful, for two primary reasons, and in this order of importance:

   a) First and foremost, we want to repair the damage we have done to the fullest extent possible in order to help the person we hurt heal and recover as quickly and completely as they can.

   b) Second, we do so because we know that addressing our behavior is the only way to alleviate our feelings of remorse.

5. Because we addressed our behavior and took full ownership of and responsibility for it, we are able to bring a significant degree of closure to it, perhaps even complete closure, so that we can start fresh and strive to make a contribution in present time, even though some feelings of remorse may crop up from time to time when we recall what we did.

We want to stress that motivation matters. In number four above, we can certainly address our behavior because we want to reduce or eliminate our remorse-filled feelings. However, if that is our primary reason when apologizing or making amends, then it is likely that neither our healing nor the injured person's healing will be as complete as when we place the needs of the injured party ahead of our own desire for emotional pain-relief. We can certainly desire both, but healthy remorse is most concerned about helping the person we harmed recover and get on with their life. The relief we get from feeling remorseful is a byproduct and not a primary goal in and of itself.

Also, even when operating from a remorse-based system, we might not be forgiven by the other person. We may have injured them so deeply that forgiving is not possible or desirable. Nonetheless, addressing our behavior, either with the person we harmed or with someone such as a therapist when it is not feasible or beneficial to be in contact with the person we hurt, will help to set ourselves free from remorseful feelings so that we can start fresh and make a contribution again in present time.

Breaking free from a shame-based system so that healthy remorse can work for you in the manner described above is not something that is done overnight. It, like many significant undertakings, is a process. We return to an analogy from Chapter Six, in which we suggested some practices to help you break free from orbiting around "Planet Offender" so that you could begin to orbit around "Planet My New Life," to help convey how you can break free from being based on "Planet Shame" so that you can visit "Planet Remorse" on your way home to the center of who you are and your core values.

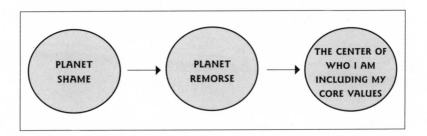

The counterclockwise rotation we used in Chapter Six to illustrate how focusing on "Planet Offender" takes you hopelessly back in time is applicable to shame as well. In a shame-based system, all you can do is look back at your wrong or hurtful behavior and feel endlessly bad about it, while simultaneously being attacked and punished by the external shaming voices that judge and condemn you for what you did, which you have now internalized. There is no going forward again, no coming home, no fresh start. Remorse, on the other hand has a clockwise rotation similar to "Planet My New Life," and allows you to move forward again as you address your behavior. It also allows you to set some limits as to how long you are going to feel remorseful.

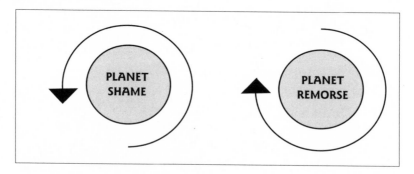

Of course, if you have been orbiting around "Planet Shame" for years or decades, you can expect to make a lot of figure eights as you go back and forth between the deeply entrenched orbits around "Planet Shame" while trying to establish a new orbit around "Planet Remorse," as portrayed by the diagram below.

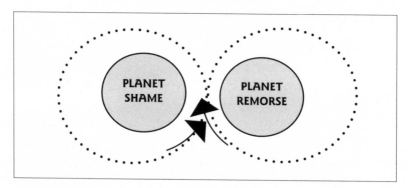

Just as we offered three specific practices in Chapter Six to help you break free from orbiting around "Planet Offender" so that you could begin to orbit around "Planet My New Life", we offer you three practices to help you break free from orbiting around "Planet Shame" so that you can begin to orbit around "Planet Remorse," and from there, let go of *feeling* remorseful and head home again.

1. **STOP calling yourself names, engaging in global self-putdowns, and endlessly focusing on your faults and failing, both real and overblown.**

   - I was a terrible father/mother/teacher/boss
   - I am a horrible person because I _____
   - I never do anything right.

2. **START referring to your wrong and hurtful behavior in *behavioral terms* rather than in terms of your personhood by using a word such as "remorseful" or "regret" or "sorry" instead of "I feel bad," as "I *feel* bad" language opens the door for shame's primary lie: "I *am* bad."**

   - I feel remorseful when I recall the time when I (name the behavior)
   - I deeply regret the time when I (name the behavior)
   - I feel very sorry for the time when (name the behavior)

3. **START considering whether you would mercilessly punish a friend or loved one who was feeling as "bad" (remorseful) about what they did as you feel about what you did, and whether anything more can be gained by continuing to punish and beat yourself up.**

281

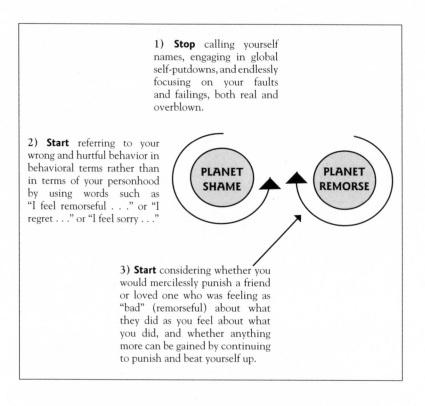

1) **Stop** calling yourself names, engaging in global self-putdowns, and endlessly focusing on your faults and failings, both real and overblown.

2) **Start** referring to your wrong and hurtful behavior in behavioral terms rather than in terms of your personhood by using words such as "I feel remorseful . . ." or "I regret . . ." or "I feel sorry . . ."

PLANET SHAME

PLANET REMORSE

3) **Start** considering whether you would mercilessly punish a friend or loved one who was feeling as "bad" (remorseful) about what they did as you feel about what you did, and whether anything more can be gained by continuing to punish and beat yourself up.

It is very likely that you will be able to begin to break free from the power of debilitating shame and move toward healthy remorse as you practice the above. The third practice, especially, is one that will launch you away from the strong gravitational pull of "Planet Shame" and all its toxicity so that you can head toward "Planet Remorse" where true healing can begin to take place.

Three more practices that are critical to breaking free from the power of shame include the use of your intellect, activating your sense of humor, and seeking healthy touch.

Using your **intellect** to challenge and reframe "I am bad" self-talk, and its endless variations, is absolutely critical to breaking free from shame. You can't afford to be an emotional thinker when dealing with shame, even though that's what shame, personified, is counting on you to do: remain stuck in feeling emotionally bad about yourself. We invite you, gently urge you, to continually counter slanderous self-talk, global putdowns, and endless self-fault-finding with the intellectual choice to refrain from all three of these shame-deepening practices. You might even need to adopt a code of ethics in which you clearly state how you are going to try to treat yourself from this day forward (we say more about this in our workbook).

The second antidote is **humor**, especially the ability to laugh at yourself, or at least smile, in a light-hearted and playful self-deprecating manner. Shame-based people tend to take themselves and life way too seriously. Instead of berating yourself when you mess up, poke a little bit of fun at yourself by saying something like, "Well, I guess being a little grouchy this morning is not a level four violation of my values; level three, maybe, but not a level four." Sometimes by sharing your story, and your shame, with others, though it is a painfully serious topic, you will find yourself laughing at some of the absurd elements of it.

We know of one person who intended to set some healthy boundaries with a relative and ended up losing his composure completely and saying some things he wished he hadn't. When talking about it with a friend, his friend quipped, "Your intention was good but your delivery was *just a little bit off*," to which our shame-threatened boundary setter replied with laughter, "Just a little bit. Not much, though."

The third and most powerful antidote is **touch**, which has two elements. One, you need to literally seek out healthy human touch, as it heals the depths of shame that neither the use of your intellect nor humor can reach. We are beings, human beings, fragile yet remarkably resilient human beings who began our life journey with a great need for physical touch. This need is still far-reaching, especially for historically shame-based non-self-forgivers who are often touch-deprived if not touch-starved. Two, you need to share yourself, including your wounds, with others through the touch of communication, especially verbally, but also nonverbally (e.g., eye contact). Encasing your shame in the darkest most private regions of your heart and mind keeps it alive and well, while you remain firmly in its insidious grip. Sharing your life, your story, and your wounds, including the wounds of how you feel "bad" for hurting others, with someone who is safe and respectful is an element of touch that is incredibly healing and liberating. This might be a pastor or priest, a counselor or therapist, a sponsor if you are in a twelve-step program, or a friend.

As you activate the three antidotes of intellect, humor, and touch, and as you incorporate the three aforementioned shame-orbit-breaking practices into your life, you will find yourself departing "Planet Shame" and refueling at "Planet Remorse," which will then allow you to come home to yourself and make a fresh start in life. In the next and final section, we offer some additional thoughts and suggestions regarding how you can make peace with the past, including the importance of making a contribution in present time, for you are still very much needed and you have much to offer.

When a remorse-based system is your
behavioral foundation, there is always a way
to make it back to the center of your being,
to the core of your personhood, which is good,
even when your behavior has been very poor or hurtful.

Making Peace with the Past

We begin this final section of Chapter Seven by saying that much of what we wrote in Chapters Four, Five, and Six can help you make peace with the past and move on. We start with Chapter Four, which is about the power of using alternative language if forgiving, in this case forgiving yourself, is something you can't seem to do. Fifteen of the healthy alternatives that we presented in the first section of Chapter Four ("Some of the Healthy Alternatives to Forgiving"), without any modification, can be just as helpful when we can't forgive ourselves as when we can't forgive others (e.g., #3: "Releasing the pain of the past to God, my higher power, or the universe"). The remaining ten, which are listed below with their original numbering at the end of each, have been reworded to help us heal when, for whatever reason, we just can't forgive ourselves. You might turn to the complete list of twenty-five to see if one or more of the ones that are not listed below appeal to you in your quest to make peace with the past. Here, then, are the slightly altered ten:

- ◞ Moving on as I keep the focus on my life, my needs, and what I have to offer in the here and now. (#1)

- ◞ Freeing myself from the remorse I have about the past and for a new beginning in life. (#2)

- ◞ Coming to terms with what I have done as best I can. (#4)

- ◞ Cutting the cords that have kept me bound to a painful past that I can't change no matter how much I would like to. (#5)

- ◞ Accepting that what I have done cannot be changed, so that I can move on and live the rest of my life in a positive, creative, and respectful manner. (#7)

⋄ Affirming my strength to move beyond the pain of the past, and to use the wisdom I have gained to share my gifts and talents more fully with others. (#11)

⋄ Disengaging from the person I was at an earlier time in my life so that I can freely love the person I have become today, which will enable me to engage my life as it is, while making positive choices in the here and now. (#14)

⋄ Letting go of remorseful thoughts and feelings about the past, each day if necessary, so that I can reach out and love and be loved. (#18)

⋄ Managing my painful thoughts and feelings of remorse, while taking small steps and risks to help me move forward and share my goodness with others, and in turn enjoy the goodness they have to share with me. (#20)

⋄ Affirming that I *can* move on with some feelings of remorse, which will decrease *as* I move on, rebuild, and make a contribution. (#25)

The phrases above, as well as the others from Chapter Four, are not the only possibilities; you can certainly create your own. The point is that if forgiving yourself is something you can't seem to do, then it might be helpful to explore some alternatives. The ultimate goal is to heal the remorse you feel for hurting someone else – or yourself – so that you can move on and be happy again. If that sounds selfish, it's not. In order to make a contribution again, and to be of benefit to others and to ourselves, we need to make peace with the past. Remaining stuck in remorse, or worse, in shame, and staying unhappy is not beneficial to anyone.

Another point from Chapter Four is that you can activate any of these alternative approaches as often as needed to help you manage your thoughts and feelings of remorse. Forgiving, on the other hand, even forgiving ourselves, seems to come with an expectation that we complete it at some point in time, which can result in confusion or discouragement when we *do* feel remorseful again, even long after we thought we had forgiven ourselves.

From Chapter Five, the following may be helpful to keep in mind as you seek to make peace with your past, whether by self-forgiveness or one of the healthy alternatives:

- ✤ **Healing is a process that involves enjoying progress, suffering setbacks, and making comebacks.** Even when you find yourself making great progress, you may have days in which you are quite hard on yourself, especially if you have had a lifelong tendency of doing so. When you are aware of treating yourself harshly, you can make a decision at that time to stop, and to replace self-abuse with self-gentleness. Revisiting old ineffective ways of treating ourselves can be but a reminder that self-abuse is not very effective, in which case, we recommit to being gentle and self-encouraging.

- ✤ **Expect to get stuck in the pain of the past from time to time, *and* expect to heal and move forward.** Getting stuck and reverting to self-punishment is typical for many who have struggled to forgive themselves or otherwise make peace with the past, so expecting it will enable you to say something like the following to yourself: "Getting stuck and beating myself up for what I did in the past is something many people struggle with, not just me. I'm down on myself now, but this will pass." And having that simple awareness will help you to expect to heal and move forward: "I am going to put this chapter of my life behind me and move on, because I have a lot to offer. The world needs me and my gifts, so I am going to treat myself gently in order to foster my healing in this moment."

- ✤ **Activate your seven intrapersonal allies as well as your interpersonal allies.** Relying on emotional reasoning, which of course isn't reasonable at all, is perhaps the single greatest trap for people who can't seem to forgive themselves. Activating your *intellect, spirituality, attitude, body, heart*, and taking positive, self-caring *action* will help you to manage your feelings of reawakened remorse so that you can release them once again in a timely manner. Also, because it is so easy to lose perspective and to revert to the old familiar ways of beating yourself up, you need the support of others. Reach out and share what is going on in your heart and mind with others, especially when you are getting down on yourself. Nine times out of ten you will feel better as a result, and be able to quickly return to self-gentleness and to what is possible in the present moment.

❖ **Do a hurt-healing cost analysis.** You can assess what your wrong or hurtful behaviors have cost you, so as to be able to grieve your losses and set them behind you. Perhaps the most important of the three cost analysis areas to consider is what price *refusing* to be self-merciful and gentle will exact from you (e.g., unhappiness, depression, going through the motions rather than living, missing out on new opportunities, etc.). No one wins if you refuse to be kind to you, and you are the only one who can do self-kindness. Of course, there is also a cost in choosing to ease up and be kind and gentle with yourself. You will have to pay the price of giving up the habit of beating yourself up, putting yourself down, and feeling excessively sorry for yourself. You will need to learn and practice some new behaviors (e.g., affirmations, accepting compliments, striving to be more positive and hopeful, etc.). And new behaviors don't fall on you from above; instead, they rise up from within as you practice them. Making peace with the past, again whether through self-forgiveness or via one of the healthy alternatives, takes effort. You are the star, because it's *your* life; everyone else in your life plays but a supporting role. The story of your life is far from over, so we urge you to get out and help create what you would like to see unfold, whether it is a new relationship, a new career, or a new way of treating yourself.

- ✒ **Set an intention to heal.** Being intentional provides you with direction, a focus point for your energies each new day, each new moment, and inspires you to take tiny actions on your own behalf. Consciously, purposefully, setting an intention such as "I intend to close this chapter of my life, which I regret, and begin writing a new and better chapter one day, one choice, at a time," or "Even though (name) still hates me and will never forgive me, I intend to love myself by letting go of the past so that I can love others and be happy again," is a powerful practice that will help you manage your feelings of remorse and move forward with your life.

From Chapter Six, accessing and activating your healthy adult power is critical to making peace with your past. Self-forgiveness or activating one of the healthy alternatives is an adult undertaking. And part of being adult is accepting that nothing in the past can be changed, and the sooner you can learn from it and let it go, the sooner you can be of help, both to others and yourself. A child can be inconsolable in their misery; as an adult you can be self-consoling when it comes to how you respond to your own emotional pain, and self-controlling when it comes to taking a single step to move forward again.

An adult practice you might consider is that of writing a letter of goodbye to the person you were at the time you hurt someone else. Many of us have a before and after, someone we once were at an earlier point in our lives and who we are today. In some cases, it even seems like two different lives if not two completely different people. Yes, we regret with all our heart what we did to hurt others and ourselves, but now it may be time to say goodbye to that person and the things we did at that time that were wrong or hurtful. Doing so via a metaphorical letter may result in greater freedom, and with greater freedom comes the ability to be more response-able, better able to respond both to yourself and those around you.

Of course, self-acceptance, of which we said much in Chapter Six, is critical to your ability to heal and make peace with your past. Many who can't seem to forgive themselves have mastered self-rejection, and our basic position is that if you've mastered something that doesn't result in you being happy and at peace, perhaps it's time to consider a new path. The more you accept yourself the more peace you will have, and the more peace you have the more you will have to offer others, and the more you offer others the more unencumbered you will be to receive the gifts of others.

The practice of refuting powerlessness, relinquishing pain, and reclaiming possibilities is as important in making peace with the past as it is in coming to terms with how you were hurt by others. You are *not* powerless over your feelings of remorse, though it may seem that way at times, and you *can* take steps to process and relinquish your painful thoughts and feelings regarding what you have done in the past. As you relinquish or give up your emotional pain, you can begin to reclaim all that is possible, and in a world that is inherently abundant, much is possible. However, in order to live into what is possible, you need to continually challenge and refute any notion that you are powerless to rebuild after making wrong or hurtful choices. Then you, like all of us, need to relinquish the emotional pain which is so easy to become accustomed to.

Finally from Chapter Six, staying in present time is key. The present moment is where your life is today. When you find yourself thinking about events in the past that do not need to be thought about again, you can refocus on what is in front of you in the present moment. You can do so by focusing on your breathing in a mindful, attentive manner or by paying the utmost attention to what you are doing, whether it is walking up a flight of stairs or folding laundry or reading a book to your kids or grandkids.

We want to close this chapter, and this book, by talking a little bit about making a contribution. Studies show that when people find a way to contribute, they feel good about themselves. Being hurt by others, or feeling the pain of remorse because we hurt others, tends to pull us inward. And going inward is necessary, but so is going out into the world again. Too much inwardness can result in a collapse of self, which is inherently unhealthy because we are by nature creative and social beings. The whole rhythm of life entails a cycle of going inward to reflect and learn, and going outward to practice and gain experience. Even the greatest spiritual masters come down from their mountain retreats in order to reengage life and be of service to others.

If you are struggling to forgive yourself or make peace with the past, making a contribution in the here and now is as powerful a practice as any we have mentioned. It pulls you out of the past and puts you back in the present, and the present is where life happens, *where* **your** *life happens.*

By making a contribution we are not talking about something huge, for it's the little things that count and which quickly add up: a smile, a hello, a good effort at work, a helping hand, mentoring, volunteering, coaching, reading to kids at a neighborhood school, befriending an outcast, complimenting someone, a prayer, warm thoughts. . . . As you practice looking for opportunities, you will come to recognize the nearly numberless ways in which you can make a difference in your corner of the world, which will make all the difference in your own life.

We are not talking about give, give, give, as many women have been trained to do from the earliest age on at the expense of their own needs. More to the point, we are inviting you to find *your* unique ways of contributing that are in line with *your* gifts, talents, and interests. We want to leave the world a better place than we found it. From our perspective, that is a healthy summation of what contributing is all about.

You may even have *more* to contribute because of the wrong and hurtful choices you have made in the past, because you have likely gained some invaluable wisdom as a result, wisdom that could benefit others. Who better to mentor young parents than seasoned parents who have made some mistakes? Who better to model a healthy and positive attitude in a workplace that is filled with chronic complaining and negativity than a transformed complainer and former master of negativity?

Here's a formula: EXPERIENCE + KNOWLEDGE = WISDOM. You have gained invaluable life experience, in part through your wrong and hurtful choices. Add what you have learned as a result (knowledge) and you have wisdom. A great question to ask yourself in order to make peace with the past so that you can make a contribution in present time is: **What did I learn from my wrong or hurtful choices?** That's where the knowledge comes in, which, when tied into your experience, leads to wisdom. And with wisdom, there are many ways for you to make a contribution in the present. And the more you contribute and give to life, the more will come back to you. And the more you live fully in the now, the less power the pain of the past will have over you. We wish you both more and less: less painful thoughts and feelings about the past and more peace and happiness as you write the next chapters of your life.

Making peace with the past, again whether through
self-forgiveness or via one of the healthy alternatives,
takes effort. You are the star, because it's *your* life;
everyone else in your life plays but a supporting role.
The story of your life is far from over, so we urge you to
get out and help create what you would like to see unfold
in your life, whether it is a new relationship, a new career,
or a new way of treating yourself.

The Forgiveness Myth
WORKBOOK

A Practical Guide to
Help You Heal Your Hurts,
Move on and Be Happy Again
When You Can't – or Won't –
Forgive Others or Yourself

Gary Egeberg • Wayne Raiter, M.A., LICSW

For more information, including the availability of quantity discounts
for your group or organization, please visit

www.theforgivenessmyth.com

or

www.originalpathways.com

Look for these books by the authors of
The Forgiveness Myth

FROM THE CO-AUTHORS OF THE FORGIVENESS MYTH

KILLING SHAME

So That You Can Live

Gary Egeberg · Wayne Raiter, M.A., LICSW

Loving Yourself First

*For Those
Who Are Last
in Their Own Heart*

Gary Egeberg · Wayne Raiter, M.A., LICSW

Available September 2008

Shame is a "killer" in that it destroys the human spirit and causes enormous suffering. Shame-based people feel like something is horribly wrong with them at the very core of their being that can't ever be fixed. Shame can even cause some to seriously contemplate taking their own lives. Tragically, too many have either attempted, or succeeded, in doing so.

If someone broke into your home with the intent of seriously harming you and your family, you would take any measure necessary to stop them. Because shame is like a relentless killer intent on doing you and your loved ones great harm, and may have already caused immeasurable suffering, it needs to be destroyed.

Killing Shame explores the destructive power of shame and how to eradicate or "kill" it so that you can live fully and freely.

Available February 2009

Loving Yourself First may be the most important invitation you ever accept in your entire life. This book is for you if you . . .

- ~ Believe that others must always come first
- ~ Have ignored your own needs, wants, and feelings most of your life
- ~ Often feel unworthy, unlovable, and undeserving
- ~ Tend to be extremely hard on yourself
- ~ Suffer from perfectionism
- ~ Assume responsibility for pretty much everyone and everything
- ~ Would *never* treat others the way you treat yourself . . .

If any of the above ring true for you, it may be time to discover that you *are* worthy, deserving, and lovable *just exactly as you are.* Don't deny yourself the love you may have been missing—and longing for—all of your life: **your own!**